STREET *by* STREET

IPSWICH

STREET *by* STREET

IPSWICH

CAROL TWINCH

breedon **books**
PUBLISHING

First published in Great Britain in 2006 by
The Breedon Books Publishing Company Limited
Breedon House, 3 The Parker Centre,
Derby, DE21 4SZ.

ISBN 1 85983 501 5

Printed and bound by Cromwell Press, Trowbridge, Wiltshire.

CONTENTS

INTRODUCTION

Ipswich, or 'Gipeswic' to use its Anglo-Saxon name, was founded in about 600 AD. The derivation of the old name is said to be owed to the freshwater of the River Gipping – 'Gip' – and 'wic' or 'wick', referring to a saltwater creek or bay. It appears as 'Gippeswiche', 'Gypewici' or variations thereof, gradually changing to 'Yppyswyche' and eventually Ipswich. Some interpret 'wic' as being the 'corner of the mouth' of the Gipping, while 'wick' also refers to the 'wicks' or hamlets of the Anglo-Saxon town, a name still found in Wicks Bishop Street.

People have lived on or around Ipswich since before the first century AD, making it one of England's earliest sites of habitation and continuous occupation. Its origins are older than Norwich, Thetford or Bury St Edmunds and excavations over the last 50 years have started to give a picture of the town's beginnings. Exciting new information is constantly emerging about the people who have lived and worked in the town for two millennia. An important Palaeolithic site was discovered in the brickfields on the Foxhall Road and was found to be a lake-side settlement, which has produced Acheulian hand axes. Palaeolithic flints have been discovered south of the river in the Maidenhall and Stoke Hill area as well as Bramford Road and the Hadleigh Road gravel pits. Neolithic, or 'New Stone Age', axes have been found near Ipswich, and in the late 1960s six Iron Age 'torcs', each weighing about 2lbs, were found on the Belstead Hills estate. In 1974 the Suffolk County Council's Archaeological Service was formed and the Origins of Ipswich Project began, since when some 30 excavations have been undertaken.

One of the first known inhabitants of Ipswich, from before the Stone Age, was buried close to what is now Dales Road. He lived just above the Gipping Valley, where the freshwater of the River Gipping meets the tidal waters of the River Orwell, an ideal site for building a shelter and utilising the hospitable vicinity for hunting, fishing and trading.

Evidence for early settlement stretches back to the Stone and Iron Ages, its population surviving the Roman occupation to become one of the earliest known Anglo-Saxon settlements. It was attacked repeatedly and ferociously by the Vikings, and the prime river location that had worked so well for 'Gipeswic' then made it vulnerable to the invaders, who sailed up the Orwell to plunder and colonise the river-side communities. The Anglo-Saxons had no standing army, which meant that the Danish hit-and-run tactics gave them the element of surprise, thus making their raids highly successful. Viking warriors believed they were possessed by the spirit of the god Odin and in battle were noted for their ferocious fighting.

At first they came in their hundreds, in small groups of ships, to steal whatever riches they could find and then return home with the spoils. They raided ships that were loading and unloading at the Stoke crossing, easy pickings for such uncompromising pirates. Later, in the mid-ninth century, they became more organised and came in their thousands, not just to steal goods but also to gain land and the rights of settlement.

'Gipeswic' survived until the Norman invasion in 1066, but following the Conquest it fell into a period of severe impoverishment before recovering to consolidate its position as a major port and trading centre.

As the 12th century drew to a close the town became fully established as an urban entity that played an important role in the life of the nation. It had survived invasion by the Celts, Romans, Saxons and Vikings before adapting to Anglo-Norman rule. However, another influence also had its effect on the town and it is one that has left monuments of the most profound and enduring kind – church buildings and street names.

Christianity reached East Anglia sometime during the seventh century and, as Dr Taylor remarked, 'like all new converts, those who embraced the new faith wished their friends, and compelled their enemies, to do likewise'. The new religion not only replaced paganism but also converted many of its traditions to suit the new regime and, like the later Norman invasion, its effects on the town proved irrevocable. A goodly proportion of the street names seen in modern Ipswich bear witness to the Christian influence: Christchurch, St Lawrence, St Margaret, St Mary, St Matthew, St Stephen, Holy Wells, Lady Lane, Franciscan Way, Grey Friars and others.

From the beginning, 'Gipeswic's' inhabitants have been in continuous contact with the rest of Europe and its growth built on the maritime industries of trade and shipbuilding. However, although Ipswich is among the most ancient boroughs in England it has less to show for it than some others. Ipswich is as famous for what it has destroyed over the centuries as it is for what can still be seen, which illustrates the unsentimental nature of the place. If old houses need knocking down to make way for a new road, then down they go. The word demolish and its derivatives feature largely in the history of Ipswich. It is not only antiquities that suffer the chop; a lot of the redevelopment that took place in the 1950s and 1960s was pulled down in the 1980s and 1990s, most famously the concrete Greyfriars complex that became not so much a white elephant as a grey monstrosity and had to be drastically redesigned in the late 1990s.

Such character derives from the grit of a commercial town and port: Ipswich changed because it could afford to. Through its commerce it had the resources to alter its circumstances and did so as proof of its prosperity. Those towns that fell into poverty or lost their earlier status and wealth remained as they were; that Ipswich does not now attract the modern tourist to view its fossilised, 'twee' exterior does not mean it has no history.

Another important influence on the character of Ipswich derives from the 400 or so years spent here by the mendicant orders of friars. Mendicant friars (from the Latin 'mendicare' meaning to beg) had a different role to monks, namely their refusal to hold permanent endowments and depend entirely on voluntary contributions or alms. Several orders sprang up during the early years of the 13th century and out of necessity needed to live in towns where alms were plentiful. They owed their popularity to their preference for going out into the world instead of withdrawing from it, as did the Benedictines or those who sought the agrarian solitude of the countryside, the Cistercians. The mendicant orders – Dominicans, Franciscans, Carmelites and Austin Friars – did not build fabulous abbeys or glorious cathedrals financed by rich patrons; instead, their poverty contrasted with the rapidly increasing wealth of the monastic foundations.

There were so many friars here in mediaeval times that they were a frequent and inescapable sight on the streets and lanes of 'Gipeswic' as they moved among the townspeople, preaching, teaching and ministering to the sick. Indeed, it was their popularity as preachers that caused jealousy among the ordinary lay clergy, who resented the crowds that flocked to the Priory Halls, halls that they did not own but were provided by philanthropic trustees for their use.

None of the friaries survived Henry VIII's Dissolution of the Monasteries, and now there is little physical evidence of their time here. Only a few stones of the Greyfriars complex survive and nothing is left of the mediaeval Chapel of Our Lady, which brought certain kudos to the town until the 16th century. That Ipswich had the mixed blessing of having Cardinal Thomas Wolsey as the 'local boy' meant that Ipswich experienced its own mini-Reformation some years before the real thing, in preparation for what was to be a college rivalling that at Oxford. The rise and fall of Wolsey, at one time the most powerful man in England, is part of Ipswich history and all that is left is for us to wonder what the town might have become if his college had become established and the events of Henry's split with Rome in 1538 had taken a different turn. The example set by Wolsey in his dissolution of the small, local monasteries to finance his college gave confidence to Henry in the 1540s to do the same, albeit for other reasons. Although Wolsey himself had already been dead for 10 years, his influence was on the Dissolution of the Monasteries and is of pivotal importance in British history.

The most significant influence shaping the character of Ipswich is its maritime commerce and, from the very beginning, its access to the world beyond East Anglia. The great scholars of the day did not make for the hallowed portals of Ipswich, but the merchants, traders and craftsmen did, bringing with them practical applications of trade and commerce. With merchant shipping at its height in the second half of the 16th century, the town flourished. Elizabeth I visited it three times, in 1561, 1565 and 1577, with possibly two visits in 1561. This was not necessarily welcomed by all the townspeople, though it undoubtedly enhanced the town's prestige as the inhabitants were taxed to pay for it, or 'assessed to the cost and charges for the entertainment of the Queen'. In 1561 one burgess was assessed at £8, and on hearing this he refused to pay. The Great Court promptly exercised its power and disenfranchised him. The man was so scorned that he finally paid not only the £8 but also the additional fine of £6 to restore his standing in the community.

In return for this hospitality, the Queen reaffirmed the town's charters of liberty and freedoms, partook of what 'entertainment' was on offer and made disparaging remarks about the 'slackness of the clergy' and the disgusting state of the Ipswich streets. Following her somewhat petulant remarks, the town, slighted by regal disapproval, made arrangements in 1571 to begin paving the town's streets which, as it happened, was the earliest such act to be obtained by any borough in England.

In 1784, Francois de La Rochefoucauld visited Ipswich:

'The town is badly built, the streets narrow, without any alignment, and the road-surface as bad as could be. As England is short of stone, the towns that are paved are paved with cobbles tightly packed, which present the foot with a series of bumps, as disagreeable when you are riding in a carriage as when you are walking.'

The radical parliamentarian William Cobbett visited in 1830 and found the town 'substantially built, well paved, every thing good and solid, and no wretched dwellings to be seen on its outskirts'. The town suburbs were still in the future. *Pigot's Commercial Directory* for 1830 says:

'The streets do not run regular, and, being rather narrow, are not particularly striking; but many of the shops being very elegant, and the town well paved, and lighted with gas, make up in a great measure the deficiency.'

During the 19th and 20th centuries much of the destruction of ancient streets was done to accommodate modern transport, although such adjustments were not a new concept. Muriel Clegg writes:

'A mediaeval street had, by law, to be sufficiently broad for two loaded carts to meet, and for sixteen armed knights to ride abreast'.

In our own time it is cars and lorries that dictate the route and width of streets and are wholly responsible for much of the destruction of the town's narrower streets and lanes. If only we had known that by the 1990s the car would no longer be king, and that much of the town would be pedestrianised, there could well be more of the beautiful and historic structures left than is the case. But, as the author of William Hunt's 1864 guide wrote:

'Ipswich is a progressive town and the need for improvement and enterprise has effaced the traces of antiquity, the signs of our fore-fathers left of their existence and their doings, more quickly and more completely than in almost any ancient town you may visit.'

So, with much of the physical evidence gone, where better to look for clues of well over 1,000 years of history than using its present street and road names to mark known but unseen sites and scenes of the past? In Ipswich, where so much has been wiped away by evolving urbanity, history is not at all obvious, although there is considerable documentation to assist in finding out how the town arrived at the 21st century looking as it does.

John Wodderspoon (1806–1862) compiled *Memorials of the Ancient Town of Ipswich* and observed that, while the chief memorials of antiquity had been 'enumerated and described', there were changes taking place even as he wrote. There were extensive alterations and 'improvements' constantly going on and, to his regret, 'involve, in many instances, an entire removal of the few remaining memorials of olden time'. Wodderspoon, writer, artist and journalist with the *Suffolk Chronicle*, rightly deemed it necessary to record in detail what 'under less changeful circumstances, would meet with but a passing notice'.

Similarly, when Dr J.E. Taylor wrote *In and About Ancient Ipswich* (1888), he was moved to carry out a similar recording of what was left of Ipswich's past, bemoaning the day by day 'improvements' that were imposed on the 'quaint ancient streets and picturesque old houses,' removing them from the face of the earth. Almost in desperation, he wrote:

'Even since these sentences were written, one old Ipswich street (Carr Street), and some old houses on the quay and other parts of the town have been modernized.'

Arthur Mee looked kindly on Ipswich in 1941 and rejoiced in the fact that, in spite of its old age, Ipswich had refused to grow up and 'keeps its poky little streets and passages so that they are choked with traffic and people'. They were crowded and 'so narrow that the noise cannot escape from them'. He wondered how many towns there were with so many 'old-world peeps just round the corner, so many quaint little places to excuse our sauntering'. You only had to walk down any street in the heart of Ipswich, he wrote, and there is something old in them.

It has not been possible, by any means, to include all streets in this book but those selected will, it is hoped, tell at least part of the story of Ipswich.

Grateful thanks are extended to all the people I met along the way who were kind enough to pass on their memories of the town, especially the Blue Guides, who share their interest and knowledge with numerous visitors each year, Brian Dyes at the Ipswich Transport Museum and Sally Dummer at the Ipswich Museums & Galleries. Thanks also to:
Archant (Suffolk)
Bill Barton
Dr John Blatchly
Anthony Coe
Hazel Clover
Vi Congalton
Elizabeth Crawford
Kenneth J Goward
Ipswich Arts Association
Ipswich Borough Council
Ipswich Borough Council Museums & Galleries
Ipswich Transport Museum
Dr Priscilla Silver
Robert Simper
Roy Tricker
And to my husband, Christopher, who took some of the photographs.

IPSWICH STREET BY STREET

The Romans undoubtedly had a certain influence on the origins of Ipswich, but the town is principally Anglo-Saxon, its street patterns set down by the end of the eighth century. The nature of Ipswich could also be described as Anglo-Saxon, in the sense that these were the first people to truly colonise the land, and they bestowed on it a character steeped in practicality and a Germanic lack of sentimentality. The town's vulnerability to attack led to a certain stoicism in the Ipswich character and a resignation that each time it was ransacked it would, in due course, be repaired and restored. Dr Taylor thought that 'Ipswichians must have been a plucky people' since they spent much of their time restoring the fortifications.

Whatever structures the Romans left behind in 400 AD became the nucleus for the new town. It began to develop near the quayside, where traffic to and from the port made it one of the most important centres in north-west Europe, and during the eighth century fanned out northwards. Long before the mid-ninth century, when the Danes began to attack East Anglia in earnest, the basic shape of the town's lanes and streets was already laid down.

Many street names are mediaeval in origin and invariably refer to the nature of business carried on there – such as Cornhill, Buttermarket, Cooks Row, Curriers Lane, Tavern Street and Rope Walk. Three mark the mediaeval town entrances – North, South and Westgate Streets. Others take the name of a popular or convenient inn or tavern, although occasionally it works the other way round.

Several did not come into being until first the Georgians then the Victorians embarked on urban expansion. The Victorians commemorated local benefactors or dignitaries and, naturally, immortalised their Queen and the Prince Consort. For most of the time, in true Ipswich fashion, the townspeople were not slow, or even reluctant, to accept the altered nomenclature. By adding Fonnereau, Cobbold, Anglesea and the rest they were claiming their own immortality.

Information about street origins is invariably gleaned from maps, beginning with John Speed's 1610 plan, which is the earliest known town map and lists five streets, including 'Kinge Stret', 'Corne hill' and 'Broke Stret' (King Street, Cornhill and Brook Street). Although Speed's map contains some mistakes in the key, it is nevertheless an invaluable guide to mediaeval Ipswich. After John Ogilby's 1674 town plan came Joseph Pennington's 1777 map which, for the first time, had street names inserted in it and began the move for the names to be properly displayed 'after the manner of those in London', which would 'give Ipswich an ascendancy over other places'.

Later mapmakers, such as Edward White (1867), and numerous other antiquaries, notably Dr J.E. Taylor, J.W. Wodderspoon and G.R. Clarke, have all added to the picture. Towards the end of the 19th century the borough itself began to draw up plans in preparation for road-widening schemes and 20th and 21st-century planners produced a prodigious quantity of paperwork.

The first permanent fixing of nameplates began in 1778. Irritated by the old joke that Ipswich was a town of streets without names – resurrected by Sir James Thornhill in 1711, referring to the derisory remarks allegedly made by the Duke of Buckingham to Charles II – town leaders raised a subscription to give Ipswich its 'ascendancy over other places', at least in the matter of street plates. The fashion of street numbering did not begin until the second half of the 19th century, but became a necessity when census enumerators and tax administrators needed to fix properties more precisely.

ANGEL LANE

Angel Lane took its name from the Angel inn that stood at the corner of Fore Street and Angel Lane, but it was redeveloped in the 1970s when the new

Star Lane road system was built. A small part of Angel Lane became part of Waterworks Street. All that is left is a spur off the north end of Fore Street, although the pub that lent its name has gone.

The name Angel indicates an inn of some antiquity and originally represented the Archangel Gabriel in the days when pre-Reformation Catholicism ruled everyday life, and inns catered for pilgrims as well as travellers. The earliest inn sign would have shown the Archangel with a scroll in his hands, which contained the words he spoke at the Annunciation.

G.R. Clarke writes of a very early malt kiln on Common Quay that was reputed to belong to a house of Cistercian monks and was called 'The Angel'. There is no subsequent history of the Cistercians in Ipswich since they were an order that preferred the isolation and self-sufficiency of the countryside, but it could be the root of the name.

ANGLESEA ROAD

The 17th-century name for Anglesea Road was Peddars or Pedders Lane, and it forms the western end of a continuous thoroughfare, the eastern side of which is Fonnereau Road (then called Dairy Lane). In the 1880s William Budden remembered with fond nostalgia when 'Anglesea Road, in my school days, was the favourite country lane walk from the Norwich Road to old Tacket Street Chapel, with green hedges and pollard oaks'.

On John Kirby's 1755 plan of the Christchurch Estate the entire area north of Pedders Way to the present Henley Road consisted of fields.

The spelling of Anglesea seems to have no significance, as observed by A.A. Moffat:

'In the old records the custom was for the scribe to spell a name according to his own fancy, as to how it sounded. There was little or no uniformity of spelling and consequently it was not always easy at first sight to recognise a name. One that kept me guessing for some little while was Sanicolastreet [St Nicholas Street].'

White's Directory recorded the hospital as 'a handsome structure' and built 'upon a bold eminence, overlooking the town and a wide extent of the surrounding country'. This aerial view also shows the playing fields of Ipswich School.

The road was named for either Sir Henry William Paget (1768–1854), 1st Marquis of Anglesey, who fought at Waterloo, or his son, General Lord George Augustus Frederick Paget (1818–1880), who gave Lord Cardigan 'his best support' and led the 4th Light Dragoons in the Charge of the Light Brigade in 1854.

A short way along Norwich Road is the Inkerman public house, named in celebration of Lord Paget's command at the Inkerman Battle in 1854, plus a Paget Road leading off Anglesea Road, as well as Redan Street and Cardigan Street (also with Crimean War association).

General Henry Paget commanded the 7th Light Dragoons, which regiment was among those garrisoned in Ipswich early in the 19th century. Under his direction, the dragoons became a highly respected unit, and in 1808 Paget led the British cavalry 'with distinction' during the Peninsular War. In that year George Elers, Captain in the 12th Regiment of Foot, wrote in his memoirs:

'The town of Ipswich at this time was full of military – the 10th Light Dragoons, the 7th ditto, under Lord Paget, the West Suffolk Militia, the Hertford ditto, etc.'

In 1963 the writer Michael Brander added:

'As we know that Peter Hawker's regiment, the

14th Light Dragoons, were also stationed there the town must indeed have been "full of military". The streets must have presented a vivid spectacle with the militia in their scarlet coats and buff waistcoats and the light dragoons booted and spurred in their gorgeous gold trimmed uniforms.'

Sir Henry was later to be second-in-command to Wellington at Waterloo, but his 'career' with the General came to an abrupt end when he eloped with the sister-in law of his commander.

The proximity of Barrack Corner and Barrack Lane are reminders of the heavy military presence thereabouts, and Ipswich remained a barracks town until the 1930s when the main garrison between Anglesea Road and Norwich Road was closed.

The barracks did not spread as far up as 'Peddars', and in the 1850s Charles Fonnereau proposed that Peddars Lane should be developed to make 'a good wide road from Norwich Road past the front of the Hospital to Globe Lane', a proposal readily accepted by the council, who abandoned the green hedges and pollard oaks to their fate in the name of progress. Work was carried out to make the new road, though it was almost permanently in a bad state of repair, and even seven years after it was widened it needed constant attention.

In 1880 Anglesea Road was among the first to be laid by a tar path, a road surface which was to cause the Ipswich Authority no end of trouble. A steamroller was required to complete the tar surface, but the street committee considered a roller was not required. Obviously, though, the road did need rolling as eventually a 10-ton roller was purchased. It was tried out first at Barrack Corner where it was drawn across a thick layer of Cornish granite. Unfortunately the roller was not sufficiently heavy, and the *Ipswich Journal* reported that the stone 'rolled up in front of the roller as if it had been passing over a feather bed'.

The East Suffolk & Ipswich Hospital and Dispensary was founded in 1835 and the original building cost around £2,500. It was built of white brick and stone 'overlooking the town and a wide extent of the surrounding countryside'. It stood in the centre of about two acres of land, purchased by the Trustees of the Revd W.C. Fonnereau, and 'tastefully laid out in lawns, gardens and shrubberies'.

In 1918, as a practical part of the Ipswich War Memorial to the Great War, a new wing was added to the hospital on adjoining land on what had been the Victorian Militia Depot. Plans were raised for the new extension, and by 1924 the amount subscribed was £50,846 (of which £5,000 was allocated to the Memorial in Christchurch Park).

During 1987 an 8-feet high tunnel was discovered running from Anglesea Road to Christchurch Park. Its precise origins and use were not discovered, although it had once been used as a cellar for the barracks.

The hospital served the town well until the new hospital was built on Heath Road in the 1970s. The building is now the Anglesea Heights Nursing Home.

ARCADE STREET

Arcade Street was developed in the mid-19th century and takes its name from the archway that stands at the junction with Elm Street and Lion Street, continuing on to King Street.

Woodcock & Son frontage before the 2004 renovations. The suffragette Constance Andrews was feted here after her release from gaol. (photo: Woodcock & Son)

Two years after the Museum was built in 1850, the Paving and Lighting Committee agreed to construct a link road between Museum Street and the ancient Thursby's Lane (shown on Ogilvy's map as extending to Elm Street, then Boat Lane). A cut was made through the house and one-time offices of the Ipswich and Suffolk Banking Company and the road was built across the garden, the rest of which gave way, in time, to houses built on both sides of the street. Although the buildings look Georgian, they date from the 1840s, when the new street was made.

One of these is Birketts, the solicitors, and it was here that Wallis Simpson came after she had obtained her divorce on 17 October 1936. Bessie Wallis Warfield was born in Baltimore, US, in 1896 and was on her second marriage, to Ernest Simpson, when she met Prince Edward, heir to the throne of England. The two embarked on a relationship that was to rock the British Empire and eventually cause the abdication of the king. It was Wallis's 17-minute court hearing at Ipswich County Hall, at which she obtained her divorce from Ernest, which made it possible for Edward VIII to tell the nation in his abdication speech:

'You must believe me when I tell you that I have found it impossible to carry the heavy burden of responsibility and to discharge my duty as King as I would wish to do, without the help and support of the woman I love.'

The premises now occupied by Woodcock & Son once housed the Ipswich branch of the Women's Freedom League (WFL). Here the suffragette and tax resister Constance Emily Andrews was brought after her triumphant release from gaol after refusing to pay her dog licence.

Constance lived at 160 Norwich Road and was secretary of the Ipswich and County branch of the National Union for Women's Suffrage Societies (NUWSS) before moving over to the more militant WFL where she was secretary from 1907 until 1913. Constance owned a dog and, although very fond of

it, resented the fact that while she was forced to pay a dog tax she had no say in parliamentary elections. In May 1911 Constance came up before the Bench for non-payment of the fine and the magistrate sentenced her to a week in gaol. The *East Anglian Daily Times* (*EADT*) declared:

'At last an Ipswich Suffragette has brought herself within the meshes of the law … for some time it appeared as if the authorities did not wish to take drastic steps for the incarceration of the fair Suffragist, who had taken care to make over all her effects to her sister, Mrs Pratt, so that officers of the law would have to imprison her in the end.'

She was, said the editorial, one of the pioneers of the movement in Suffolk and one of the first 'martyrs' of the cause, even though she was 'a lady of culture and well versed on many social questions, especially those relating to women's industry'.

Police went to 160 Norwich Road, but were told that Constance and Miss Lily Rowe were 'perusing a magazine in the Mechanics Institute'. There she was apprehended and 'the two ladies walked from the room and took the cab that was waiting to take them to the prison'.

Sentenced to seven days without hard labour, Constance made further trouble for the authorities by declaring herself a vegetarian. As they were 'somewhat puzzled as to what constituted

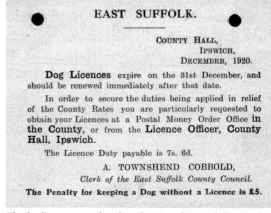

EAST SUFFOLK.

COUNTY HALL,
IPSWICH,
DECEMBER, 1920.

Dog Licences expire on the 31st December, and should be renewed immediately after that date.

In order to secure the duties being applied in relief of the County Rates you are particularly requested to obtain your Licences at a Postal Money Order Office **in the County,** or from the **Licence Officer, County Hall, Ipswich.**

The Licence Duty payable is 7s. 6d.

A. TOWNSHEND COBBOLD,
Clerk of the East Suffolk County Council.

The Penalty for keeping a Dog without a Licence is £5.

The dog licence was enforced until 1988 and cost 7 shillings and 6 (old) pence for the whole of its statutory duration.

vegetarian dietary', they readily availed themselves of the Home Secretary's discretionary powers and allowed Constance's meals to be brought into prison by her sister, Lilla Pratt. In fact, Lilla was not her sister but had been the family housemaid when Constance, together with her mother and sister, had lived and worked at Cheltenham Ladies College.

However, as she was only allowed 'family visits' she might have found herself on short rations if she had no family. Also it no doubt amused Constance to put one over on both the press and the prison authorities.

On 27 May 1911 the *EADT* reported:

'Immense gathering assembled outside the gates of Ipswich Prison in Grimwade Street on Friday morning in the hope of witnessing the release of Miss Constance Andrews, after undergoing a week's imprisonment.'

Among the gathering was Mrs Charlotte Despard, 'that grand old lady of the women's movement', who was a high-profile celebrity and her presence was a feather in the cap of Ipswich suffragists. Mrs Despard, President and founder of the WFL, led a rousing cheer when Constance appeared, and after a brief rally she and Constance were driven at walking pace along St Helens' Street, Carr Street, St Matthew's Street and down Museum Street to Arcade Street, accompanied by women carrying banners and chanting slogans. There the party was given breakfast, with Mrs Hossack, one of the Ipswich pioneers, saying that they all felt very proud of the activities of the local suffragettes and that Constance was the first Ipswich woman to be imprisoned for her beliefs.

In reply, Constance said that, as far as it went, Ipswich prison 'was very satisfactory, clean, well ventilated and everything was as good as a prison could be, though very little air came in.' She added that no woman should pay the dog licence and that if they did not have a dog they should buy one so that the prisons would be full.

That evening there was a meeting in the Old Museum Rooms (next door, in Museum Street) with Mrs Despard as the main speaker on the Women's Enfranchisement Bill, then before parliament. It was noted in the press that Constance was among those who 'dodged the census' in 1901 by being in the Old Museum Rooms.

Woodcocks are an old-established firm, founded in London in 1850. They opened an office in Aldeburgh in 1890 and came to Ipswich in the 1920s, first to offices on Princess Street and then to Museum Street in around 1926. Although the firm now specialises in 'classic homes in Ipswich, period and country property', their root business lay in agriculture and farming.

The offices were not far from the Corn Exchange or the cattle market, so on Tuesdays (market day) Woodcocks welcomed plenty of their customers taking the opportunity to transact this or that business. John Woodcock, the fifth generation of the family to run what is still an independently owned and managed family firm, remembers that in the days before the market closed for good they had plenty of 'mucky and muddy boots over the threshold'!

ARRAS SQUARE

Arras Square was created and named when the Buttermarket Shopping Centre was built in 1992 and is named for the town of Arras in Pas de Calais in the north of France, with which Ipswich has a Charter of Cooperation. Since 1993 the town was 'twinned' with Arras, but in 2003 the new Charter was signed and the communities of Ipswich and Arras agreed to cooperate on the mutual objective of promoting education, economic development and cultural, sporting and social exchanges.

Here is a true mixture of old and new as the modern symbol of European friendship has on its edge the 15th-century Church of St Stephen, which, in its new incarnation as the Tourist Information Centre (TIC), welcomes visitors from all over the world. There are places to sit in tree shade and, although the hustle and bustle of the town is nearby,

There is a plaque in Arras Square dedicated to M Bernard Durot who was the prime French force for establishing the link with Ipswich in the 1990s. (photo: Ipswich Borough Council)

there is no immediate traffic noise, and it is a favourite place for buskers.

Since 1993 many Ipswich clubs and societies have visited Arras, including the Triangle (Ipswich) Motorcycle Club, Ipswich Rugby Club and several local football teams. A group of singers who gave the first provincial rendition of Haydn's 'Creation' in their first concert, and who arrange performances with their French counterpart, is the Ipswich Choral Society, founded in 1824 and one of the oldest choral societies in England.

Inside the Buttermarket Shopping Centre is a yellow French post box (from which collections are made by the Royal Mail), and at the Place d'Ipswich in Arras can be found a red telephone box.

Students from the Suffolk College work in cooperation with French schools and each year the borough council arranges and plays host to work placement students. The spirit of 'entente cordiale' became a visible reality when, in 2004, the

placement students were set to work in the Tourist Information Centre.

St Stephen's now faces the vast, glazed edifice that is the Buttermarket Shopping Centre, and in spite of contrasting symbols a thousand years apart it retains its dignity. Arthur Mee wrote of it as 'an oasis of silence in the noisy streets', and in 1982 Roy Tricker thought St Stephen's 'a humble building, situated in a quiet lane, amongst trees. The churchyard has been made into a place where people can sit in peace and quiet'.

The church structure is 15th and 16th century restoration, but a church was founded here before the Domesday Book was compiled in 1086. It has a false floor because when it was converted to the TIC visitors had to step down into it as the street level had risen since its foundations were laid down. It is mentioned in Domesday as being held by Godrick and had a small parish, consisting mostly of the residents of Brook Street. Excavation in the nave in

St Stephen's Church is now the Tourist Information Centre, opposite the Buttermarket Shopping Centre. (Ipswich Borough Council)

the 1970s suggested the core of a Norman tower in the south porch. In the 15th century the Ipswich Corporation granted a piece of land on the west of the churchyard to the church, in consideration that a red rose was yearly rendered, if demanded, and is, says Wodderspoon, 'fortunately almost the only association Ipswich has with the famous and fatal Wars of the Roses'.

Inside, the church contains several memorials, including that of Robert Leman (one time Lord Mayor of London) and his wife, Mary. Their son and four daughters are beneath the kneeling couple, both having died on the same day, 'the same sun that closed her eyes in the morning shutting up his in the evening'. They are remembered in a poem that reads:

'Beneath this monument entombed lie
A rare remark of a conjugal tye.
Robert and Mary, who to show how neere
They did comply, How to each other deere.
One loath behind the other long to stay
(As married) Died together in one day.
  3rd Sept 1637'.

There is also a monument to Miss Clara Reeve, the 18th century author of 'The Old English Baron' and 'Exiles', whose father was perpetual curate of the parish of St Nicholas. Clara was said to be a 'woman of considerable literary attainments'. *Hunt's Guide* said:

'The few interesting incidents of her life may be found in a short biographical account of her career by Sir Walter Scott. She died in 1807 and was buried in St Stephens'.

BARRACK CORNER and BARRACK LANE

Barrack Corner is applied generally to the busy junction where Norwich Road meets Clarkson Street, London Road, Burlington Road, Portman Road, St Matthew's and Barrack Lane. The name Barrack is a reminder of the huge military presence here after the cavalry barracks were built in St Matthew's parish. During the Napoleonic wars, temporary barracks were set up near Stoke Bridge and on Woodbridge Road but more permanent arrangements were made in the area around Barrack Corner, which turned Ipswich into a garrison town.

In 1759 the War Office wrote to the Duke of Grafton that it was the King's command for the militia of the County of Suffolk to be embodied in two battalions, the 1st or Western Battalion, under the Command of Colonel the Honourable Nassau, to march to Bury St Edmunds, and the 2nd, or Eastern Battalion, commanded by Colonel Francis Vernon, to Ipswich. The Militia were, however, only to be paid from the day of marching and there was a certain pecking order in arrival and it was first come, first served in respect of barracks:

'The regiment of Militia which first arrives in camp, or quarters, shall have seniority there, the next which arrives being deemed junior, and so on, as they march in successively.'

Muriel Clegg writes:
'In 1786 the Government purchased a large house at the far end of St Matthew's Street, with grounds extending to Angelsea Road. Construction of the barracks which were to contain 1,500 men proceeded rapidly.'

By 1795 a permanent base was established for the cavalry called Horse Barracks, and the first regiment to move in were the 2nd or Queen's Regiment of

View across Barrack Corner from the GFS in the 1960s. Where Barrack Lane meets St Matthew's is the Old Half Moon and Stars public house, restored in 1999 by the Ipswich Building Preservation Trust, which is now a private residence.

Dragoon Guards, nicknamed 'the Bays' because in 1762 they were mounted for the first time on bay horses.

In October 1805 the Duke of York arrived in Ipswich to inspect the troops and stayed the night at the house of Lord Paget, Marquis of Anglesea. The following morning, in heavy rain and 'amidst a multitude of spectators', he inspected the troops on Rushmere Heath:

'The Royal Berkshire, Shropshire, R E Middlesex, Hertford, and W Suffolk regiments of militia; a detachment of the Royal Artillery, Royal Horse Artillery, British Dragoons, (the Greys) and the 7th and 21st Light Dragoons, amounting to 8,000 men.'

Some years later it was decided to extend the accommodation in the town. In 1830 G.R. Clarke wrote:

'In consequence of the introduction of a great many troops during the late war, the place being considered as a garrison town, it was roused from its apathy and dullness, and quickly became the scene of bustle, business and importance; lodgings and houses were let at high prices to the officers and their families, and many new houses were erected.'

Inevitably, the huge influx of the military caused problems in the town, not least on market days, and townspeople found the noise intolerable. Writing in 1816, Sarah Trimmer declared 'you cannot get through a street without hearing drums and trumpets and meeting troops of soldiers'.

On the corner of St Matthew's Street stands Alexander House, a landmark building which was built around 1850 for the Quaker banker and noted 19th-century photographer Richard Dykes Alexander (1788–1865), son of Dykes Alexander (and later occupied by his nephew, William Dillwyn

Sims). R.D. Alexander was a partner in the family firm of Alexander and Company but retired early to devote himself to public work and photography. At one time part of the building was used as the Post Office's telephone exchange and between 1955 and the mid-1970s became the Wing Training Centre for the PO's thousands of telephonists. In 2005 Alexander House was acquired for development.

Barrack Corner was also the site for a studio used by the Victorian photographer William Vick, who for some 30 years ran a thriving photographic business. Vick took over the business that stood at the junction of Clarkson Street and London Road in about 1870 from William Cobb, a 'photographic artist'. Vick rightfully claimed to produce 'very superior' portrait and landscape photographs and, because of his proximity to the cavalry barracks, was also an 'equestrian photographer'.

Robert Malster writes:

'The works for which he is best remembered today are undoubtedly his views of Ipswich streets, which he issued both as separate mounted prints and in three bound volumes. They show Ipswich before the coming of the electric trams, and before the age of the motor car; the horse reigned supreme, hauling everything from tradesmen's carts and gentlemen's carriages to the early trams introduced in 1880.'

Just off Barrack Corner, on what was open countryside until the mid-1850s, stands 1 Burlington Road, which is the marker for the Burlington Road development that began in the 1860s. This was for many years the Girls' Friendly Society (GFS) Hostel and was home to many girls who had left their country homes for the towns in the days before they could have flats or bed-sits of their own. Board and lodging was provided, with a warden to supervise and run the establishment.

The GFS was founded in 1875 when an Irish woman living in London, Mary Elizabeth Townsend, became concerned about young girls coming to the towns to go into service. With this in mind, she founded the GFS so that the girls would

Group of girls in the GFS hostel in 1963 (author seated left of fireplace).

have friends and safe lodging, with someone to turn to if they had problems. The Ipswich residential hostel was opened in about 1925 and was an extension of Miss Beck's Burlington Sunday School. Although the GFS is still a worldwide organisation, the hostel had outlived its usefulness by the late 1980s and has been closed for some years. It is now divided into flats.

On 30 April 1915 Barrack Corner sustained a Zeppelin attack. The first bomb fell near the corner and the second at the top of Waterloo Road. Later, in March 1916, more Zeppelin damage was done in Key Street and a man was killed in Lower Orwell Street.

BERNERS STREET

This street name commemorates the Berners family, and it was built in the 1830s as an approach to the Anglesea Road Hospital from St Matthew's Street and was echoed in the Berners Arms Coffee Tavern that stood at the corner of St Matthew's Street. In the 18th and 19th century Berners Street was home to officers from the nearby Anglesea Road barracks.

In 1773 William Berners (1710–1783) bought an estate in Woolverstone, about four miles outside town, and built a magnificent hall, designed by architect and surveyor John Johnson, who had worked for William Berners on the development of the Berners estate in Marylebone, London.

William's son, Charles Berners (1740–1815), drove the first motorised vehicle, a De Dion powered tricycle, into Ipswich in November 1896. He had bought the machine in Paris several months earlier but had been unable to use it anywhere other than on his private land until the necessary laws legalised its use on public thoroughfares. He drove into town to visit Mr Popplewell's cycle shop on Woodbridge Road and in doing so made history.

In the glory days of ballroom dancing there was a popular studio of Ballroom Dancing at 75 Berners Street, offering private lessons daily and classes twice a week. The result of these lessons could be tried out at the regular 'Saturday Night at Eight' dances at the Arlington Ballroom in Museum Street, where the resident band, the Arlington Quartet, would provide 'music in strict tempo'.

BLACK HORSE LANE

Accessed at its north end from Westgate via Lady Lane or by Black Horse Walk, the Lane goes south from Westgate Street opposite the Bon Marche shop. It was part of the ancient town rampart at the point of the old West Gate, curving southwards towards Curriers Lane, and it now forms the eastern boundary of the 1960s Civic Centre development. Somehow it survived the building of the Civic Centre, Crown Court and police station, which line its western edge.

Dr Taylor recorded:

'Down the historic Lady Lane, some of the rows of cottages or 'courts' at the lower end of the street are on ground raised two or three feet above the Lane, and between it and Black Horse Lane. This is all now left here of the old Ramparts; and it would hardly be noticed except for knowledge of the fact that the ancient wall went this way.'

In the 18th century it was known as Gaol Lane and ran parallel with Lady Lane (then a much longer lane leading across the Wolsey car park). In the vicinity of the car park is the approximate site of the old town gaol, built by a town bailiff, John Caldwell, in 1448. The name Gaol Lane was obviously accurate and appropriate and continued in use as long as the gaol did, which was more or less until the new county gaol was built in St Helen's in 1786. In 1822 the premises were sold by auction for £730 and demolished.

A little while afterwards, Gaol Lane became Black Horse Lane, named after one of the many hostelries in that part of town and briefly described by Dr Taylor as 'another old Ipswich house, as the gables and yard plainly indicate'.

An old guide described the Black Horse inn as standing 'on the Mount at the lower end of the land to which it gives its name'. When it was built in the mid-16th century it had spacious grounds surrounded by open fields and meadowland, and enjoyed an uninterrupted view of the River Gipping. Like many inns, it was once the house of a wealthy merchant and became a public house in the 18th century.

The Black Horse inn has associations with the Suffolk heroine Margaret Catchpole as it was here that her brother Charles enlisted in the 33rd Regiment of Foot. Although it closed briefly in 1973, it reopened three years later.

BOLTON LANE (formerly Little Bolton Lane)
There is some confusion about how Bolton Lane got its name, but Muriel Clegg suggests it could have been an 18th-century mapping error. There was a Great Bolton Lane (close to the West Gate) and a Little Bolton Lane leading off St Margaret's Green. The road leading northwards from the town (along the Bolton Lane route) was also known as Thingstead Way and recorded by Ogilby in 1674. This is entirely logical since it crossed that part of the town known since ancient times as Thingstead (see also St Margaret's Green). However, when Joseph Pennington made his map in 1777 the name Thingstead had gone, and the lane was instead named Bolton Lane. The hamlet of Bolton was on the other side of Christchurch Park but for reasons long since forgotten, and whether by mistake or not, the old Thingstead Way also became known as Bolton Lane.

To walk along Bolton Lane is to travel in the footsteps of the Augustinians Canons of the Holy Trinity, whose presence in the town between the 13th and 16th century helped to shape both its character and appearance. Their priory stood between the present Christchurch Mansion and St Margaret's Church, just north of Soane Street and west of Bolton Lane. It was established in 1204 by a confirmatory charter issued by King John. Part of the known precinct wall of the priory forms part of the northern boundary of St Margaret's churchyard. Dr Taylor writes:

Charles May and his two sons. (ITM Collection)

'St Margaret's Church is a noble building. Its row of clerestory and side aisle windows are seen to great advantage from the Green; and the splendid arboreal foliage of Christ Church park forms a good background. The older Trinity Church formerly stood near the present edifice.'

The Trinity Church would have been for the use of the Canons and St Margaret's for the parishioners. To judge from the Poll Tax returns of 1381, St Margaret's ministered to a large parish as it accounted for 19 percent of those taxed.

The Augustinians, sometimes called the Austin Friars, wore black cassocks with a white surplice and hooded black cloak and were thus named the Black Canons. They arrived in England at the beginning of the 12th century and by 1200 had some 140 foundations, two of which were in Ipswich. The Augustinians were renowned for selecting ancient holy sites for their houses, and while it is not known precisely what stood on the Bolton Lane site it is generally thought to have been an early church. It is

probable that the first community of Holy Trinity came from the other side of town, brother Augustinians from the Priory of St Peter and St Paul, immediately north of where the Church of St Peter still stands (see also College Street).

The churches appropriated to Holy Trinity were the town churches of St Mary le Tower (already in existence at the time of Edward the Confessor and annexed to the priory at its foundation), St Lawrence on Dial Lane, St Mary at the Elms and their 'home' church of St Margaret. Of the Holy Trinity Priory, only two relics remain: a 13th-century coffin lid (near the south door in St Margaret's) and the Canon's timber-framed Guest House on Soane Street (now the Guitar Shop).

St Margaret's Church, standing prominently on the west side of Bolton Lane, dates from the 13th century and is one of Ipswich's greatest treasures. H. Munro Cautley called it 'probably the finest church in the town' and suggests that it might have become the town's civic church, instead of St Mary le Tower, if it had been in the town and not outside the ramparts. D.P. Mortlock thought it 'undoubtedly the town's most handsome church' and Pevsner pronounced it to be 'certainly the most spectacular church in Ipswich'.

Its chief glory is the double hammerbeam nave roof, which was added at the close of the 15th century. The hammerbeam concept meant a tie beam was no longer necessary, the thrust of the roof's weight being taken on 'hammer' brackets. The ends of the hammers bear cut-out cartouches of arms with pierced tracery above the beams and wall posts. The posts are carved with figures, made headless by the iconoclast William Dowsing.

In the late 1980s an extensive programme to repair, restore and conserve St Margaret's was embarked upon and completed in 1996. During the rewriting of the new church guide, Dr John Blatchly discovered that the church was first dedicated to Margaret of Antioch, though more recently the church community has considered Margaret of Scotland to be the patron. However, the Revd David Cutts (Vicar of St Margaret's) wrote diplomatically

that they were continuing the affiliation to Margaret of Scotland, though 'we know it to be misplaced'. They had, he wrote, 'grown rather fond of the one-time Queen of Scotland and it is comforting to know that we are following a person with a more credible history!'

In the 19th century Bolton Lane was home to Charles and Nancy May, who arrived in Ipswich in 1836 to join Ransomes engineering business. In addition to being a partner with Robert Ransome, Charles May (1801–1860) was Fellow of the Royal Society (FRS), Fellow of the Royal Astronomical Society (FRAS), Member of the Institute of Civil Engineers (MICE) and a keen amateur astronomer (see Old Foundry Road).

May's family were members of the Society of Friends, or Quakers. He had gone as an apprentice to Mr Sims, a chemist in Stockport, where he married Mr Sim's daughter, Ann (called Nancy), before returning to the family business in Ampthill, Bedfordshire. Charles had visited Ipswich on at least one occasion, 'for the sale of drugs' as a pharmaceutical manufacturer, and many of the Ipswich Quakers were related to him directly or by marriage. His father's early partner, John Wise, moved to Ipswich with his young son in 1830, after his wife died, and there had been frequent visits between Ampthill and Ipswich.

Although Nancy initially missed their family and friends in Ampthill, she quickly immersed herself in Ipswich life, especially enjoying frequent invitations from the Ransomes, Dykes and Alexanders. There was a ready-made 'family' of Quaker society members, but she nevertheless wrote to her mother, betraying an attack of homesickness on the part of at least one son:

'Our dear boys are quite well, so full of life & spirits, when not at school it sometimes is as much as I can do to keep them within moderate bounds. They have lately taken a fancy to drawing which helps to pass these long evenings, they are now sitting at the table, what with shaking it & keeping up a constant chat I know I write more than usual, which is at all times poor. Robert often exclaims Ah! how I wish I could be at Ampthill.'

Soon, though, the Mays were entertaining visitors, Louise Hooper writing to Nancy in 1837:

'We were quite amused with your long company list but you will have to lengthen it yet. Really Ipswich seems in a fair way to become famous (in our society at least) as the place of resort for all. Aunt has heard that William Lucas, Joshua Ransom and Henry Brown are all Ipswich bound.'

Charles, Nancy and their four children spent much time visiting Robert Ransome, where they were 'very handsomely entertained'. There was plenty of activity in Bolton Lane, too, but all too often Nancy had to share Charles with one or other of his many interests. On one occasion 'in came George Alexander to consult him about steam navigation and bespeak his attendance at a meeting upon it this evening'.

Writing in *Astronomy Now*, Bill Barton records:

'At the suggestion of his friends Admiral Smyth and Dr John Lee, Charles joined the Royal Astronomical Society in 1836. During his lifetime Charles May engineered several telescopes, amongst which was the Northumberland refractor, the Greenwich great equatorial and the Airy transit circle.'

Charles also invented the two-hole paper punch, used for binding loose papers into a ring binder. He had seen the Astronomer Royal using a single hand punch and thought he could do better!

The Mays later moved to Carr Street, close to the Ransomes, and Charles continued as a partner in the firm, all the while developing his interest in astronomy, an interest he shared with Robert Ransome. They left Ipswich in 1851 when Charles

Seal of Trinity or Christ Church Priory drawn by Walter Hagreen for Wodderspoon's 'Ipswich'.

decided to pursue his career in London. Thereafter, he suffered a gradual decline in health and died in 1860. Their house in Bolton Lane later became a mental hospital, known as the 'Suffolk Idiot House'.

BRIDGE STREET
The seventh-century river crossing, and probably the original fording of the river, is still identified today as Stoke Bridge, at Bridge Street. This gave access from the town on the north of the river to the hamlet of Stoke ('over Stoke' in local parlance) on the south side and enabled access to Stoke Mills (see also Stoke Hamlet). It was also the mediaeval route south out of 'Gipeswic'. During excavations for the second Stoke crossing in 1981–82, several river banks were uncovered, each protected by a timber 'revetment' and identified as early eighth or ninth century.

Keith Wade points out that the river banks were

On the dock side of the bridge is the Trinity House buoy, in the traditional red and white colours of a middle ground buoy, marking the division of the Orwell into two channels. Painting by Charlotte Harvey who specialises in capturing the evolving landscape of the Ipswich Waterfront. (WAG Visual Arts)

roughly in line with College Street in the seventh century, and during excavations in 1981 the river was discovered to be wide, shallow and tidal, 'as it is further down the Orwell estuary today'. Land reclamation began in the eighth century and was continuous, each waterfront constructed nearer to the middle of the river and the land behind filled in, raised and developed.

There have been several bridges at that point over the centuries, and one is recorded in the Little Domesday Book of 1086. There is also a 14th-century reference to 'Peter's Bridge,' which might be Stoke Bridge. The height of the early bridges would have prevented river traffic from going up the Gipping and, because of the depth, the boats were of shallow draft. Only simple quays were needed for the boats to tie up and unload, although international trade was carried out throughout the eighth and ninth centuries. Keith Wade includes 'imported Norwegian hone stones, Rhenish lava

millstones and Frankish pottery', evidence of which have been discovered on sites along the ancient waterfront. The main trade link was with the River Rhine as well as with Belgium and Northern France and the whole of East Anglia.

John Wodderspoon listed several different bridges at the Stoke crossing, including one in the town books of 1300 when a town property holder, Thomas Alvarde, left 20 shillings a year 'for ever' for the maintenance of the bridge. During the reign of Henry VI, John de Caldwell offered to make a bridge at Stoke at his own cost, provided that the townspeople would pay pontage. A new bridge was built in the reign of Henry VII and 'an order passed the Great Court that all carters going over Stoke Bridge, lately built, shall pay towards the repairing and maintaining of the same'.

A stone bridge, built some time in the early 1600s, survived until 1818 when floods swept two of the arches away. *White's Directory* reported:

Stoke Bridge around 1890. (ITM Collection)

'A handsome and substantial cast-iron bridge, called Stoke Bridge, connects the town with the parish of Stoke, and was erected at the cost of £7,000 in lieu of the old stone bridge, which was destroyed by a flood on the 12th of April 1818.'

A temporary pontoon bridge had been thrown across the river, and a civil engineer called William Cubitt was approached to come up with plans for a new bridge. He produced plans for an iron bridge with a 60ft arch. It was decided that the new bridge should be of cast iron, and the contract was awarded to Ransome & Sons.

The new bridge was opened in June 1819 and served the town for the next 100 years. A concrete bridge replaced it in the 1920s and eventually the traffic became so great that a second was built alongside in 1982.

Bridge Street has now acquired a Y shape, linking Grey Friars with Vernon Street across the river and College Street. The Old Bell inn, 'reputedly the oldest pub in Ipswich', stands calmly at what is now a phenomenally busy junction as traffic merges from all directions onto the two roundabouts at the north end of Bridge Street. The inn marked a regular stopping place for those entering and leaving the town over the centuries, especially farmers and other carriers on market days. Dr Taylor writes:

'That the Old Bell inn existed in the parish of St Peter as far back as the year 1639 is clear from the town assembly books, where it is mentioned that "the posts lately erected by John Cole, ship carpenter, in the streete before his house in Peter's parish, against the Bell, shall stand at the rent of 6d".'

Until Vernon Street was created to accommodate the increased traffic, Bell Lane formed the main thoroughfare, and the Old Bell premises once had a large yard and stables. It is reputed that both Bell Lane and the inn were named for a bell foundry that once stood near the site.

BROOK STREET

One of the longest surviving streets in Ipswich, stretching northwards from the lower end of Foundation Street to Northgate Street, Brook Street's name can be traced back as far as Henry III and the very early years of the 13th century. It is possible that the name is associated with the ancient Manor of Brooks, or 'Brokesstrete', at the north end, but just as likely is its association with the brook that ran south along the route of the modern street. Sometimes it was known as 'Broc-steet', that name hardly needing explanation, though Dr Taylor wrote:

'There was no Water Works Company then, so there was an abundant supply of water, most of it flowing down the streets. To this day, Brook Street indicates the aquatic origin of its name. The ancient town authorities appear to have watched with the utmost jealousy their "water rights".'

The brook ran towards the river and was swelled on occasions by water coming from the numerous springs in what is now the Lower Arboretum of Christchurch Park. On Speed's 1610 map, the earliest known plan of the town, 'Broke Stret' runs in a direct and straight line from St Margaret's to St Mary 'Key' (at Quay), but Upper Brook Street now begins at the Great White Horse junction with Northgate Street (previously known as the top end of Brook Street).

From the earliest times the street was divided into two, Upper and Lower. There was a convenient halfway point at the junction with Tacket Street and Dog's Head Street where a cross or stone marker stood, known as Lewes Crouch (or Lieuescros). Thus, the lower half of the street was known as 'the highway from Lewis Crouch towards the Quay' or, of course, going from south to north as 'the highway from St Mary Quay to Lieuescros'. In the days before road signs or common literacy, these crosses were essential landmarks used in verbal directions.

Brook Street has always been a commercial highway. It is now a pot-pourri of architectural styles and it would seem has always been a mix of inns, private houses and, in modern times, shops and offices. Dr Taylor wrote that in the 1880s:

'Upper and Lower Brook Streets, here and there have sprinkled among the solidly-built Georgian brick houses, a few antique, picturesque, gable-fronted dwellings of a less pretentious character. The older of the poorer houses nearly all possess mansard roofs – perhaps an architectural relic of the days of the infamous window tax.'

Mansard roofs are curbed roofs with steeply pitched or curved lower slopes, almost invariably with dormer windows, and take their name from the French classical architect Francois Mansart (1598–1666).

Upper Brook Street

Many of the merchants' houses were converted into inns during the late 17th and early 18th century, one of the most important being the Coach and Horses (or the Coach House), which later became a hotel and stood opposite where Sainsbury's now stands on the corner of Dog's Head Street. The 16th-century building was remarkable because of its 'quaint gallery, staircase and courtyard' and was once a fine mansion belonging to Charles Brandon, 1st Duke of Suffolk (1485–1545) and his wife, Mary Tudor (1495–1533), Duchess of Brandon, Dowager Queen of France and sister of Henry VIII.

The love story of the Duke and Duchess of Suffolk was very nearly one of tragedy, had it not been for the nerve and daring of Charles Brandon and the support of Thomas Wolsey. Mary, although the favourite sister of Henry, was, nevertheless, intended for a political marriage not of her own choosing. 'She is very beautiful' wrote a Venetian merchant, 'and has not her match in all England – tall, fair and of a light complexion, affable and graceful.' No wonder that the already twice-married Charles fell in love with her. The king, however, thwarted his advances, and Mary was forced to choose her 'duty' to her brother, the king, before a love match of her own.

In 1514 she was despatched to France, albeit with a retinue of 400 barons and knights, 200 gentlemen and 80 ladies, where she married the elderly King Louis of France in October. Mary was crowned in November and widowed only three months later, on New Year's Day.

On hearing the news, Charles went quickly to Paris where he and Mary were married before Henry could stop them, without heed to Henry's displeasure and probable vengeance. The deed already done, the rapacious Henry resorted to extracting £24,000 in yearly instalments of £1,000 and the whole of Mary's £200,000 dowry from Louis plus all her plate and jewellery. He eventually gave the marriage his blessing through the intercession of Thomas Wolsey, who saved them from the worst of the king's anger.

Mary preferred Suffolk to court life in London, and while their main home was at Westhorpe near Bury St Edmunds she and her husband were frequently in Ipswich. Henry was always fond of her. Soon after he came to the throne he took charge of the royal fleet and commissioned a new flagship of the English fleet, the *Mary Rose*, named after his sister and their family emblem, the Tudor rose. In 1545 the *Mary Rose* suffered the ignominious fate of sinking on her maiden voyage, only a short way out to sea and in front Henry himself. In 1982 the *Mary Rose* was raised from the seabed and is preserved in Portsmouth Dockyard, where she had been built and dedicated to Mary Tudor almost 500 years before.

After Mary died in 1533, his chameleon loyalties led Charles Brandon to repay Wolsey poorly for his support and he played a part in his downfall. The mansion on Upper Brook Street eventually became the 'Coach and Horses' and the entrance yard became a 'tap' bar. In the coaching era it became the boarding point for the 'Quicksilver' coach – which left for Colchester at 7am daily – as well as others for Bury St Edmunds, Norwich and Woodbridge.

At one time it belonged to the Tollemache brewery, which took over the Brook Street Brewery that occupied the area now the Woolworths car park. The brewery was founded in 1856 and acquired by Charles Cullingham in 1862, but in 1888 the three sons of the 1st Baron Tollemache of Helmingham bought Cullingham out. They expanded the business and in 1923 merged with the Cobbolds, the two companies operating independently until they became one company in 1957. The business moved to Cliff Quay and the Brook Street Brewery closed in the 1960s.

Yet another survivor of the 16th century is the Cock and Pye public house, still in business as a restaurant and Beer Garden. During the 18th and 19th centuries it was the 'drinking hole' of the cavalry officers garrisoned in the town and was one of the last places in Ipswich to hold cock fights (hence its name). It had its own cock pit with terraced seating and was much frequented by race goers attending the annual Ipswich race meeting, including the cavalry officers who would spend the day on the racecourse and the evening at the Cock and Pye. A ferocious blood sport, introduced to Britain by the Romans, it took place on a stage in a circular pit. Intensively trained gamecocks with metal spurs were set to fight, usually to the death, and rowdy spectators indulged in heavy betting. It was banned temporarily by the Commonwealth Government but gained resurgence in Restoration England due to Charles II's own enthusiasm for the 'sport'. Cock fighting was finally banned in 1835, but many pubs, such as the Cock and Pye, attest to the places where it was practised.

When, on 14 January 1736, George II spent a night at the Great White Horse, the festivities lasted far longer than the visit itself. The Cock and Pye, being just down the road from the Great White Horse, was well placed to take full advantage of the event and provided extra entertainment by offering performances by the Royal Company of Artificial Actors (so called because the 'actors' were puppets).

Upper Brook Street is as commercial as ever it was but, as elsewhere in the town, the nature and ownership of the shops alter with contemporary regularity. Unlike the 'old days', when established businesses were handed down from father to son, shops are here today, gone tomorrow, often victims of changing fashions. Today is found Café Nero, Scholl footwear, charity shops, building societies and, at the junction with Tacket Street, Sainsbury's supermarket.

Lower Brook Street
In the 19th century Lower Brook Street was the habitat of the professional classes and was called 'The Faculty'. The houses that line the street opposite the newspaper offices were built in the 1850s and were the first of their type to be constructed in the town. It was a new style of architecture, often with four storeys, and those who could afford it had the houses fronted with the expensive white Woolpit bricks. The very well off showed what they were made of by having the whole house built of the prestigious white bricks, though they are now a dull grey having aged badly. There are several Victorian houses on Fonnereau Road where this white-brick façade is particularly noticeable and betrays the contemporary view that appearance was 'all'.

Hunt's author wrote disparagingly of Lower Brook Street:

'We need not take Lower Brook Street into our route, for very little can be said of it, except that here stood the house Gainsborough is said to have inhabited.'

Gainsborough did live briefly in a rented house on the street before moving to Foundation Street in about 1752.

Halfway down the street is The Master's House, 19–21 Lower Brook Street, which has a Blue Plaque commemorating the physician William King (1786–1865), who was born in the house when his father, the Revd John King, was Master of Ipswich School. After becoming a physician, William King moved to Brighton, but he is celebrated as 'a

founder of co-operative democracy'. He founded a Co-operative Benefit Fund and wrote the periodical *The Co-operator* (1828–1830), which helped to inspire the pioneers of the Co-operative Movement in 1844.

The house was previously known as the Preacher's House, having been built by Dr John Burges in the 1590s, when he was Town Preacher. It was here that the famous and notorious Town Preacher (or Lecturer) Samuel Ward lived until his death in 1640. He was elected to the post in 1607 for life, or 'if he shall soe long dwell in this Towne'. In Ward's day the sermons were very long, anything from two to three hours, and it was compulsory for councillors to attend.

The Revd Samuel Ward (1577–1640) was one of the most famous of all the Town Preachers. His popular name of 'Watch Ward' comes from the following lines, quoted by Dr Taylor as occurring 'between the representation of two ancient beacons':

'Watch, Ward, and keep thy garments tight,
For I come Thief-like at mid-night,
All-seeing, never-slumbering Lord,
Be thou my Watch, I'll be thy Ward.'

Ward was a staunch Puritan and as such often found himself in conflict with Matthew Wren, Bishop of Norwich, but broadly the town approved of his principles. He was committed to prison after publishing a tract on which a drawing appeared showing the Spanish king in conference with the Devil, just at the time when James I was negotiating a marriage with Maria, the Spanish Infanta. When he was released, he said he had no intentions of meddling in the king's 'secrett affaires'.

The office of Corporation Preacher was not abolished until 1845, and Samuel Ward was its most famous holder, though whether his rantings from the pulpit had any real effect on the morality or behaviour of the townspeople is open to conjecture. There was certainly a visibly effective and traceable rule of law during his time. People were always coming before the magistrates for the illegal selling and consuming of beer and unlawful gambling (including cards, dice, slide board and bowling), but this could easily be put down to the tell-tale culture of Puritanism, whereby a man would inform on his neighbour, and even a family member on another, in order to be a good Puritan. The Sabbath was a particularly good opportunity for enforcing the Puritan ideals as such pursuits as 'unnecessary rowing of boats' or the 'riding of horses further than is necessary' were easily committed offences. One man was even reported for playing his fiddle at night 'on the fast day' and another fined for serving a subpoena on the Sabbath.

The Master's House ceased to be such in 1851 (see also Henley Road).

Before moving to Lower Brook Street in 1966, the *EADT*, *Evening Star* and associated titles operated from Carr Street, at the junction with Little Colman Street, in buildings erected in 1887. The *Anglian*, as it is known, was for many years part of Eastern Counties Newspapers but now belongs to the Archant group.

There have been many memorable characters associated with the paper, not least the one-time proprietor Ralph Wilson, who was one of the last of the old time 'Fleet Street' journalists before the Eastern Counties Newspapers takeover in the 1960s. He inspired many an aspiring journalist by his example as a dedicated wordsmith and somewhat romantic, but always professional, approach to the newspaper business, not least because most evenings he could be found imbibing alcohol in the Great White Horse and at the appropriate hour would stagger down Carr Street to put his paper 'to bed'. When he retired he was properly 'banged out' in the printing works, an honour not given to all.

One of the last agricultural editors of the Wilson era, before the advent of Peter Hopper, was Rintoul 'Rin' Booth, who was a journalist, author, sculptor and a contender for the Australian Olympic riding team. He also founded a group known as The Agricultural Gentlemen for farming 'types' with literary leanings, which is still presided over by 90-year-old Philip Wood, former books editor at

Farming Press (based for many years at Wharfedale Road). Rin Booth came to England from Australia as a young man and instead of taking up a university place decided to become a journalist. He came to Ipswich in the 1960s where he was appointed agricultural editor. His wry humour is amply illustrated in one of his books, *Farming Handbook to End All Farming Handbooks*, where he hands over to two British economists, 'Dr Ludwig Scapweed and Mr Gregorio Scales', who are required to prepare a report on the rural scene. They rely on a Mr Arthur Mardle for much of their information, a small farmer who is more than willing to discuss his not inconsiderable problems with the boffins from the training board.

The book is a sideways and humorous lampoon of farming in its many guises, which at one point ends up in the West End, where 'Arthur Mardle' loses his cloth cap to a belly dancer. This and a follow up, *Horseman's Handbook to End All Horseman's Handbooks*, were dedicated to all Mardles who have to endure the army of government departments and Boards which assail them, together with 'levies, legalities, technicalities, New Town developments, reservoirs and the weather'.

Rin retired from the *Anglian* in 1969 to become a sculptor. His most famous piece is the Black Bull of Otley that stands outside Otley College. It is three-quarters life size and based on a triangular concept, and modelled on a Friesian bull named Sutton Hoo Idena Dividend, which belonged to Mrs Barton of Sutton Hoo.

BURRELL ROAD

It followed that immediately as the railway reached Ipswich the town layout would need alteration to accommodate it, and the location of the station would affect the way people went about their business. No one was surer of this than Peter Robert Burrell (1810–1909); in July 1860, as part of his alterations to the thoroughfares leading to and from the new railway station, he required a more direct road. He also wanted to stop up a bridle way, which led from Belstead Road to the station and for which

Great Eastern Railways' open-topped bus on the fore court of Ipswich station in 1915. (ITM Collection)

consent had to be sought. Permission was granted and the new road, with its primary access to the railway station, was named Burrell Road.

Peter Burrell lived at, and rebuilt, Stoke Park Mansion and his contribution to Ipswich and Suffolk was considerable. As well as being High Steward of Ipswich and a magistrate, he also served as High Sheriff and Deputy Lieutenant of Suffolk.

He was a man in the forefront of both national and local affairs and succeeded to the Gwydyr barony after the death of a cousin in 1870. Living at Stoke, it was inevitable that he should take a keen interest in the development of the railway (see Stoke Hamlet). Willoughby Road is named for Burrell's son, as is Willoughby Terrace (on Burrell Road).

Until the middle of the 19th century the river had been the most effective means of communication, trade and travel. Even when sail gave way to steam, and the steamers took both passengers and cargo, the sea was still the chief entrance into and out of the town. There had been an inland road system for centuries, along which people had walked or ridden to and from all parts north, west and south. But in 1836 Royal Assent was given to a bill that would allow a railway link, which was to alter forever the nature of Ipswich and herald the end of the mail and passenger coaches such as the 'Quicksilver' and the 'Retaliator' (see also Tavern Street). The *Ipswich Journal* mourned the passing of the 'Golden Path'

Forecourt of Ipswich station. (ITM Collection)

Colchester-London coach, which ceased running a few years later in 1843:

> 'We cannot but regret the disappearance of a class of vehicles which might be regarded as a connecting link between the present rapid transit of the railroad carriage and those earlier modes of public travelling, when it was customary to announce that the "Ipswich Machine", or the "Colchester Stage", or the "Harwich Flying Machine" would perform the journey in one day, adding, with a reverential regard to an over-ruling Providence, not fashionable now-a-days, "if God Permit".'

Ipswich was not among the railway pioneers and, indeed, the railway came late to East Anglia in comparison with the rest of the country. Possibly because Ipswich and Norwich had fewer inhabitants than the northern towns, there was no local coal and its local industries had no real need of improved transport (being river-orientated), the first proposal of 1834 gained no support. It was resubmitted two years later, this time successfully, and the Eastern Counties Railway was granted Royal Assent for a Bill to connect London and Yarmouth via Ipswich. However, it was not until 1838 that work actually began on the line, and in the first year only 11 miles were opened and the line terminated at Colchester without reaching Ipswich. Financial considerations were weighing heavy on the company and there was no support to extend it beyond Colchester.

The businessmen of Ipswich quickly saw that without a rail link the town would be commercially and politically isolated, and John Chevallier Cobbold (1797–1882) set up a new company, the Eastern Union Railway Company (EUC), to complete the line from Colchester to Ipswich. John

Ipswich Station, 1960s. Ipswich is the last place in the country to retain the practice of naming its buses. Many are named after local schools, town personalities and after Ipswich barges, including the 'Mirosa' which is at the Ipswich Transport Museum. (ITM Collection)

Chevallier Cobbold was a man described as 'so closely mixed up with the social and public life of the town as to be inseparable from the actual identity of Ipswich', and on 11 June 1846 the new Colchester to Ipswich line was opened. The Mayor declared a town holiday and 600 ladies welcomed the first train, waving 'snowy kerchiefs'.

The original station was in Croft Street (commemorated by the parallel Station Street) as it was the first convenient point east of Stoke Hill and, because of the river to the north, the closest it could get to the town. When a line to Bury St Edmunds was mooted the engineer Peter Schuyler Bruff (called 'the Brunel of the Eastern Counties') opted to connect the two lines, not by a viaduct, as had been proposed, but by driving a tunnel through Stoke Hill. Bruff (1811–1800) had indeed rubbed shoulders with such pioneers as Brunel and Robert Stephenson and received his engineering training under Joseph Locke (1805–1860).

Bruff's extraordinary tunnel, considered by connoisseurs to be a superb feat of engineering, was the first railway tunnel to be constructed on a continuous curve and is unique in East Anglia in that it is in close proximity to a depot and a station. Thus, in 1860 the new station was opened at the north end of the tunnel and the line was continued to Bury St Edmunds and Norwich. In 1864 *Hunt's Guide* announced:

'The Ipswich Railway Station is open to the public, except on occasion of the arrival and departure of very heavy excursion trains, when precautions are taken to prevent the overcrowding of the platform.'

Although the station is now on Station Road, the road immediately in front of the station is now a bus stop, taking the place of the old tram stops which first ferried passengers up into the town. It was initially an open space and called The Station Yard. Here the omnibuses for the White Horse, Golden Lion and the Crown & Anchor queued to take passengers to their respective accommodation.

For those not going into town there was the Station Hotel at the south side of the Princes Street bridge, a 'creditable building and accords with the architecture of the Station. Very good house and its charges are reasonable' said *Hunt's Guide*.

BUTTERMARKET

The Buttermarket is one of the town's oldest thoroughfares and, as its name suggests, was once a market for selling butter, although on White's 1867 map it appears as 'St Lawrence Street'. It was one of the streets that gained importance when the traders were forbidden in 1285 from carrying on commerce in the nearby St Mary le Tower. At one time it had been the fish market, and in 1635 was described as 'the fish market now used as the butter market'. During the 18th century it became 'the street from the Butter Market to Brook Street', but when a name was needed in the 1860s Butter was chosen over Fish, though it had been some time since butter had been sold on the street.

There was a market of sorts here from at least Anglo-Saxon times right up until 1810, when trading ceased, although the earliest find came only in 1863 when a coin hoard was found that dated to around 979 AD. It was probably buried during one of the innumerable Danish onslaughts into 'Gipeswic' and, since it was not retrieved, its owner likely perished. The hoard consisted of about 500 silver pennies, many struck in the Ipswich mint (see Orwell Street).

Just south of the Buttermarket, towards the old cattle market (now the Eastern Counties bus station), a bronzesmith's workshop was unearthed, complete with crucible and moulds, indicating the area's long standing contribution to the town's industry.

Little evidence of the bustling mediaeval market is left, but we can imagine it in those times as little more than a country lane, dusty in summer and muddy in winter, boarded on both sides by stalls in front of rough dwelling houses. The hustle and bustle was accompanied by the smells from the various stalls – meat, fish and all manner of dairy

The Ancient House with its ornamented front, bold bay windows and pointed gables. On the west front (right hand corner) is a shepherd and flock of sheep, representing the valuable mediaeval wool trade, of which Ipswich was the centre.

products – together with the waft of rotting waste at intervals along the street making for a rich mediaeval stew of life in the raw. For hundreds of years it echoed to the sounds and smells of a busy market place: it was where the women from the country came into town with their dairy produce and, no doubt, where local rivalry was alive and well and the sounds of street cries would fill the air.

The 13th and 14th centuries saw an expansion of industry and commerce across England. In addition to everyday trading and buying provisions, Ipswich had, from Saxon times, held a regular market to which sellers and buyers would travel not just to trade but to socialise. Here, as in other towns at the time, these gatherings were boosted by the extra jollifications and attractions of the annual fairs, at least three of which – St George's Fair, the Lamb Fair and the Cheese and Butter Fair – continued into the 19th century. All ancient English towns had a weekly market and invariably those engaged in the same trade, fishmongers, dairymen, butchers, etc, set up their stalls in proximity to one another as it was always the custom that traders should, as much as possible, carry out that trade in the vicinity of like-traders.

When, in the 1720s, Daniel Defoe visited Ipswich he recorded:

'A person very curious and on whose veracity I think I may depend, going through the market in this town, told me that he reckoned upwards of 600 country people on horseback, and on foot, with baskets and other carriage, who had all of them brought something or

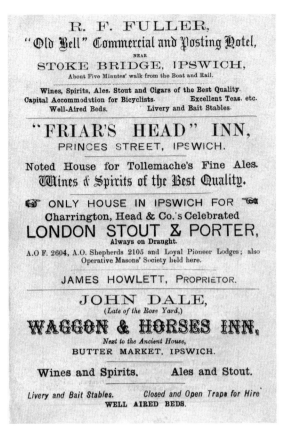

In 1897 John Dale of the Waggon & Horses inn advertised 'well aired beds' as well as stabling and bait stables.

other to town to sell, besides the butchers and what came in carts and wagons.'

In earlier times this curious person would also have seen the travelling showmen, musicians and entertainers mingling with friars from four different houses, itinerants, street entertainers, buyers and sellers of all kinds of goods and produce and, in pre-Reformation times, pilgrims visiting the Chapel of Our Lady in Lady Lane and visitors to the numerous religious houses.

In Ipswich, market days were Tuesday and Saturday. Even in the 1960s people from the outlying countryside would 'go to town' on a Tuesday, the men congregating at the cattle market and the women doing the rounds of the shops. Tuesday continued to be a special day in the town long after provision or cattle and stock markets had ceased. Today a mixed market is still held on Cornhill every Tuesday and Saturday. Market days

are a hard habit to break when they have endured for hundreds of years, although stalls held on Cornhill today are mostly fruit and vegetables, clothes and household goods, and those selling a variety of goods from pet food to children's toys.

Few early structures survive but one of the town's most famous buildings, the Ancient House, is the final version of a long succession of different versions of one house on that site. Its old name was Sparrow or Sparrowe's House, the Sparrow family living there from the 1600s until 1898. Though it grew piecemeal, it is a Grade I listed building and contains evidence of at least six earlier structures, the earliest dating from the 15th century. When Thomas Fastolf had it in 1483 he added a strip of common soil, which fronted onto what was then the fish market. The structure seen today was built in about 1567 by George Copping, a fish trader who lived in it until 1570. It is now occupied by Lakeland Limited.

Its first incarnation was as a replacement for an earlier, primitive dwelling and is, as Dr Taylor remarked, 'perhaps the most beautifully ornamented and best-kept old house in England. It has been painted, sketched, photographed, lithographed, and etched, times innumerable'.

In the 1850s R. Makilwaine Phipson wrote an account of the Ancient House, adding:

'I may perhaps be permitted to express a hope that so curious and interesting a structure, setting forth as it does the excellent knowledge and good taste of our ancestors, will not be allowed to fall into decay, or what is, I fear, more probable, be swept entirely away by the ruthless march of so mis-called modern improvement'.

Mr Phipson's entirely likely prophecy was, fortunately, not fulfilled and Ipswich still has its Ancient House.

Shortly after George Copping died the house was bought by William Sparrowe who promptly removed the fish market eastwards towards Brook

Street and converted it into an altogether more fragrant smelling grocery and spice store. Perhaps this coincided with a general smartening up of the Buttermarket, as it is doubtful if the highly ornate house would have appeared among hovels or traders' stalls. The long occupancy of the Sparrowe family caused the property to be known as Sparrowe's House, or Mr Sparrow's House (the 'e' being dropped in the 19th century).

A poem attributed to Charles Partridge sums up the highlights of its history:

'The Ancient House, you glibly dub me now;
But, had you liv'd four hundred yeas ago,
You would have call'd me new; young Wolsey watch'd
Them build my timber frame; George Copping me
Enlarg'd when great Queen Bess through Suffolk pass'd;
And Francis Bacon (whome you 'Shakespeare' call)
Was here in James his time; and, later on,
The poet Milton from Stowmarket came;
And after Worcester fight I hid King Charles -
Yes, I am ancient; but, my friend, when you
Lie low in grave, I still shall carry on.'

The Sparrowe family, who were ardent Royalists, commissioned the pargetting ornamentation seen on the exterior. Conspicuous above the main doorway are the Royal Arms of Charles II, placed there at the Restoration and in time for the king's visit to Ipswich in 1668. A tradition exists that Charles II himself lay concealed in the labyrinth of rooms at the Ancient House after the Battle of Worcester, but this is as resolutely discounted among local historians as it is believed. However, in 1801 a chapel was discovered in the oldest part of the house when a concealed loft was revealed. Arched timbers in the roof bore traces of ornamentation and 'there were found stored therein wooden angels and other figures such as usually decorate a Catholic place of worship.'

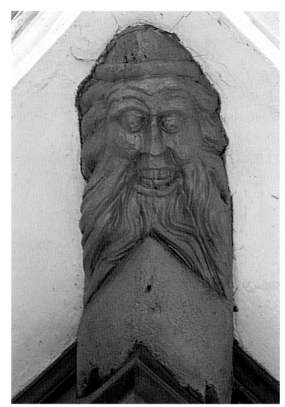

Part of an ancient angle beam survives on the corner of the Buttermarket and Dial Lane.

The Buttermarket frontage contains emblematical symbols of four continents – Africa, America, Europe and Asia. Australasia was, in the 16th century, yet to be discovered.

In the early 1800s the Ancient House was one of the first venues used by Madame Tussaud (1760–1850) for her travelling exhibition of wax models, before it found a home on Baker Street in London. The exhibition was advertised as being in 'Mr Sparrow's Upper Ware Room'. Madame Tussaud came to Ipswich a second time but on that occasion she used the Assembly Rooms.

During World War Two, by which time it was a bookshop, the cellars of the Ancient House were used as an air raid shelter so that customers did not need to go out to a public shelter. There were chemical toilets and even a dartboard for the men!

In 1965 Mr Harrison (of W.D. Harrison & Son, booksellers, stationers, newsagents and printers) hired a television so that his staff could watch Sir Winston Churchill's funeral.

Godfrey Green, brought up in the rectory of St Stephen's, where his father was Rector, worked at the Ancient House as manager of the book department in the 1950s. His first job had been in Norwich, to where he had cycled daily, and he had started work at the Ancient House as an assistant in 1938. Even after he retired in December 1973 he continued working part time until 1981, when he was 73-years-old, making his service at Ancient House a total of 43 years. Georgina Abbott, who worked there for 30 years, remembered that he often reminisced about the changes he had seen, in particular when the Waggon and Horses inn was pulled down in the 1930s and the Ritz cinema (afterwards the ABC, which closed in 1986) put in its place. The site is now part of British Home Stores.

Georgina also recalls that Mr Green would often work late, catching up on his work, but said he never heard or saw any of the ghosts associated with the house. However, few of the staff would go to the attic stock room after dark!

The Waggon and Horses was one of the most famous among the town inns. Dr Taylor wrote:

'The quaint Interior of the adjacent "Waggon and Horses" inn and yard are more than worthy of inspection … [it has] an old-fashioned courtyard and rooms. Three centuries ago this was known as the "Waggon".'

Presumably someone added the horses at a later date.

At the junction with Dial Lane is the Edinburgh Woollen Mill shop that has an easily-missed carving from an ancient wooden corner post still visible, once such a common feature of Ipswich's mediaeval buildings and now a cherished rarity. It is of an old, bearded man who seems to be smiling at something, but no one knows at what!

Between the Buttermarket and Falcon Street, previously the printing works of W.S. Cowell Limited, the Buttermarket Shopping Centre was developed. It coincides with the area that was once the pre-Reformation Carmelite Friary, founded in 1278, which eventually extended south from the Buttermarket to Falcon Street and from Queen Street to St Stephen's Lane (see Queen Street).

CANHAM STREET

This was laid out on a piece of land always known as Canham's Marshes and was one of the Corporation marshes west of Portman Road. Canham was probably a one-time Portman of the town who exercised his charter rights to graze the town marshes.

CARR STREET

The origin of 'Carr' is uncertain and the name does not appear until the late 1500s, but there is little doubt that it is one of the oldest streets. For some years part of it was known as Cross Keys Street after a long-gone inn. In G.R. Clarke's time it was spelled 'Car'.

Muriel Clegg writes that this is one of several cases in Ipswich where a street name and a surname are recorded at very nearly the same time; in the reign of Edward I the principal resident of 'Karistrete' was William Kaa. It appears in 1402 as 'Carystrete' and no doubt had other (verbal) names over the centuries. The Latin prefix 'car' relates to various words associated with carts and waggons, while 'carr' in Old English is an area of boggy land; either, or both, could have been influential.

In *Hunt's Guide* Carr Street 'was made in the days when no one thought of introducing uniformity or structure into a street, or of classifying localities according to the conditions or occupations of men.' Indeed, the Cock & Pie inn was separated only by a wall from the 'pretty garden of Mr James Allen Ransome'.

The first hint that 'Gipeswic' had a much older foundation than was thought came in the 1950s when some of the pottery stored in Ipswich Museum was studied for the first time by John Hurst and Stanley West. It had been discovered on the south side at the eastern end of Carr Street. The pottery, renamed 'Ipswich Ware', dated from the mid-seventh to the mid-ninth century, and while

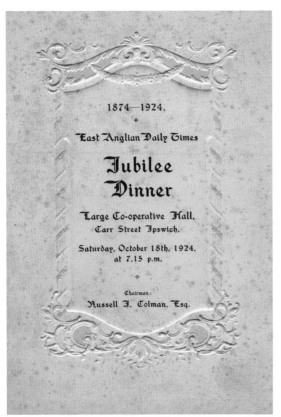

1874—1924.

East Anglian Daily Times

Jubilee Dinner

Large Co-operative Hall,
Carr Street Ipswich.

Saturday, October 18th, 1924,
at 7.15 p.m.

Chairman:
Russell J. Colman. Esq.

In 1924 a Jubilee Dinner for the EADT *was held at the Co-operative Hall, presided over by the chairman, Russell J Colman. The six-course menu included a 'starter' of 'Clear Tapioca' and 'Pudding Mercedes' as 'Sweet'.*

much of it was made locally there was also imported Rhenish amphorae, which indicated trade in the eighth or early ninth century. By way of confirmation, a wine barrel discovered in Lower Brook Street was dated by dendrochronology to around 871 AD and matched a tree ring pattern of the Mainz area of Germany.

Carr Street pottery was sold throughout the East Anglian Kingdom and exported as far away as Yorkshire and Kent, and it was the only wheel-made and kiln-fired pottery made in England between the seventh and ninth century. Such a flourishing industry would certainly have attracted immigrants to the area, perhaps from the Rhineland, and brought prosperity and kudos to Ipswich. Carr Street is one of the town's most historic sites, and walking down it now, past Woolworths to the 1960s Eastgate Shopping Centre, it is worth a thought for the generations of Ipswich people making and

trading their wares along that route for more than 2,000 years.

It was also another meeting place of sorts. *Hunt's Guide* said darkly and not a little mysteriously:

'There are houses here where pedlars and travelling street musicians, and men who hang strangely on the outskirts of society, know where to find each other.'

The name of the Salutation inn at the east end gives away its mediaeval origins when the sign would have represented the Angel Gabriel saluting Our Lady. It is unusual for the name to have survived since the Puritans at the time of the Civil War changed it in most places to Soldier and Citizen. This is doubly surprising, perhaps, since during the Civil War soldiers were billeted at the nearby Cross Keys inn. Dr Taylor writes that the Salutation was 'a quaint, low-roofed, wood-carved, and wall-frescoed ancient public house'.

In the 1920s the landlord, Richard Morbey, was a well-known promoter and host to travelling sports personalities, especially boxers, and competition bouts were held in the pub yard. At the time Ipswich had its own boxing hero, Harry Rednall, who was landlord of the Bridge Tavern. When the Bridge closed in 1917, Harry, who boxed under the name Harry Marney, became a promoter and encouraged the various training establishments that sprung up in the town at the time.

Carr Street is much altered from how it was, even in the 1960s, the biggest change being the demolition of the area originally named the Carr Precinct, now renamed Eastgate Shopping Centre. One of the saddest farewells was to the quirky, red-brick building that was home to the *EADT* and stood at the junction with Little Colman Street.

The *EADT* was founded in 1874 but moved to the Carr Street offices in 1887 and stayed there until the move to Lower Brook Street. Its unique red-brick, five-sided corner turret, displaying the names of its main titles, was a landmark building. Newspapers, by their nature, are at the heart of day-to-day events,

Facsimiles of the first issue, together with a cartoon card by E.H. Banger, were presented to the Jubilee Dinner guests who were entertained by a series of musical recitals and speeches. (Archant)

and during the 1926 General Strike the *EADT* produced daily emergency issues, printed on old-fashioned flat bed machines, which used type set by a jobbing printer. Police protection was needed for the vans bringing the type to Carr Street.

The Lyceum Theatre, a 1,300-seater auditorium, was built in Carr Street in 1890–91 at a cost of £9,000. It was described as 'a confection of yellow and gold, liberally sprinkled with Shakespearian mottoes', such as 'All The World's A Stage', and was a popular venue with its Italian-style architecture and the novelty of mass entertainment. Its fortunes waned when the new Hippodrome, the 'Theatre of Varieties', was opened on St Nicholas Street and, even after the Hippodrome's owner took it in hand for a while, the writing was on the wall for the Lyceum. It became a cinema in the 1920s and then a department store (at the time a new-fangled and expansive idea of a store having more than one department) but closed in 1936, after which it was demolished to make way for the Great Universal Stores of Manchester.

At the time the Lyceum became a department store it stood opposite the new premises of F.W. Woolworth, who have occupied their current site since 1924 when they boasted that they sold 'Nothing Over 6d' (six old pence).

It is still possible to see reminders of an earlier Carr Street by looking above the shop fronts at pavement level. The extensive Co-operative building bears its banner message '1908 Each for All and All for Each' and marks the long association of the 'Co-op' with Carr Street.

Chartism had been strong in Ipswich, and in the 1840s there was a Co-operative society with a shop at 34 Carr Street, but it did not take off. In 1875 a second attempt was made to establish the society at 38 Carr Street, formerly the Wellington inn. The reading room was open to members on Saturdays from 3 to 10pm and was advertised as 'well lighted and warmed' but only lasted about five years. However, in the history of the Ipswich and Norwich Co-operative movement, *People & Places*, the author writes:

Cartoon card by E.H. Banger. (Archant)

The EADT *offices moved to Carr Street in 1887. (W. Vick Photo from ITM Collection)*

'By the 1880s the first wave of East Anglian co-operative societies had put their early troubles behind them and were firstly established … the Ipswich Society had gone on to establish a bakery, clothing departments, a butchery shop, four branch stores and its own coal depot by 1880.'

In 1886 the new Ipswich 'Central Premises' store opened and was one of the largest buildings in town. Ipswich was the strongest society in East Anglia, with its own farm, Boss Hall, on the outskirts of town. Boss Hall was described as 'about sixty acres and situated a mile-and-a-half from the Cornhill' and is marked by Boss Hall Road (now a supermarket and Business Park). The first branch store was opened on Vernon Street in 1878 and 'when first opened the store was only a few minutes from the countryside and there was little traffic passing by; children could safely amble across the

road'. In 1932 the society built its Model Dairy beside the old, original farmhouse and was reported to be the first in the area to provide pasteurised milk.

In 1908 the society purchased property in Carr Street, Cox Lane and Union Street for the erection of a second grand building, a new central drapery and furnishing premises. The original, somewhat

A 1980s advertisement for the Ipswich Co-operative Society.

grandiose, plan for a completely new store had raised much concern among members, and the eventual building was smaller than initially envisaged. However, its modern style was appreciated by some, 'being built on steel stanchions and girders of British manufacture' and the Ipswich Co-operators were justly proud of their building.

The Co-op has been a large part of the nation's life for over 100 years, and in 1929 the popular entertainer Gracie Fields put it on the Music Hall circuit. The first verse of 'Stop and Shop at the Co-op' went:

Carr Street in 1888, drawn by Percy E. Stimpson for Dr J.E. Taylor's Ancient Ipswich.

'There's a shop called the Co-op in High
  Street,
By Gum! It's a great idea;
For out of what you spend, you get a dividend
Three times ev-ry year.
When Ma takes two shillings for her share,
She shouts feeling like a millionaire.'

Gracie visited Ipswich in August 1941 when she took part in an ENSA concert at Ransomes Sims & Jeffries. It was in 1960, at the Co-operative Hall, that The Ipswich Society was founded at a public meeting convened by local architects, historians, councillors and interested members of the public. One of the first projects the Society got involved in was a modest transformation of Fore Street in preparation for the visit of the Queen, who was to open the new Ipswich Civic College. In 1968 it helped to defeat the proposal to demolish the Great White Horse and over the years since has been involved in all manner of conservation and planning issues. Members were involved with the riverside tree planning along Ranelagh Road and in creating a path along the river, upstream from Stoke Bridge.

As well as organising the annual Heritage Open Day programme, the Society has launched a blue plaque scheme to commemorate notable people with Ipswich connections.

CASTLE HILL (Whitton)

Although somewhat north of the town, and, therefore, beyond the original Anglo-Saxon settlement, the Castle Hill area deserves special mention as the site of a Roman villa and, some say, is named for the lost Ipswich Castle. Another Castle Hill, alongside Henley Road and close to the arboretum, is also thought to indicate the site of the 12th-century castle. However, it is generally agreed that, although it is on high ground, the site would have been too far from the town to provide effective fortifications. The third site, that of Elm Street, is a better contender for the castle site.

Wodderspoon, however, makes a case for Castle Hill by pointing out that occasionally 'masonry and other remains are turned up by the plough [which] points to the conclusion that on this spot the castle of Ipswich once stood.'

Similarly Dr Taylor suggests 'there was some kind of a stronghold on the Castle Hills, beyond Brook's Hall.'

Until the Romans imposed the formality and structure of a town on the native population, who lived mostly in groups of huts within protective dykes or ramparts, there were no permanent urban sites and no central controlling bureaucracy. Essentially town dwellers, the Romans imposed the idea of a township, or vill, in order to civilise it with organised government. They made their settlement on high ground at Castle Hill, east of Whitton, where a Roman villa was first discovered in 1854. It was, says Nikolaus Pevsner, 'apparently of corridor type'. A fabulous floor mosaic was discovered as well as pottery and coins from the second and fourth century AD, which indicates a long period of habitation.

Following the traditions of tribes who had buried their dead in the Dales Road valley, the Roman settlers at Whitton also buried their dead there for some 200 years. Thus, it has been suggested that the town of Ipswich had its origins in a Roman cemetery.

CIVIC DRIVE

The construction of Civic Drive took place in 1966 as part of the phenomenal development of the town throughout the 1960s and was designed to take traffic away from the town centre. The dual carriageway runs northwards from the junction with Princes Street and Franciscan Way to the St Matthew's roundabout. As part of the development, the Civic Centre, police station and large office blocks were built alongside on an area known as The Mount (Mount, Perth and Stirling Streets disappearing).

The Ship sculpture, executed by Bernard Reynolds in 1971, now stands in the centre of the Civic Drive Roundabout. Originally in front of the Civic Centre, it was moved for convenience as it was

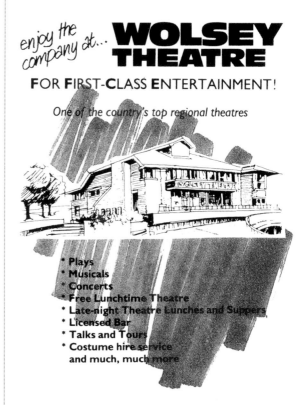

A 1980 advertisement for the Wolsey Theatre, shortly after it first opened.

WOLSEY THEATRE

CIVIC DRIVE, IPSWICH

SUMMER SEASON DEAL
A discount when you book
both productions

ROOKERY NOOK
By Ben Travers   6 Aug—23 Aug

BLITHE SPIRIT
By Noel Coward   28 Aug—20 Sept

AUTUMN SUBSCRIPTION SEASON 1980

CAMELOT
By Lerner & Lowe   24 Sept—25 Oct

NIGHT & DAY
By Tom Stoppard   29 Oct—22 Nov

THE CURSE OF THE WEREWOLF
By Ken Hill   26 Nov—20 Dec

MURDER AT THE VICARAGE
By Agatha Christie   6 Jan—31 Jan

CHRISTMAS CHILDREN'S PLAY

THERE WAS AN OLD WOMAN
23 Dec—17 Jan

IPSWICH'S NEW THEATRE
BOX OFFICE: 53725

The Wolsey Theatre opened on Civic Drive in 1979.

Paul Leonard and Simon Clarke in Sweeney Todd, *the opening production at the New Wolsey Theatre in 2001. Andrew Clarke told* EADT *readers 'Attend the tale of Sweeney Todd – that was the cry of a chorus of powerful voices which soared above a packed foyer at the Wolsey Theatre. Outside, a cloud of orange balloons filled the air to celebrate the re-opening of the Ipswich theatre.' (M Kwasniak)*

thought to be too close to the entrance to the underground car park. In July 1994 the *Evening Star* reported a borough spokesman as saying that the sculpture had been 'in the wrong place for years' and not in a good situation 'for being seen'.

The police advised that it was not considered 'jazzy' enough to distract motorists and could be moved to the roundabout.

The aluminium, steel and fibreglass sculpture won the Sir Otto Beit Medal for Sculpture in 1972. Bernard Reynolds has two other sculptures in the town, one in the Wolsey Gardens behind Christchurch Mansion (Triple Mycomorph) and the other at the entrance to Suffolk College (Pylons).

The municipal building that is the Civic Centre is due to be demolished to make way for a supermarket, with council offices moving to Russell Road, opposite Endeavour House (the new home of Suffolk County Council), in what is to be called the 'Ipswich Village'. When the move takes place the Civic Centre will have lasted only 40 years.

One of the most striking modern buildings is the AXA centre, which curves its way down Civic Drive. AXA is one of the largest insurance companies in the world and one of the biggest employers in Ipswich.

A year after the last performance took place, in the Tower Street Theatre, the Wolsey Theatre opened in September 1979 and quickly became a well-established facet of town life. It continued with considerable success until beset by problems in 1998. The final show before going 'dark' was an amateur production of the Rodgers and Hart musical *Pal Joey* put on by the Appeal Theatre Group. It was to be 18 months before it reopened as the New Wolsey Theatre, when Sarah Holmes told Carol Carver of the *Evening Star*:

> 'We want to emphasise that we are new. We couldn't and wouldn't ever lose the name Wolsey, we just want to make it plain that we are not the same as before.'

In 2001 the theatre reopened 'under new management, with a new name and in the new millennium'. The opening production was *Sweeney Todd, the Demon Barber of Fleet Street* by Stephen Sondheim, starring Paul Leonard, Joanna Mays and Robert Irons.

COBBOLD STREET

The name Cobbold is woven inextricably into Suffolk's history and appears in several street stories. The family were principally farmers and brewers but during the 18th and 19th centuries became industrialists, philanthropists and members of the town's gentry. John Chevallier Cobbold was responsible for the opening up of railway communications, and it is thanks to Felix Cobbold that Ipswich now has Christchurch Mansion.

Cobbold Street is now mainly residential with the Royal British Legion headquarters on the corner with St Margaret's Green.

COLLEGE STREET

College Street does not seem to have had an ancient name, though it was once a westward extension of Key Street. It is undoubtedly as old as any in that part of town and might well have been named at one time in relation to the Church of St Peter or with the Augustinian Priory of St Peter and St Paul, which grew up behind St Peter's and flourished there from the 12th century. The name College Street appears

Wolsey's Gateway as it looked in the 18th century.

on Joseph Pennington's map and is taken from Cardinal Wolsey's 16th-century college, built on the site of the Augustinian Priory that was dissolved to make way for the proposed college. All that remains of the college is the south gate now leaning drunkenly towards the busy street that takes the traffic westwards, badly eroded by the acidic exhaust fumes and traffic vibration that have assailed it for years.

Nearby associated street names are Cardinal Street, New Cardinal Street, Wolsey Street and Cardinal Park, to the west of Grey Friars Road. St Peter's Street, leading northwards off Star Lane, once led to the church.

St Peter's is recorded in the Domesday survey as holding large possessions including three acres of meadowland, in addition to '6 caructes of land'. By the time of the Conquest, Christianity had long replaced paganism as the popular religion, and although it is not possible to say precisely when the first church was built in Ipswich it is generally thought to have been one dedicated to St Peter, which stood on the site of that now seen on College Street.

St Peter's is one of the 12 surviving mediaeval churches, though its position today, on a noisy traffic island overshadowed by the huge docklands building of R. & W. Paul, is in stark contrast to the previous church. An earlier building was built when

*Wolsey's Gate and St
Peter's Church in the
1920s.*

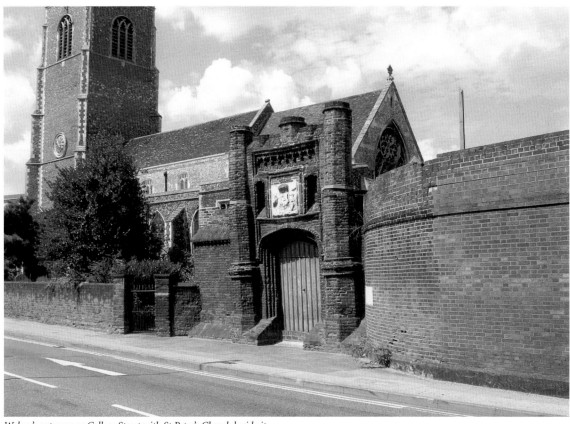

Wolsey's gateway on College Street with St Peter's Church beside it.

the river was much wider than it is now and the church would have been closer to the water's edge, though on more substantial ground than St Mary Quay to the east, which was built on marshland.

Entry is via the west doorway, made larger by Wolsey when the church became the chapel for his proposed college. Inside, its greatest treasure is the 12th-century Tournai marble font, which has a Tudor base that was commissioned by Wolsey at the same time as he enlarged the west doorway. The square bowl, made of black polished Tournai marble, was brought here from the banks of the River Scheldt, near Tournai in Belgium. Each side has three carved lions and at the four corners are tiny columns, which date the bowl from 1150 or thereabouts. There are only 10 such fonts known to exist in England, and it is thought to be all that is left of the earlier church.

The Ipswich Historic Churches Trust now has St Peter's in its care, together with the other redundant Churches of St Clement and St Lawrence.

St Peter's is intimately associated not only with the rise and fall of Wolsey's doomed college (see St Nicholas Street) but also with the Augustinian Priory of St Peter and St Paul. The priory was founded in 1130 and occupied land immediately north of St Peter's Church. In 1527 it was suppressed by Cardinal Wolsey to make way for his aforementioned college. With little or no regard to the Canons, their property or their rights, Wolsey requisitioned the priory and all its entitlements, and on 15 June 1528 John Longland, Bishop of Lincoln, laid the first stone of the college, dedicated to the Blessed Virgin. Richard Taylor records in *Index Monasticus*:

'The Cardinal, with the permission of Pope Clement VII, and the concurrence of King Henry VIII, had built and founded the college of Ipswich; the monastery of St Peter, in Ipswich, of the order of St Augustine, with all its dependencies, having been suppressed.'

As well, several parish churches, with their rights and emoluments, which were attached to the monastery, were also requisitioned, including St Peter's. The parishioners were, therefore, left without a church in which to worship but were instructed by Wolsey to attend one of the other churches nearby.

Alas, the college, its dean, 12 secular canons, eight clerks and eight choristers lasted only three years. Wolsey fell from grace and died soon afterwards, and his college was not well enough established to survive. Henry VIII was said to have taken offence to the fact that Wolsey had placed his own arms above that of the king's on the Gate House, and most of what occupied the six-acre site was 'razed to the ground'.

G.R. Clarke described the remnant of Wolsey's Gate:

'This gate, with the exception of a square stone table on which are carved the arms of Henry VIII, is entirely of brick, worked into niches, wreathed pinnacles, flowers and other decorations, according to the fashion of the time.'

Although the Gate is said to have been the entrance to the College, it is not likely that it was the main one so it will never be known if, in fact, Wolsey had placed his arms above the king's or whether this was just one of the many charges laid at the Cardinal's door when he fell from favour. In 1830 James Bird wrote:

'All, all are gone, with Cardinal, and King!
And thou, old Portal! Art but left to show,
That withering Time, with his relentless wing,
Sweeps, like a pestilence, o'er all below'.

In the 19th century College Street was dominated by E.R. & F. Turner's works. Founded in 1837 as iron founders and general engineers, the Turners set up shop in the St Peter's Works, next to Wolsey's Gateway. By 1849 they had expanded into Greyfriars

Works and there they prospered until well into the 20th century. In 1969 the company split, one part became Bull Motors and operated from Foxhall Road until 2004.

The only relic of past industry left on College Street, just east of St Peter's, is a row of forlorn, empty buildings that once formed part of Burton Son & Sanders Limited, established in 1824. The factory site, cleared but left bare for some years and now colonised by Buddleia bushes, is earmarked for an apartment block to be named Cardinal Lofts.

CORNHILL

There is no record of exactly when the Cornhill was so called, but there is no doubt that this was a central market and meeting place from very early times, fixed first by custom and then regulated by law. Certainly the name was established by 1610 when it appears on Speed's map as 'Corne hill'. It is said that, due to soil build-up, Cornhill is some 5ft higher than it was several hundred years ago.

The oldest buildings on Cornhill are Mannings and the Golden Lion, both timber framed with later façades, the rest are Victorian. Clinton's Cards was for many years Grimwades Clothier's shop (built in the 1870s). All traces of mediaeval 'Gipeswic' have gone, but it remains the heart of the town and an observation in an old guide remains as true today as it was in the 19th century:

'No native or old inhabitant can glance across this open space without recurring to scenes

Cornhill in the 1890s before Lloyds Avenue was cut through. (ITM)

Cornhill from Lloyds Avenue by L.R. Squirrell, painted in 1935.

and events he has witnessed there, never again to be repeated'.

In 1888 Dr J.E. Taylor made reference to the Palaeolithic (or 'Old Stone Age') dwarf men who once lived in and about Ipswich even before Neolithic man. Their contemporaries in the animal world were the woolly-haired elephants, and he imagined them in hand-to-hand fights on the site of the present Cornhill 'which took place perhaps fifty thousands year ago, between the probably hairy and black dwarf Palaeolithic men and equally hairy mammoths'! A mammoth (an example of which is seen in the Museum) would provide Stone Age man with the everyday necessities for some time and were worth the considerable effort to catch and kill one.

Cornhill grew from being a piece of high ground east of the marshes to become the centre of 'Gipeswic'. From ancient times, produce would be brought from the surrounding countryside for sale

in the town, and in return the farmers would buy goods and chattels either made or imported by the townspeople. This trade was an important source of revenue for the authorities and from at least the time of King John there was an efficient and organised system of market tolls, a tax or charge paid by the buyer on the purchase of tollable goods.

The market was always a failsafe way for the authorities to raise money since it was impossible for the town to function without the flow of traffic both in and out, especially goods intended for import and export via the port. In 1352, for example, the bailiffs lost no time in raising a tax to pay for strengthening the earthen ramparts during a time of unrest. Tolls of halfpennies and farthings were levied on goods entering the town gates so that all cartloads of corn, meat and other provisions were taxed, as were the hundreds of lamb, hare, rabbit, fox, cat or squirrel skins coming to the Ipswich tanneries. Two pence was levied on every 2,000

Cornhill and Tavern Street, 1904.

A very congested Cornhill at the turn of the 19th century.

The Old Post Office (left) and town hall.

rushes, used for strewing floors or thatching roofs, and a similar amount on each bundle of cloth and other goods destined for sale.

The importance of the Church of St Mildred, which once graced the south side of Cornhill, is belied by descriptions of its small size. It stood at the Golden Lion corner of the town hall, and what is now Lion Street was once called St Mildred's Lane.

Described variously as a parish church and a chapel, St Mildred's was built in around 700 AD alongside a hall belonging to the Wuffinga kings and purposely on the central market and all-important town meeting place. They laid down the precedent that Cornhill was thereafter the site of civic administration. The naming of St Mildred's also indicates the hand of the Wuffingas as royal patrons.

In about 550 AD the new kingdom of East Anglia emerged, whose kings were called the Wuffingas. While these new rulers established their power-base beside the River Deben at Sutton Hoo, they were fully cognisant of the potential advantages to be had from the commercial town and port of 'Gipeswic'. Depicted on the reverse of the official town seal of 1200, St Mildred's is one of the earliest recorded

buildings on Cornhill and the dedication to a seventh-century Saxon saint of royal birth again reflects the interests of the Saxon Wuffingas.

St Mildred (died *c.*700 AD), the daughter of the King of Mercia and Princess Ermenburga of Kent, retired to a convent in France to avoid the attention of an unwelcome suitor, where she met the mother of Aldwulf (664–713), King of East Anglia. Mildred was described as 'ever merciful, of easy temper and tranquil' and said to be generous to the poor, taking special interest in widows and children, and when she died her tomb became a place of pilgrimage. She became a popular saint of early mediaeval England and with so many royal connections was a suitable choice for the 'Gipeswic' chapel.

The chapel lasted until some time in the 14th century, when it was converted into the first town hall. As a church, it had been in decline for some time. Its small capacity would have precluded large congregations, and low attendance numbers meant correspondingly low income for the priests. The change of use of St Mildred's from church to town hall (or moot hall) demonstrates an early example of the pragmatic nature of 'Gipeswic' townspeople.

The old Corn Exchange and Cornhill in 1865. (W. Vick Photo)

The Westgate corner of Cornhill in the late 1950s taken either early in the morning or on Wednesday afternoon half-day closing. (ITM Collection)

Old Waterloo House (now Debenhams) and Mumford's Passage, which in the 1930s became Lloyds Avenue.

JAMES BEART.

WATERLOO HOUSE

GENERAL DRAPERY & COSTUME WAREHOUSE.

The moot hall was the original meeting place for the Corpus Christi Guild, the 'guild merchant' of the 1200 Charter, and recast as the Guild of Corpus Christi in 1203, under the patronage of the Corporation. Guilds began in the 12th century as religious fraternities, a kind of mediaeval trade union, which revolved around parish activities. Within the community, they made provision for their members who fell on hard times and promoted the interests of their common trades, including the provision of apprenticeships. Corpus Christi Guild played a key role in social, religious and commercial life, and although it had no real say in the town administration it was inextricably linked in practice. Its business was civic and not restricted to church matters, though religion was at the heart of all their functions. St Mary le Tower became the guild's church and its chief festival was the annual procession on Corpus Christi day (see Tower Street).

The town's right to hold a fair or market was confirmed by a series of royal charters. Attached to this was provision for a court, which became known as the Pie Powder Court (a corruption of the French *pieds poudreux*, the 'dusty footed'), whose officers met in the moot hall. The officers dispensed swift justice: injuries, disputes, illegal trading or the regulation of measures was decided before 'the dust can fall from the foot'. When it came to trading laws, the town had both the authority to ensure the rule of law and the means to punish those who offended.

Other forms of justice were dispensed from here, too. In 1450, in the days before glazed windows, a shoemaker called John Maughteld was fined 20 shillings for eavesdropping. People would creep around the town at night to stand below the overhanging upper storeys and listen for scandal or secrets. Personal space was as much an issue then as now, and in 1332 John Bande the Elder had to pay Geoffrey Costyn £10 in damages as he had built a windmill on a mound that overlooked his land, thus encroaching on his privacy.

Since the law was administered from Cornhill, it is logical that here also was its physical embodiment – notably the stocks – an ancient punishment for petty criminals. The unfortunate offenders were subjected to public ridicule by having their feet, and sometimes hands, locked into a wooden structure. The use of stocks died out in the 19th century but the image of those miscreants in the stocks being pelted with rotten fruit or similar endures in the public memory. Dr Taylor commented in 1888:

'The Ipswich Stocks were in use in the borough until a comparatively recent period. They may now be seen at the borough police station. This kind of punishment has been in vogue in England from Anglo-Saxon times to the present century. Although the Ipswich Stocks are in good preservation, it is evident they have been used.'

Close by the stocks was the pillory, where the offender was secured by the neck and arms in a standing position, thus rendering him vulnerable to objects thrown by passers by. In the 13th century the pillory was prescribed for selling tainted food or for re-selling goods bought outside the town. Millers were put in the pillory for charging more than the regulated price; for two hours on a first offence, seven hours for the second and third offence, but the third offence meant they had to give up trading forever. The pillory was finally abolished in 1837, but not before it had bequeathed the expression 'pilloried' to the language.

There was also 'Whipping at the Cart Tail', where the miscreant was tied to a horse-drawn cart with a bare back and taken three times round the Cornhill, being whipped with a cat o' nine tails throughout. Other miscreants were paraded around the town in a tumbrel – a punishment invariably for anyone working in or keeping a 'bawdy' house – accompanied by a boy banging a drum to draw the attention of bystanders.

In front of the Hall of Pleas public hangings took place and, in the 16th century, the burning of heretics. It was decreed, however, that burnings had to be done before 10 o'clock in the morning as the

market opened then and the town authorities knew any overlapping was not good for business.

Among the first to be burned was a man known only as Kerby, in 1546, who was 'brought to the market-place, at Ipswich'. A stake was ready with wood, broom and straw, and poor Kerby, with only his shirt and nightcap on, was fastened to the stake with irons and the fire lit.

Protestants, known as the Marian Martyrs (and for whom there is a memorial in Christchurch Park), were burned at the stake for their faith after the Catholic Queen Mary ascended the throne in 1553. One of the first was a minister of East Bergholt, Robert Sammuell. The following year two women were also burned on Cornhill, 'being fastened with irons to a sixpenny stake and surrounded with piles of broom and faggots'.

White's Directory records the burning of Nicholas Peke:

'When the faggots were blazing about Peke, Dr Reading called out – "Peke, recant thy opinion, and I have thy pardon in my hand"; but he answered, "I defy it and thee, and withal spit out a mouthful of blood". Hearing this answer, Dr Reading promised in the name of the bishop of Norwich, 40 days' pardon for sins to all those who would cast a stick in the fire. Whereupon Sir John Audley, kt, Mr Barnes, Mr Curson, and divers others of reputation, there present, cut down boughs from the trees with their swords, and threw them into the fire.'

In 1588 a Catholic Priest, Father John Robinson, was hanged, drawn and quartered.

At least two cases of 'Delapidaretur' were carried out on Cornhill in 1519, which consisted of pressing the miscreant to death under heavy weights or stones.

In 1898 an independent company, the Ipswich Omnibus Service, commenced operations. Eighteen buses, known as 'Penny Omnibuses', offered the fare of '1d all the way'. (ITM Collection)

Grain trading at the Corn Exchange in the 1930s. The last corn market was held on 29 June 1972. (ITM Collection)

The Cornhill is the one part of the market that has never changed its name, and it has more or less kept its original rectangular shape. If we could take just one part of Ipswich that would best reflect its evolution it would be the Cornhill. As R.A.N. Dixon put it, 'it has seen tragedy and gaiety, processions and fairs – clowns, conjurors, performing animals, giants and dwarfs; bull baitings, the burning of heretics at the stake, and the whole quasi-sided gamut of mass emotion'.

In 1698 the traveller Celia Fiennes visited Ipswich:

'This is a very clean town … their streetes of a good size well pitch'd with small stones, a good Market Cross railed in. I was there on Saturday which is their market day and saw they sold their butter by the pinte, 20 ounces for 6 pence, and often for 5d or 4d. They make it up in a mold just in the shape of a pinte pot and so sell it.'

She observed that the Market Cross 'has good carving' but thought there were only '3 or 4 good houses in the town'.

The Market Cross was built in 1629 and replaced an earlier one given to the town in 1510 by Edmund Daundy, a notable local benefactor. It is thought that some Market Crosses were erected to commemorate the granting of a market's charter, and thus there might well have been a Market Cross of some description standing on Cornhill since the 13th century. Were it still there, it would show a very

different character than the present arrangement and would, without doubt, be the town's mascot such as those at Salisbury, Chichester or Winchester.

The Market Cross was an important town landmark, and it was here that proclamations were made as well as it being a focal point for the town, situated as it was at the heart of the town's commercial, administrative and judicial centre. It also stood close to where offenders against the laws of the market and town were punished, it being as public a place as possible and serving as an example to the many who passed by. Later it was used for public meetings and for election speeches and rallies.

The Market Cross was removed in 1812, said by Robert Malster to have been 'to the regret of some townspeople at the time and of many more since.'

Barnard Barton, wrote some verses in *The Suffolk Garland*, lamenting its demise:

'Lost to our view that ancient Cross, so fair,
Its timeless fate full oft we must deplore;
Regret shall breathe her murmuring in the air,
And anger loud her rage indignant pour'.

The health or otherwise of the Cornhill trade reflected the ups and downs of agriculture, on which so much of the surrounding county depended, and which can be tracked using the borough's income from market tolls as a guide. In the 1300s, for example, poor harvests brought near-starvation, while the Black Death, or bubonic plague, brought havoc to the town, and few traders wanted to risk paying the market tolls without prospective customers. Things picked up during the Hundred Years' War and variations in commercial and political life continued to be reflected on Cornhill throughout the centuries.

Although the corn market lent it its name, there were numerous commodities sold on Cornhill, including meat and livestock, with an apple market to the north-east of St Mildred's. A timber market occupied a comparatively large area south-east of the church. The herb market, behind the Shambles,

Sketch of the Rotunda by George Frost, which was removed in 1812 to make way for the first Corn Exchange. (Ipswich Borough Council Museums and Galleries)

was once an important feature and was still there in 1792 when new market commissioners were appointed to reshape the area.

As part of the reorganisation, the commissioners ordered that the Shambles be taken down and replaced by a Rotunda. Corporation records point to there having been a Shambles on that site since the 13th century. They were described as 'newly built' in 1583, and it is likely that those removed in 1792 were the result of reshaping of several earlier structures.

The Old Post Office building (now Lloyds TSB) was where the mediaeval Shambles stood and was that part of the market place where the butchers and fishmongers ('fish and flesh') plied their trade and often lived, too. Here they also slaughtered the

beasts, the blood running down the open drains along with the waste and general town refuse. Their stalls or shops fronted the messy and smelly business of preparing the meat, and the word shambles has come to mean scenes of chaos or mess, as such places, of necessity, became.

Close by the Shambles was the bull stake, or 'ringle', where the bulls were 'baited' before slaughter. Bull baiting is mentioned as far back as the reign of Edward III, when there was a strong feeling that beef could not be wholesome unless the animal had been baited. In 1468 'every butcher shall be amerced 12d for the sale of bull's flesh not bayted', and no beef was allowed to be sold that had not 'been baited by dogs at the bull ringle'. The practice continued until 1676.

The Georgian Rotunda that replaced the Shambles was short lived even by Ipswich standards. It had been so badly constructed and with such appalling ventilation that it was unusable for the purpose for which it had been built, namely as what we would recognise today as a shopping centre. It was considered that no modification was possible and in 1812 the Rotunda was demolished to make way for the first Corn Exchange.

The most significant building on the Cornhill, in terms of its name, was the Corn Exchange. It opened in March 1812 but had a 'forbidding appearance'. Its exterior was said to be 'jail-like' and the openings in the walls were grated with heavy iron bars. Inside was an open market so that when it rained, as of course it often did, the grain traders had to huddle round the sides. Around 1849 the council was requested to raise the walls, roof it with glass and get rid of the iron bars. The number of stands for the corn merchants was increased to 90 but, although the scheme was eventually agreed and implemented, the result was only a temporary improvement.

By the 1860s the Corn Exchange was extremely crowded on market days, and the council was urged to consider alternative venues, including converting the public hall in Westgate Street. However, in 1879 the council acquired the King Street site at the rear of the town hall and earmarked the old Corn Exchange site for a new Post Office.

The Old Post Office was built in 1881 as part of the sweeping changes that took place in the town in that year, including the building of the new Museum (see High Street). Part of the imposing architecture has female figures representing industry, electricity, steam and commerce, all the things that went to make Victorian England great.

A major upheaval was carried out on Cornhill at the start of the 20th century, when Ipswich Corporation embraced the innovation of the electric tram, which was partly responsible for the

Artistic licence is used, by George Frost to show (left to right) the Market Cross, Rotunda and St Mildred's, the latter already in use as the town hall. The figure of Justice on the Cross was moved to the Corn Exchange and re-christened Ceres. (Ipswich Borough Council Museums and Galleries)

construction of the electricity generating station in Constantine Road (also the site for the necessary tram depot). More than 10 miles of track were laid, and in 1903 the main terminus on Cornhill was constructed, eventually calling time on the horse trams that had run from Cornhill since 1800. The new tram system was to benefit those workers who were housed in the town's environs but whose jobs brought them to the new factories and dockside business and to the growing number of offices in the town itself. For a time, both types of trams operated alongside one another, and photographs of the early 1900s show Cornhill to be overcrowded and chaotic with barely enough room for pedestrians to make a dash for it between the clanking trams and the numerous horse-drawn vehicles. Gradually, though, the horses were squeezed out and the rows of horse-drawn public transport dwindled away.

In 1893 a Cabmen's Shelter was erected on Cornhill, but it was removed after a very short life of only two years after complaints from would-be passengers that the drivers would not come out if the weather was wet. The shelter was moved to Christchurch Park where it still stands near the Bolton Lane gateway, though at time of writing it is boarded up after being partially destroyed by arsonists.

By 1923 the trams had been superseded by the railless trolley bus and the coming of the era of motorised transport was heralded by the first engine driven taxis taking their place on the Cornhill cab rank, although motor buses did not come in until 1950.

The town hall, with the police station in the basement, was built in 1868 'in yellowish Bath stone, red sandstone from Mansfield and Portland limestone'. Built in the Venetian style, it incorporates five figures on its roof, all female, representing commerce, justice, law, learning and agriculture. The portrait heads are of Richard I, who first promised the town a charter, Cardinal Wolsey and King John. It served the town well until the 1950s, by which time it was severely inadequate with various departments having moved out to offices dotted across town. In the 1960s the bulk of the civic administration, the police and the law courts all moved to Civic Drive.

The town hall, though, remains the heart of the town and houses the offices of the Mayor. A Royal Commission had found 'deplorable corruption and inefficiency' in the old administration and, under the Municipal Reform Act of 1835, a new Corporation emerged consisting of a mayor, aldermen and councillors. This saw the end of the ancient role of the Portmen but greatly contributed to the enlargement of the electorate. The office of Mayor continues to this day.

COX LANE

Part of the Cox Lane car park, south of Carr Street, was the centre of an extensive pottery industry for almost 500 years and Cox Lane was extensively used in pre-Norman times as access for all aspects of the pottery business (see also Carr Street). The lane led directly south onto Foundation Road and so to the quayside, where the pottery could be loaded or unloaded. Excavations in 1958 led to the discovery of the now famous 'Ipswich ware' and evidence that in the Middle-Saxon age, from around 700 AD to 850 AD, pottery was the major industry of the town.

Cox (or Cock's) Lane has had several names over the years and it is unclear why it was so called other than speculation that cock fighting took place thereabouts, as it did at the Cock and Pye in nearby Upper Brook Street. It was known as 'Warrockes-lane' in the 16th century, for which no explanation is forthcoming, and in 1315 it was 'the lane leading from the Friars Preachers to Caristrete' (Carr Street). The Friars Preachers were the Dominicans, who established their friary in Ipswich in the 13th century. Muriel Clegg writes:

'In 1402 it appears as "the lane from Carystrete to le Cay" (Carr Street to the Quay). The evidence of a number of mediaeval deeds makes it possible to identify this lane as Balmannys Lane (1480), Baldman's Lane (1542), Baleman's Lane (1552) until in 1609 we know exactly where we are, for we are in "the lane heretofore called Ballman's Lane" now Cocke's Lane.'

In the early 19th century Cox Lane was heavily populated, and in 1874 there were plans to built more cottages on Cox Lane and they were to have 'a back way'. *Hunt's Guide* described it as 'an old fashioned avenue leading to Carr Street, containing many varieties of dwelling houses and small shops, but not a good one.'

Cox Lane is now little more than the entrance to the large car park that backs onto the Co-op, but it is probably one of the town's oldest routes. There was once a Pottery Street and a Potter Street nearby, but these are long gone and there is nothing now in the way of street names to commemorate the great pottery-making era. In its day it must have been a highly important and commercial thoroughfare for an industry that provided the town with much of its wealth and trading status throughout the seventh and eighth centuries.

In the 1920s the Ipswich Co-operative's butcher shops were started in Cox Lane, in buildings previously used as the hardware department. The top end of the old lane is now the covered walkway between the two Co-op buildings, its original route obliterated by the open car park.

A small street claimed by the Cox Lane car park was Permit Office Street, which is explained by White's 1844 directory that says the occupier was an official who issued Custom and Excise permits.

On the west side of Cox Lane is Christ Church Joint Baptist and United Reform Church and on the east side is St Pancras Catholic Church.

COYTES GARDENS

Look in vain for the gardens that at one time inhabited this tiny corner of Ipswich, once the pride and joy of one Dr William Beeston (1671–1731) who was, wrote Daniel Defoe, 'exquisitely skilled in botanic knowledge.' All that remains is a small byway linking Princes Street and Friars Street that once ran through Dr Beeston's garden. The name

should, perhaps, be Beeston Gardens, but at his death Dr Beeston willed it to his nephew, Dr William Beeston Coyte, his sister Frances's son. Dr Beeston Coyte died in 1810 and his daughter sold the property for development in 1824. It was considered 'most eligible' for building plots and by 1837 there were 28 houses. By the 1850s, however, this was reduced to 20 when Princes Street was cut through and the road was paved with broken stone. It was Dr Coyte, therefore, not Dr Beeston who was fresher in the memory when it came to naming the byway in 1878.

Dr Beeston's was typical of many such gardens that were dotted around the town in the 17th and 18th centuries, occasioning John Kirby to observe that 'most of the better Houses, even in the Heart of the Town, have convenient Gardens adjoining to them, which make them more airy and healthy, as well as more pleasant and delightful.'

When Daniel Defoe visited the town he noted that there were some 'things very curious' to be seen, though 'some superficial writers have been ignorant of them'. One of these things was the garden of Dr Beeston, an eminent physician who 'began, a few years ago, a physic garden adjoining to his house in their town, and as he is particularly curious and, as I was told, exquisitely skilled in botanic knowledge, so he has been not only very diligent, but successful too, in making a collection of rare and exotic plants such as are scarce to be equalled in England.'

On Pennington's map the garden is shown as an extensive area just north of Boat Lane (its only surviving part is, more or less, Friars Street). There were shrubberies marked out by paths and places to sit and enjoy the diverse range of rare and exotic plants. Places, too, for Dr Beeston to contemplate the storm he had whipped up by championing inoculation. When, in 1724, he inoculated three people, he was subjected to vociferous protest from those who believed that far from preventing the onset of disease (especially the dreaded plague) it actually caused it. In response, Dr Beeston suggested that his accusers, whom he called the 'bigotted high

Churchmen' and 'Dissenters' who had stirred up the trouble, to use reason on the subject. The accusers sentenced to 'damnation' all who were concerned in the 'heathenish' practice of inoculation.

However, Dr Beeston's example inspired Robert Sutton to do smallpox inoculation trials and he advertised in the *Ipswich Journal* that he had hired a house for the 'reception of persons who are disposed to be inoculated'.

Coytes Garden is unique in retaining part of its old road surface of small paving setts and central guttering, which Muriel Clegg thought indicated an early date before side guttering was common practice. Such paving probably covered a larger area but was replaced by broken stone at the time of the housing development.

The Revd Richard Canning, in his 1764 edition of Kirby's *The Suffolk Traveller*, made the observation:

'One favourable circumstance is almost peculiar to this place, which is that most of the better houses, even in the Heart of the Town, have convenient Gardens adjoining to them, which makes them more airy and healthy, as well as more pleasant and delightful.'

Perhaps it was these same gardens that inspired John Glyde to write in *The Suffolk Garland*:

'Oh Ipswich! Sweet, scene of my juvenile years
Thy pleasure recede from my view,
To thy grass cover'd meads, embroidered with
    flowers,
I bid a reluctant adieu.'

Another to remark on Ipswich gardens was Francois de la Rochefoucauld:

'The town gives the impression of being empty: one sees hardly anyone in the streets, and this impression derives a little from the spread of the town which is much increased by the large number of gardens within its bounds. They boast that this makes the air very salubrious.'

A memorial to Dr Coyte, his two wives and three children was erected in St Nicholas' Church by their grandson, William Coyte Freeland.

Coytes Gardens was once famous for its stamp shop, which operated for many years before its final closure in 1985. The premises now house a sandwich shop.

CROWN STREET

Crown Street is now characterised by the prominent Crown Pools and the Corporation bus depot, but it was once home to numerous stables servicing the many inns on Tavern Street. Here the horses were harnessed and prepared for a quick changeover on the arrival of the mail coaches. There seems to be no definitive reason for its name, other than it literally 'crowns' the old town, making a small arc above the northern ramparts, or it took its name from a lost Crown inn.

Many changes have taken place on Crown Street and nothing is left of the houses, inns or stables that once lined it. It lost its importance once the mail coaches gave way to the railways, although several rows of shops kept it busy until the 1960s.

The name of Egerton is synonymous with 20th-century Ipswich, and the huge rectangular building built on the north side of Crown Street was famous in its day for the ramps that drivers had, somewhat nervously, to negotiate to get to the top-floor

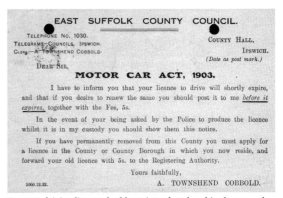

By 1903 driving licences had been introduced and in that year the speed limit was increased to 20mph.

The Egertons advertisement on the end wall of Yates's public house informed motorists they were en route for Egertons garage on Crown Street.

servicing area above the showrooms. The only reminder of Egertons is a sign painted onto the east wall of Yates's public house (previously Colchester Carpets and, before that, Egertons car showroom), visible on the approach from St Margaret's Street, indicating 'Egertons (Ipswich) Ltd, 100 yds'. Careful examination of the paintwork reveals that it replaced an earlier wall painting, which said simply 'Egertons the Garage'.

The Egerton and Botwood 'empire' of motoring engineering, which held sway in the town for most of the 20th century, were pioneers in what was perhaps the most significant step along the way of motorised transport. The Locomotive Act of 1878 was blamed for the slow start of the British motor engineering industry. The Act restricted mechanical road vehicles to 4mph in open country and 2mph in towns. Three drivers were required for each vehicle, two to travel in the vehicle and one to walk ahead carrying a red flag. Thus, the Act became known as

the Red Flag Act. Even for the solid-tyred 'horse-less carriages', 2mph was very slow, yet it was 1896 before the Act was repealed and the *EADT* was able to announce that 'motor carriages may use highways at a maximum speed of 12mph – an added peril to life and limb'!

By 1900 it was clear that the motor car had captured the imagination of a new generation of men and women looking for fresh and exciting diversions in their already rapidly changing lives. World War One saw an acceleration of the developing technology, and by the 1920s the public's fascination for motoring had taken hold. A band of entrepreneurs sprung up to cater for the market. One of these was a young engineer, William Botwood, who had moved to Ipswich in the 1860s and got a job with Henry Bennett, who had a coach-building business in St Clement's Street (off Fore Street). By 1868 the firm had become Bennett & Botwood, although a few years later the partnership was dissolved and William set up business close to his own home on Woodbridge Road. He manufactured top of the range coaches and opened showrooms in St Matthew's Street. Unfortunately, William's health gave out but his two sons, William and Samuel, took over and built up the business into a successful venture. They manufactured 75 different kinds of carriages, gigs, broughams, shooting wagons, two types of rickshaw and exported not only to Europe but also to American, Japan and all parts of the Empire. The Botwood brothers astutely picked up on the new motor vehicle potential and by the turn of the century were manufacturing car bodies as efficiently and profitably as they had carriages.

Keen to keep ahead of the game, Samuel Botwood went to Paris to negotiate with the De Dion Bouton Company over taking on an agency for their cars. He was successful, and in 1902 was joined by Justin Reginald Egerton (always called Reggie) in founding a new company, Botwood & Egerton.

At the time Reggie moved to Suffolk a new era in motor engineering was just beginning. The Egerton brothers saw huge commercial opportunities

Egerton's showroom in the early 1900s, photographed by Adolphus Tear. (ITM Collection)

opening up and the more adventurous of the two, Reggie, took to motoring with the enthusiasm of his generation, eager to push out the boundaries and unafraid of the consequences. Hubert, though, was not to be outdone, as in 1901 he was the first person to ride a motorcycle from John O'Groats to Land's End, a feat that inspired Reggie to try the same with a 'Primus' car in 1903.

The Egerton brothers were born at Weston Longville, Norfolk, where their father was Rector. Leaving home aged 18, Reggie farmed in Canada for a few years before returning to England to find that his brother Hubert had, in the meantime, entered into partnership with Gerard Mann, so founding the Norwich firm of Mann Egerton. With Hubert forging ahead in Norwich, and Reggie building up Botwood & Egerton, those who had initially thought that motoring was just a new craze soon became aware that the car was here to stay. Motoring became the 'in' thing, though Brian Dyes of the Ipswich Transport Museum points to the names given to early motoring events. Since a relevant vocabulary

had not then been invented, any gathering of cars was called a 'gymkhana', borrowed from the horse world.

Reggie's motoring exploits were to be infamous and his name became familiar throughout the new motoring world and to the local constabulary. His regular brushes with the law, mostly in respect of speeding or dangerous driving, regularly made the newspapers and *The Motor* magazine.

Inevitably, perhaps, the partnership between Reggie and the Botwoods foundered, and in 1910 the directors of Egerton & Botwood went their separate ways. When Samuel Botwood died at the early age of 44, Botwoods was taken over by Mann Egerton (though the name was retained), which gave both Egerton brothers business interests in Ipswich.

After World War One trade picked up rapidly and the post-war years saw the burgeoning of private motoring, although people still had to be persuaded to part with their money in the post-war depression. John F. Bridges writes in *Early Country Motoring*:

CROWN STREET

'The late '20s and '30s were difficult times for most companies, and Botwoods were no exception. Their main agency was by now Austin, which was heavily promoted by events such as "Austin Week", when the cars were paraded through the streets of Ipswich. The local authorities co-operated in this exercise by putting the traffic lights out of action so the procession could proceed smoothly.'

When the new showrooms and repair workshops were built at Major's Corner in 1924 the old Woodbridge Road Works was sold off, thus ending the association with the coach-building days of Henry Bennett. In 1928 the Crown Street premises were built and Reggie extended the number of car agencies. Gradually, other premises across the town were brought into the Egerton umbrella, including the workshops on Great Colman Street.

In the 1950s Egertons were the only firm to employ a night watchman, who used to make an hourly call to Ipswich police station saying 'Humber reporting'. Humber cars were one of the main makes of car sold by Egertons and used as a codeword.

After a series of takeovers and amalgamations, the Crown Street site became redundant and in the early 1960s was sold for a new town swimming and leisure facility. The Mayor, Mrs Anne Smith, laid the foundation stone for the Crown Pools on 24 April 1982, and two years later, in May 1984, the Mayor, Mr Peter Gardiner, opened it for business.

One of the few surviving landmarks of the 19th century on Crown Street is the Cricketers Hotel, now owned by Wetherspoons, which stands beside Crown Pools. It is built to emulate the style of Helmingham Hall, home of the Tollemache brewing family.

A Temperance Hall once stood on the corner of

A 1909 Renault car, under the direction of Ernest Prettyman's chauffeur, photographed at Orwell Park, Nacton. Gillian Bence-Jones remembers that her grandfather Prettyman 'once went round the stable yard seventy-three times backwards being unable to take his hands off the wheel long enough to change gear'! (ITM Collection)

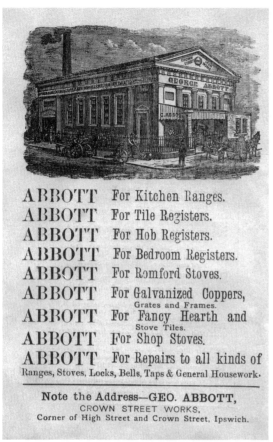

ABBOTT For Kitchen Ranges.
ABBOTT For Tile Registers.
ABBOTT For Hob Registers.
ABBOTT For Bedroom Registers.
ABBOTT For Romford Stoves.
ABBOTT For Galvanized Coppers, Grates and Frames.
ABBOTT For Fancy Hearth and Stove Tiles.
ABBOTT For Shop Stoves.
ABBOTT For Repairs to all kinds of
Ranges, Stoves, Locks, Bells, Taps & General Housework.

Note the Address—GEO. ABBOTT,
CROWN STREET WORKS,
Corner of High Street and Crown Street. Ipswich.

George Abbott's Crown Street Works advertisement for 1897.

Crown Street and High Street, built in 1840 at the expense of the Quaker banker Richard Dykes Alexander. It was a 'large and handsome building, of Doric architecture' and could accommodate 800 people, 'being 68 feet long' with a spacious gallery and platform. It was here that members of the Ipswich Total Abstinence Society held their meetings. Drunkenness was a serious problem in the 19th century and many were called on to 'sign the pledge' of total abstinence. The Ipswich Temperance Society was formed in 1836 and between 1840 and 1850 they published 200 temperance tracts, ranging in length from 2 to 20 pages each. Many were written by Richard Dykes Alexander, who was also a noted photographer and philanthropist.

The Hall was also the venue for talks, the *Ipswich Express* announcing in November 1851 that 'Mrs Henry Knight and Miss Charlotte Knight will lecture on Dress Reform in full Bloomer Costume at the Temperance Hall, Ipswich on Saturday 8th'.

The ladies Knight, no doubt, caused something of a stir in their bloomers!

In 1890 the hall was taken over by George Abbott, who set up his Crown Street Iron Works on the site. Abbotts was famous for the 'Victoria' cooking range, together with lawn mowers, palisading, gates, railings, boiler repairs and all makes of bicycles, tricycles and perambulators 'repaired and made equal to new at reasonable cost'.

In 1964 the old Temperance Hall was demolished to be replaced by an insurance office and is now called Churchill House.

CURRIERS LANE
As the name suggests, this is one of the old town lanes and is associated with the considerable tanning industry known to have flourished in mediaeval times and which continued well into the 20th century. Raw hides were first stripped of fat and then soaked in lime pits before they could be called 'leather'. A 'curryer' was the man who 'finished' the dry leather by greasing it to make it flexible, when it was then sold to the town's craftsmen, such as saddlers and harness makers.

Its earlier name, Barkers Street, also has tanning connotations as the 'barker' was a man working in the 'barking house', where fishing nets were steeped in a solution made from oak bark, the tanning of which helped to preserve them from saltwater. The barkers were also leather tanners and until the 1960s, when it was swallowed up by the Civic Drive development, Tanners Lane was nearby.

Hunt's Guide says of what was then called Currier's Arms Lane, 'of this we need only say that it contains several poor cottages, the old sort, and that it leads to the Railway Station Road.'

In addition to its traditional uses, leather was also used in book coverings. The town's first printing press is credited to Anthony Scoloker who, together with the physician-schoolmaster-priest, Richard Argentine, began work in Ipswich in the 1540s and printed the works of Luther and Zwingli. In 1548 another Ipswich printer, John Oswen, produced

Exhortation to the Sick. Thought to have been written by Richard Argentine, it gave advice for those afflicted with the plague. In preparation for his new college, Wolsey encouraged several printers to settle in Ipswich.

Leather was also needed for making pails, which in the 16th century were necessary to put out fires. In Bacon's *Annals* he notes that in the year 1537 'Henry Burgess, being admitted a freeman, shall provide Bobbets and pailes of leather before Christmas next, for danger of fire'.

A few years later, in 1564, it was ordered that 'every burgess have one leather bucket in his house' and four years later 'every burgess of this towne shall have their bucket or buckets ready before a certaine time, and the treasurer shall provide for every ward a crome and a ladder, convenient, at the town's charge'.

The crome was a long pole with a hoe blade at the end and when fitted with hooks could pull away the burning thatch, which was the primary roofing material. A crome, a ladder and a leather bucket would seem poor weapons in the defence against fire, but Ipswich was blessed with numerous springs and the ready availability of water added considerably to the fire fighter's arsenal.

An even older name for Curriers Lane is seen on Ogilby's 1674 survey, when it was named Pudding Lane and, had it survived until Victorian times, might have fallen prey to prevailing niceties, as 'pudding' in Middle English meant entrails or guts, which had come to also apply to the scrapings from the hides being cured in the lane. Not only would a foul and oppressive smell have hung over the area, but it would also have attracted huge numbers of flies and rats, both of which were loathed by town dwellers but were very much a fact of life. Muriel Clegg observes:

'Refuse from the fish and cattle markets, from the slaughtering of beasts on the Cornhill and elsewhere with the consequent flooding of gutters with blood and entrails together present a horrifying picture.'

Larger conurbations would have had more than one Pudding Lane, invariably close to the Shambles, where the meat was prepared; London has five but the most famous one, where the 1666 Great Fire of London broke out in a bakery, is erroneously thought to get its name from pudding makers.

As late as 1844 there were five listings under 'Curriers and Leather Cutters' in *White's Directory* – Henry Bond and Thomas Shuttleworth (St Helen's Street), Thomas Corder Jnr (Buttermarket), William Frith (Woodbridge Road), William Garrard (Back Hamlet) and Walton Turner (Elm Street). One of the last tanneries to close was that of W. & A.J. Turner, in Bramford Road, which closed its doors in 1991. Turners was founded in 1716 and as late as 1946 one of their two factories, though modernised, still retained some of the old methods by 'pit tanning' the leather. The factory's output of leather, principally for shoe manufacturing, was 1,200 hides a week.

The local inn was the Curriers' Arms, and in 1881 Dr Taylor wrote:

'I do not know how long the Curriers' Arms has been a public house but both the present inn and the house adjoining are very ancient wood and brick buildings, and were once handsomely kept, as the outside architectural details prove.'

It is not clear where the Curriers' Arms stood but it seems to have survived until at least the 1850s when it appears in the Ipswich directories.

Curriers Lane was also where Church of England 'worthies', such as 'gentlemen and clergymen', founded a Grey Coat School for boys in 1709. It was an attempt to provide education for poor children and the curriculum was based on the tenets of Christianity. By the 1840s the Schools of Grey Coat Boys and Blue Coat Girls had attracted many benefactions and bequests together with an annual income of around £300 from Pemberton's Charity.

The Board School is now the offices of Gottelee & Goldsmith, solicitors.

CUTLER STREET

The route of this street was once that of a lane leading to St Nicholas Church. However, in the late 19th century the Paving and Lighting Commissioners gained permission from the feoffees of Cutler's Charity for a strip of land to be used to enable the new street to be created, hence its name.

William Cutler endowed Cutler's Charity in 1620 that left money to the borough to provide an amount of '2 l' for 'three poor persons.' Under the Municipal Reform Act of 1835, Ipswich Corporation became trustees for a number of charities, including Cutler's.

The St Nicholas Centre has its main entrance on Cutler Street.

DIAL LANE

A narrow lane giving a glimpse of old Ipswich, Dial Lane links the Buttermarket with Tavern Street and it, too, is undoubtedly an ancient thoroughfare. It crosses the Buttermarket alongside the Ancient House and merges with St Stephen's Lane and Arras Square.

Previously known as Cook's Row (or Cook Row), this was the mediaeval equivalent of a row of fast food providers, where the ready-made pies were sold. Following the custom of trading as close to other cooks as possible, this must have been one of the most fragrant – or perhaps pungent – smelling lanes in town. Food sold or supplied by the cooks later came to be called victuals and the cooks themselves victuallers.

Just as we now change the use of buildings, market traders moved their stalls to different streets when circumstances dictated. In 1447 the cloth market moved from St Lawrence Street up to Cornhill and the fruit market moved into St Lawrence Street, so it was with the cooks, who in the 17th century moved to Dial Lane, which for a while also became known as Cook Row.

In 1864 *Hunt's Guide* said:

'This Lane has an old look about it, but a fire that occurred opposite the Church, last summer, has been the means of letting in the modern builder; who have found some human skulls among the old foundations, and who has set his stamp in white brick facia upon the west side of the Lane.'

It is probable that the premises were originally part of the mediaeval churchyard.

The name Dial Lane came about in the 19th century and took its name from a clock that projected from the Church of St Lawrence, before the tower's reconstruction in 1882. The old clock had stuck out as an odd angle and 'rocks in every high wind'. It was still known as Cook Row in 1844 but soon became 'Cook Row alias Dial Lane' and soon simply Dial Lane. Charles Borrett, the builder, removed it when he restored and enclosed the church tower in 1882.

Looking to right and left along Dial Lane, it is still easy to imagine it in former times as some of the timber-framed buildings jut out over the walkway, like Chambers Gallery and Chocolate Boutique, where the jetty is clearly seen. It is not always easy to tell the fake buildings from the genuine ones, but the John Michael hair salon and Soletrader (on the corner of Tavern Street) have examples of bow-fronted 'Ipswich' windows, which sit on corbels that project from the face of the wall and consist of a block built into the wall that supports the window. These were replica Ancient House windows copied by several Victorian architects and used on several buildings around the town. The 'Ipswich' window became very fashionable and was taken up by architects in other towns.

This was not the first time that Dial Lane had seen innovation in the matter of windows. In the 14th century even wealthy men were only just beginning to have glazed windows, and in 1307 the widow of a merchant, Phil Harneys, prized her windows sufficiently to mention them in her will. Alice Harneys left a large house, containing two shops and 'two solars', to her grandson, John Harneys.

Dial Lane was always busy as people pass between

The tower and south side of St Lawrence's Church.

Although the panel showing carved stone shears on the east end of St Lawrence's Church is Victorian, it replaced a decayed original and reflects the influence of the town's mediaeval drapers.

the Buttermarket and Tavern Street or to attend services at St Lawrence's. What they might not have known, or indeed those who walk along Dial Lane now, is there are said to be one or even two 'subterranean chambers' running under the street. They are believed to have been underground communication tunnels that led to and from the Carmelite Priory, which for several hundred years occupied part of the Buttermarket (see Queen Street).

The 1920s 'art nouveau' shop front of what is now the Pickwick Coffee Shop recalls the timeless traditions of providing 'victuals' and is housed in what used to be Scarborrow's Opticians, signalled by the spectacle-like front windows and a pair of frames incorporated into the wrought iron gate. In Edwardian times the frames projected out over the pavement from a lantern.

The most significant edifice on Dial Lane, however, is the 15th-century Church of St Lawrence with its highly decorative tower and flint exterior, built in the perpendicular style. Its construction began through the good offices of one of the town's drapers, John Buttold, who provided the initial funding and built the nave at his own expense. Buttold died in 1431 and is said to be buried

somewhere in the church. In the mid-19th century Hunt recounts the precarious state of the tower:

'The gigantic patchwork steeple has been seen to rock to and fro in every high wind for the last 50 years; yet, at every fresh hurricane, the passers by in Tavern Street will stop to watch it, and point out to others how it sways backward and forward, and so a small crowd will be formed, diminishing and renewing as long as the wind continues to blow.'

The money to build the chancel was provided by John Baldwin, a draper, who died in 1449. The church that stood here at Domesday is said to have had 12 acres of land, though it is not clear if they were all in the Dial Lane area. St Lawrence was one of the churches of the Holy Trinity Priory.

DOGS HEAD STREET

One of the most unusual street names in Ipswich is named for a public house that formerly stood at the corner of Upper Brook Street called The Dog's Head in the Pot. It stood by the entrance to the Provision Market, which operated from December 1810 until its demolition in 1897, and the east end of Falcon Street was generally known as Dogs Head Lane (minus apostrophe). Later names for the same pub seem to be the White Hart and the Punchbowl.

The offices of the Ipswich Building Society now occupy the site and have done since the early 1900s. Established in 1849 as the Freehold Land Society (FLS), it was formed by the lower middle and working classes of the 19th century, who pooled resources to buy plots of land for house building. It became a building society in 1866 and is one of the longest serving such societies in the country. The letters FLS can be seen on the name stones of houses around the town.

Origins for the name of the Dog's Head pub are, thought the Revd C.H. Evelyn White, probably Dutch, since there was considerable traffic over the centuries with the Low Countries and many Dutchmen lived or settled in Ipswich:

Eastern Counties Omnibus Company began operating from derelict land near the old cattle market in the 1930s. Notice the crest which belonged to the public house called the Ipswich Arms. (ITM Collection)

'A "dirty, slovenly housewife" was supposed to be characterised by such an epithet. In Holland, when one is late for dinner, he is said to "find the dog in the pot", viz the empty pot, which, true to Dutch manners, would be consigned to the dog after the meal was served.'

It also served as a warning to husbands who tarried too long in the pub: they should hurry home or else the dog would get their supper!

Dog's Head Lane was widened in 1876 when John Chevallier Cobbold offered to finance the work in memory of his deceased son. Since the lane was only 15 feet wide the offer was accepted, and in 1881 Lane was changed to Street. A few years later yet more changes were made and the entire length of one side was moved back. A house at the corner of Brook Street was removed and by then the Dog's Head in the Pot inn had also gone.

The Plough public house, also known as the Old Plough, is still functioning though it has lost part of its premises to redevelopment at the time when the Provision Market was created in 1810 (see Falcon Street). It is now on the borough council's list of Ipswich Buildings of Special Architectural or Historical Interest.

EAGLE STREET

The Spread Eagle inn gave this street its name though it was once part of the western end of Rope Lane (now Rope Walk). It is now a small access road between Orwell Place and Bond Street. The Spread Eagle, which in the 19th century was a combined butcher's shop and inn, is the only survivor of four inns that once stood at this crossroad and was completely rebuilt in the 1850s to match the style of older buildings nearby. The Bull's Head stood on the opposite corner and later became Martin & Newby's ironmongery, the Eclipse was at the corner of Fore Street and Orwell Place and the Shoulder of Mutton close by.

A plaque on 9 Eagle Street marked the home of John Glyde (1823–1905), an author of historical books which are still standard reference works on the social and economic aspects of the town and county of Suffolk. He was described as a radical thinker and was involved in many organisations working for the social and cultural improvement of the town.

ELM STREET

The row of elms that stood for many years in the churchyard is the origin of the street name and the name of the church, St Mary at Elms (St Mary Elms for short). It was described by Dr Taylor as 'one of the most picturesque churches in Ipswich … its square embattled, red brick Tudor tower is half grown with ivy and with the old gabled houses at the

bottom of Black Horse Lane, makes up a very pretty picture'.

Built on the site of the older church dedicated to St Saviour, the Norman doorway in the south porch, parts of its stone discoloured by the touch of countless hands, is a clue to its age. It is likely that it remains from the earlier building. The brick tower was added in 1443 and bears the 'diaper' pattern, made by using bricks with burnt ends alongside lighter bricks and commonly found in Tudor brickwork. It is thought that Cardinal Wolsey brought the bricks from the Netherlands for use in his proposed college, but at its – and his – demise they were diverted to St Mary's. Its present shape, however, dates from the 1880s when the church was enlarged and the north aisle was extended and the present chancel added.

Close to the tower base, on the triangle of grass at the junction with Black Horse Lane, is Tam, a bronze sculpture by Honoria Surie. It depicts a young girl, the artist's daughter, sitting cross-legged and working a lump of clay.

Inside is a haven of peace and quiet from what

The cottage behind St Mary Elms dates from the 15th century and is one of the oldest houses in the town.

'An old corner of St Mary Elms' by the Victorian photographer William Vick. The site later gave way to the extensive premises of R.D. & J.B. Fraser. (W. Vick Photo)

D.P. Mortlock refers to as 'the strident traffic outside' where there are some decorative wall monuments, the largest to William Acton, who faces his wife across a desk, erected by his son John whose wife died in childbirth. She is shown separately, reclining with a skull at her elbow and a book in her hand.

The Huguenot weavers of the 1680s worshipped here. They were Calvinist Protestants who were constantly at odds with the Catholic majority in France, Spain and the Low Countries, many arriving in Suffolk as refugees. They found employment in Ipswich in the weaving industry of the day. Daniel Defoe wrote:

'The French refugees when they first came over to England began a little to take to this place, and some merchants attempted to set up a linen manufacture in their favour, but it has not met with so much success as was expected, and at present I find very little of it. The poor people are however employed, as they are all over these counties, in spinning wool for other towns where manufacturers are settled.'

St Mary Elms is High Anglican and its congregation have a special affection for Our Lady (venerated not far away in Lady Lane). In 1977 the Guild of Our Lady of Ipswich was founded and under the auspices of the Revd Haley Dossor the Shrine of Our Lady of Grace of Ipswich was re-established in the church. A replica of the Nettuno statue, carved by Robert Mellamphy, stands in the niche created in the old priests doorway on the south side of the nave. Exchange pilgrimages take place between the congregation at Ipswich, who visit the Shrine of Our Lady of Grace at Nettuno (Italy), and the Italians, who visit St Mary Elms (see Lady Lane).

On the north side of the church is The Cottage, dating from 1487, which is the oldest occupied house in Ipswich. It once stood in the grounds of Thomas Seckford's estate and housed those who looked after his stables (see Westgate Street). The cottage was restored during 1984–85 and now has a Parish Room on the ground floor and a flat on the first floor.

Speculation about the location of Ipswich Castle continues unabated but Elm Street is a strong contender. Ipswich Castle was one of several built in Suffolk by the conquering Normans, although it is difficult to say whether it was built for defence or merely to show the local population who was in charge (see also Cranfields Yard).

The Castle was deliberately destroyed in 1176 by order of Henry II, though the reasons are unclear. However, if Elm Street is the correct location then the site of a razed castle becoming available for the construction of the nearby Church of St Saviour (now St Mary's) is a possibility. How much of the castle was stone and how much wood is unknown, and there is no great evidence of recycled materials in the present Church of St Mary. However, it has been speculated that rubble from the Castle was used to build the Holy Trinity Priory (in Christchurch Park), which would account for the lack of appreciable evidence of any stone and masonry in Elm Street.

At 2 Elm Street, now Morgan's Bistro, is an Ipswich Society plaque commemorating a celebrated Victorian author, Jean Ingelow (1820–1897). She was a bestselling author and, though almost forgotten in her native country, there is a Jean Ingelow Society in America. She was highly regarded by authors such as Tennyson and Ruskin and, in addition to novels, wrote children's stories and poems, the best known of which was *A High Tide on the Coast of Lincolnshire*.

Sir Alfred Tennyson read her first volume of poetry, *A Rhyming Chronicle of Incidents and Feelings* (written under the pseudonym of Orris), and declared that he should like to meet the author. They later met and became friends. Jean moved with her family to Ipswich in 1834, when her father was appointed manager of the Ipswich and Suffolk Banking Company in Elm Street. For 10 years they lived in the spacious first-floor rooms over the bank, where she began her writing career. When the bank failed the family moved out. To create access from King Street to the new Museum in Museum Street, part of the Ingelow house was demolished and Arcade Street built across their garden.

Another piece of literary history belongs to Elm Street in that John Bagnall established the *Ipswich Journal* there in 1720. The journal was to remain in publication until 1902, though it was produced at several different locations across the town.

FALCON STREET

Like many streets, Falcon Street began as Falcon Lane, though it is hard to imagine it now as a lane, with its north face being the border of the mighty Buttermarket Shopping Centre and the constant flow of general traffic, compounded by the to-ing and fro-ing generated by the Eastern Counties bus station. There is mapping evidence that the name Falcon Lane was in use by at least 1694 and the Falcon public house building survives. Since it was called le Falkon in 1609 and The Faulcon in 1650 (when parliamentary troops were billeted there), it is reasonable to assume that the name Falcon Lane is at least 400 years old.

Falcon Street has, since Anglo-Saxon times, been an important route linking the west and east of the town and was used by traffic headed towards the market areas of Cornhill and the Buttermarket. In 1810 the entrance to the new fruit and vegetable market, known as the Provision Market, was on Falcon Street (where the shopping centre stands), bordered on the west by the long-gone Market Lane.

The Provision Market was created as the result of two Acts passed in 1789 and 1793, which dealt with encroachments and annoyances 'where the streets, lanes, public passages and ways of the Town were rendered incommodious and dangerous'. The town's commissioners were required to regulate the various street markets dotted here and there, and so the Provision Market (and cattle market) came about.

The Provision Market was successful for some years, but by the 1880s it was tired and out-dated. *Hunt's Guide* said:

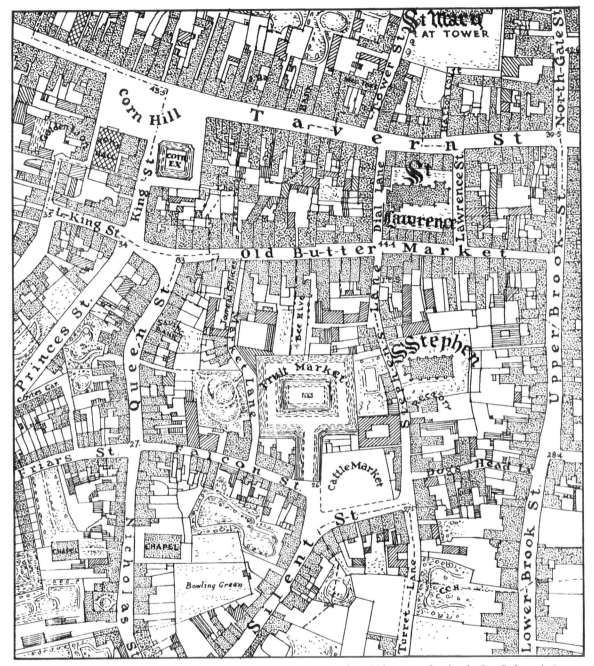

An extract from Edward White's plan of 1849 showing the Fruit (or Provision) Market, which was transferred to the Corn Exchange in August 1888. (Ipswich Borough Council)

'Once so popular, [the Provision Market] is now, almost deserted. Ten years ago, a vast quantity of fowls, eggs, butter, meat and all kinds of fruit and vegetables were sold there every Saturday and the place thronged from eight in the morning till ten at night'.

The decline was attributed to hawking, then allowed in the streets without a licence, but in truth it had just had its day. In spite of valiant efforts to revive it, the market 'ceased to be a place where men and women sold, and men and women bought'. It was moved to the new Corn Exchange on King Street and the buildings were demolished in 1897.

FONNEREAU ROAD

In the late 1880s William Budden recalled that in his school days 'Fonnereau Road was merely a footpath, with hawthorn hedges on each side – a veritable "lover's walk" in early summer. It led to the Bolton fields, which now form the Upper and Lower Arboretums' (in Christchurch Park).

The lower part of Fonnereau Road was a lane historically named 'le Deyry Lane', or Dairy Lane, and one of the earliest landowners there was Alice Tymperley, who in 1312 held a plot 'varying in width from 39 feet to 26 feet'. Whether it was the Tymperley dairy that gave the land its name, or simply that there were several dairies on what was then an area of countryside containing a number of smallholdings, is not clear.

The shaded bridleway that runs between the Lower and Upper Arboretum (sometimes called Lover's Lane, echoing Budden's 'lover's walk') is a reminder of its purely rural origins. As development progressed it was also used for carriage access to some of the larger houses.

The lower end of the street is mostly Georgian, but those were not prosperous times in the town's history, and little Georgiana exists, though what there was formed the platform for the Victorian expansion. The Victorians were in search of somewhere healthy to live, above the crowded old mediaeval town; somewhere with plenty of light and air. Dairy Lane, north of the ramparts, was just such a place. There was, happily, no shortage of water in that part of Ipswich with many springs emanating from the higher ground of what is now the Arboretum.

The development of the Dairy Lane area in the 1850s is owed to the Fonnereau family who were Huguenot refugees, descended from a branch of the family of the Earls of Ivry of Poitiers in Normandy, France (which accounts for nearby Ivry Street). Zacharie de Valliquerville, surnamed de Fonnereau, was one of those who had fled in 1685 after the revocation of the Edict of Nantes, which heralded a time of religious persecution for those of the Protestant persuasion. His eldest son, Claude (hence Claude Street), was born in 1677 and 'naturalised' as an Englishman in 1693. Zacharie made his fortune in London and in the 1730s invested in properties in Suffolk, including the purchase of Christchurch in 1735. The family proceeded to establish themselves as one of the major family players in Victorian Ipswich and, for around 150 years, owned Christchurch Mansion and Park.

Even before the shattering events of Henry VIII's Dissolution of the Monasteries, the Augustinian Priory of the Holy Trinity that had been part of town life since 1162 ceased. In 1535 Henry gave the Priory and its revenues to Cardinal Wolsey to help fund his College and, following Wolsey's fall from grace and death, the remaining fabric and property was sold in 1548 to Edmund Withipoll (1512–1582) who built a mansion on the site of the old Priory. The Withipolls had acquired great wealth through trading and Paul Withipoll, Edmund's father, had married into the Curzon family. On visiting Ipswich he decided to establish Edmund as a 'country gentleman'. An old guide records:

'Edmund continued his father's business in the City and appears to have been a typical Tudor Englishman: a successful merchant, a driver of hard bargains who aimed to extend his lands, found a line and married his children well. He was a man of letters, he appreciated art and had a measure of classical learning.'

He also possessed what is described as a 'temperamental' nature and was frequently at loggerheads with the borough authorities on account of his 'land grabbing' propensities and several times they had to resort to the law to defend the 'town rites' against his encroachments. In 1566 'the Headborough presented Mr Edmond Withipoll for taking in with hedge and gate, the way for horse and foote, from Brook's Hall to Dayry Lane (now Anglesea Road), and he was amerced three shillings, and payned to lay the same open.'

Edmund also entered into a violent dispute with

A bronze statue of Queen Victoria once graced the front of the Mansion, unveiled in May 1904, but demolished in 1942 when it was decided to contribute to the call for salvage metal for munitions and armaments.

the borough when, in 1568, he assumed the right of St Margaret's Fair, held on the Green to the south of his property. The rights pre-dated the Reformation and Edmund began demanding absolute authority over the commercial aspects and required the Serjeants of the Maces to yield up their staffs of office to signify the supercession of the bailiffs' jurisdiction for the three days of the Fair. Naturally the Serjeants and others protested and insisted on their rights to act as justices and examine the weights and measures of the vendors.

The original E-shape of the mansion, thought to have been in Edmund's original plan, reflected the courtyard style popular in late mediaeval architecture. It might also have been a compliment to Edward VI who had ascended the throne the previous year. Built of red brick, originally with stone quoins at the corners of the building, it has two matching wings very much in keeping with the Renaissance architectural principle of symmetry. Additions were made to the West Wing in around 1600 and dormers, with 'Dutch' gables, were added some 40 years later.

Edmund was not just concerned with earthly endeavours; while he neglected his obligations and liabilities in maintaining and repairing the chancel of St Margaret's Church, he nonetheless had the time and wherewithal to commission a high table tomb in the centre of the chancel in readiness for his death. Bishop Wren took particular exception to the tomb on the grounds that its sheer size divided the congregation from the Communion Table and, though he ordered action be taken, it was not until 1754 that the necessary faculty was sought to remove the tomb altogether.

The Christchurch estate eventually passed to Sir William Withipoll. During the Civil War William stood for the king, but his daughter married Colonel Leicester Devereaux, 6th Viscount Hereford, an officer in the Parliamentary army. The difficult family situation did not, however, stop the estate from passing into the hands of Devereaux on the death of his father-in-law in 1645.

It was during a visit to Christchurch Mansion by Charles II to the Herefords that the reputed comments about the state of the Ipswich streets

A rather stern Cardinal Wolsey with two Tudor roses on the wall of the Wolsey Art Gallery, Christchurch Mansion.

were made, the Duke of Buckingham also referring to Ipswich as being a town 'where the asses wore boots', a reference to the booted asses which used to roll Viscount Hereford's bowling green. However, there is some dispute over these remarks since they are often attributed to the king himself, while others deny they were said at all.

The estate remained in the Devereux family until 1735, when Price Devereux sold it to Claude Fonnereau. Generations of Fonnereaus lived at Christchurch Mansion until, in 1894, William Neale Fonnereau (1862–1904) sold it to a development syndicate who wanted to demolish it and develop the site. To the lasting gratitude of the town and all who now enjoy the Mansion and Park, Felix Thornley Cobbold (1841–1909) made an offer to the Corporation that was difficult to refuse. He offered to buy the mansion from the syndicate and present it to the town on the condition that they, for their part, purchased the surrounding park. Since all the contents had been dispersed, he also had the foresight to set up a fund to purchase items for display (which continues to this day).

The pond in Christchurch Park is thought to have once been the fish ponds for the pre-Reformation Priory of the Holy Trinity.

In the park is found the Boar War memorial (originally on Cornhill, where it was unveiled in September 1906) and the Cenotaph. On the rise behind the Art Gallery is found the Martyrs' Memorial.

A popular place of recreation, the park is enhanced by the duck pond, which is traditionally held to have been fishponds for the Holy Trinity Priory.

Fonnereau Road continues to be mainly residential, though at its southern tip is found the Bethesda Baptist Chapel. This dates back to 1829 and is still used for Sunday services.

FORE STREET

Streets named Fore are usually so called because they were the foremost or principal streets of the community. However, in Ipswich it is more likely that Fore Street was so named because of its proximity to the 'fore' or 'foreshore' of the River Orwell. Muriel Clegg wrote:

'It was much used by neighbouring parishioners who called it "the Fore", a name similar to "le For" which appears among the Petty Rentals of 1499, describing a "way" near the salt water at the western fringes of the town.'

Prior to the 18th century it was called St Clement's Street.

Curving in line with the old ramparts, Fore Street is now in three parts, beginning at the Duke Street roundabout to become part of the A1156 before branching north along its old route (where the Fore Street Pool is) before becoming the central link between Upper and Lower Orwell Street. A complicated route for an ancient and vital thoroughfare that once led from the riverside to the Blackfriars Priory and on into the commercial heart of 'Gipeswic', it is described by Nikolaus Pevsner as 'the most interesting street in Ipswich'.

One of the most famous buildings on Fore Street is Number 86, the Old Neptune inn. It was built originally in 1490, and in 1639 a wealthy wool merchant extended the house and added two floors. Dr Taylor writes:

'There can be little doubt the house was built for and inhabited by some former Ipswich merchant prince. Without and within the decorations are bestowed with a lavish hand. Over the windows the date, 1639, is carved.'

The back of the inn is even older, aiding the conclusion that there has been a merchant house of sorts here for many hundreds of years, albeit much humbler than is seen today.

The Neptune ceased to be a pub in 1937 and was used as a workplace for some years before it was bought and restored by Bodley Scott, a director of Cowells the printers, and converted back into a private house in the 1960s.

At one time the Neptune was the centre for paying off dockworkers, in keeping with the old tradition of paying workmen cash on a Saturday night. Not a popular practice with their wives, however, since much of the cash would find its way across the bar of nearby hostelries!

On 97 Fore Street a plaque marks the residency of Thomas Eldred. Although Eldred's House has been demolished, it is thought to have stood opposite the Old Neptune inn (see St Clement's Church Lane).

A few doors up, opposite the The Lord Nelson inn, is another Tudor merchant's house that bears the date 1636. The merchants' houses that once lined the south side had living accommodation and, often, a shop, with warehouses extending down to the quayside.

The Fore Street swimming baths, built in 1894 with funding from Felix Cobbold, is still going. Until the middle of the 20th century it was a popular place for those whose houses still did not have a bathroom, who could pay to have a bath.

Opposite the baths stood Herbert Wells's butchers' shops, which had a great reputation for pork sausages. In the 1940s and 1950s queues would form down Fore Street when a new batch went on sale.

In the 18th century onion growers from St Malo in Brittany off-loaded their ware into the back rooms of the Neptune inn. They would then string the onions onto long poles and hawk them round the streets.

Close to the Duke Street roundabout a row of cottages, converted into shops in 1895, when viewed from the back still give a flavour of the town in the 17th and 18th century. The Bressummer beam at first-floor level bears the date 1620.

44 Fore Street bears an Ipswich Society plaque commemorating the Dutch artist Cor Visser (1903–1982). Visser settled in Ipswich after World War Two, during which he was official artist to the Dutch government-in-exile. He lived for some years on a boat in Ipswich dock before setting up a studio in Fore Street.

FOUNDATION STREET

The name Foundation Street was adopted because here are the almshouses, built in 1552, which were known as the 'Foundation' of that great town benefactor and Portman of Ipswich Henry Tooley (see also Key Street and Common Quay). Prior to that, it was known as St Edmund Pountney Lane in reference to the Church of St Edmund de Pountney, which once stood opposite St Mary at Quay in a one-time path called Rosemary Lane (between Foundation Street and Lower Brook Street). It now stretches from Key Street, across Star Lane and thence to Orwell Place.

Tooley's and Smart Almshouses, which give the street its name, are north of the Smart Street junction. The 16th-century Tooley almshouses and Christ's Hospital (established under a Charter from Elizabeth I in 1572) were originally two separate foundations but were bracketed together as 'the foundation'. Thus, by 1745 the street had acquired the name Foundation Street.

The lower end of the street was known as Bank Street from the 18th century, marking the 'Yellow' Alexander bank (the colour denoting the Liberal politics of the Alexander family) and its adjoining Bank House. The last remains of the bank buildings were destroyed in 1973 by the Star Lane traffic scheme.

When a highway is as old as Foundation Street so much has happened hereabouts that its name recalls just one of the myriad events in this ancient part of town, not least the foundation of the Dominican Friars. They established a community in Foundation Street in 1263, after Henry III purchased a house for them, extending eventually up as far as Orwell Place (see Orwell Street).

Part of Foundation Street, like Cox Lane and the lost Balmannays Lane, was once known as 'the lane leading from the Friars Preachers to Caristrete', the Dominicans being famous for their preaching. The sight of hooded friars in their distinctive black habits would have been a familiar one along 'St Edmund Pountney' during the 13th to 16th centuries.

Whatever its name, Foundation Street has served as a route northwards towards the town from the quays on the north bank of the river and vice versa, as goods were taken to and from the town to the waiting ships tied up alongside the wharfs and merchant warehouses strung out along the quays. The most famous of these was the Tudor merchant Henry Tooley (known as The Great Tooley, or Toolie). He amassed a fortune during his lifetime, some of which he left for the setting-up of the almshouse for 10 townsmen who 'shall be tried unfaynedlye lame by occasion of the kynges warres' (unfeignedly lame, by occasion of the King's Wars), indicating a special interest in disabled or aged soldiers who he had, no doubt, seen begging in the town. If there were less than 10 ex-soldiers others could be considered who were 'aged and decrepite personnes whiche be not able to gette theyr lyke livynge'.

Since Tooley's children predeceased him, and he had few near relatives, his main beneficiaries were the people of Ipswich. In addition to the almshouses, Tooley left a further sum to be used in the upkeep of the foundation plus numerous legacies to the poor and downtrodden of the town, including £20 to those who were 'lame decretpite or impotent' and over £90 to the poverty-stricken in general. A legacy of £60 was made to provide 'poor, fatherless maids' with a dowry of 20 shillings each on their wedding day.

Although Henry Tooley died in 1551, his will was

such a long and complicated document that many of the bequests took time to realise. Some of his estate went to his widow for her lifetime while property had to be sold and the legalities completed. There was a dispute between the bailiffs and Tooley's executors over some 'ambiguities' in the will, which had to be resolved by the lord keeper, Sir Nicholas Bacon, who 'took great pains and travail in devising rules, ordinances, and statutes, and compounding the controversies between the said Executors and the said Bailiffs.'

It was not until 1562, therefore, that the Tooley bequest was securely established on a site near to the Church of St Mary at Quay close by Christ's Hospital (housed in the old monastic buildings of the original Dominican Friary but demolished in 1848).

The present almshouses were rebuilt in 1846 in the vicinity of the original 16th-century buildings. On the front wall the arms of Tooley can still be seen, with the following inscription:

'In peaceful silence let great Tooley rest;
Whose charitable deeds bespeak him blest.'

The Ipswich architect John Shewell Corder (died in 1922) left a bequest of £200 to enable covered walkways to be erected 'to the comfort of the inmates'. In 1952 the gardens were 'beautified' in memory of William S. Jewhurst, who had for 28 years been the Honorary Secretary to the Ipswich and East of England Horticultural Society.

Thousands of townspeople have benefited from the Tooley Foundation just as they have from the charitable bequest of William Smart, portman, who in his will of 8 January 1598 left several estates in trust to the town bailiffs and 'commonalty of Ipswich' for the purpose of maintaining sundry poor persons, finding them fuel and clothing. A portion of the almshouses was appropriated for those in receipt of the Smart charity, and administration of the Smart and Tooley foundations joined together.

Tooley's Court, off Shire Hall Yard, com-

Plaque to Henry Toolie on the wall in front of the Almshouses on Foundation Street.

memorates Henry Tooley and there is a Smart Street nearby.

A memorial tablet for William and Alice Smart can be seen in St Mary le Tower, which has a palisade running along the bottom 'viewed from over Stoke and taking in the town from Broomhill on the left to Bishop's Hill and the Common Quay on the right', as it was in 1600.

These men lived through times of tumultuous social and religious change yet they accepted the challenge of maintaining the commercial prosperity of Ipswich while forging the new society forced on them by circumstances beyond their control. In Tudor England there was no room for open dissent, and men like Tooley and Smart had to be circumspect in their dealings and entrepreneurial in spirit.

Opposite Tooley's Court, at 32 Foundation Street, is a plaque marking the residency of Thomas Gainsborough (1727–1788), who moved to Ipswich in 1751. He lived for a time in Lower Brook Street but then rented 34 Foundation Street, a house similar to 32, which was demolished in the early 1960s.

Gainsborough was born in Sudbury, the fifth son

of John Gainsborough, a clothier, and Mary Burroughs. After being sent to London to study art, he returned to Suffolk in 1749 and moved to Ipswich in the same year that his youngest daughter, Margaret, was born. It was during his sojourn in the town that Gainsborough developed his familiar style and began to make his way in the art world. While at Foundation Street, he completed a masterpiece of portraiture, purely for his own enjoyment, a magical image of his two *Daughters Chasing a Butterfly*. Malcolm Cormack writes:

> 'Such a personal evocation of the fragility of childhood had no parallel except, perhaps, in the moving studios by Chardin during the eighteenth century.'

It is thought that the painting was first given to the Master of Ipswich School, the Revd Robert Hingeston, who was a neighbour and friend of Gainsborough. Later it passed to the Master's son, the Reverend James Hingeston, Vicar of Reydon with Southwold. Gainsborough painted both Robert Hingeston and his wife, Catherine, and shared a mutual interest in music, and both attended a weekly music club in the town.

Richard Felaw (*c.*1420–1482) was another Foundation Street resident with altruistic leanings and was a leading light in town affairs. He was twice the town's representative in Parliament and eight times bailiff, and as a merchant traded in salt, iron, tallow, hides and corn. As a Member of Parliament, he served on a commission of inquiry into the evasion of customs duties in 1449 and in 1458 became Comptroller of Customs and Subsidies for the port (see also Felaw Street).

Felaw left his house on the west side of the street, known as Felaw's House, to the Grammar School. It consisted of five two-storey, dwellings, which were added to and altered over the years, so much so that when it was demolished in 1963 it was thought that only the foundations of the kitchen were contemporary with Felaw's occupation. Dr John Blatchly laments the demise of Felaw's House, not

least because the site remained waste ground for 30 years, 'well into the era when conservation would have been automatic. What a tourist attraction a 15th-century schoolhouse would be today!'

In 1612 the Grammar School moved from Felaw's House to the old Blackfriars complex off Foundation Street, bought by a merchant, William Sabyn, after its dissolution in 1541. It remained there until 1842. By 1851 it had become Queen Elizabeth's Grammar School and was moved to purpose-built premises on Henley Road.

FRANCISCAN WAY

This modern carriageway commemorates the Franciscan, or Grey, Friars who from the 12th century to the Reformation had their friary in this vicinity (see also Friars Street). It formed part of the 1960 inner ring road scheme, designed to take traffic away from the town centre. Inevitably its construction destroyed some of the town's old buildings and streets, but its final route was toned down from the original plan to cut a far wider swathe through what is one of the town's oldest inhabited areas. It runs south from Civic Drive to the St Peter's roundabout and so to the ancient river crossing at Stoke Bridge.

FRIARS STREET

The former name for Friars Street was Boat Lane, though in its previous incarnation it ran from the town to the marshes that in 1200 were granted to the portmen for grazing their horses. Boat Lane formed the western approach to the town with a bridge, marked by the name Friars Bridge Road, but was cut up when Princes Street was created to form a north-west access after the coming of the railways. It now runs between Princes Street and Falcon Street.

The friars were the Franciscan Friars, who arrived in Ipswich in 1297. Their friary extended south-west from St Nicholas Church, in the parish of St Nicholas. Dr Taylor wrote:

> 'All that is left to suggest the former existence of religious houses hereabouts, is the name

Princes Street reflected in the Willis Corroon building.

Friars' Road, Priory Street, etc. Fragments of the ruins remain in the garden of Mr Frederick Messent's house.'

Needless to say, Mr Messent's house is long gone and so is all evidence of the friary.

The Greyfriars, or Friars Minor, were established by Sir Robert Tiptot and his wife, Una. At first they, like all Franciscan and Dominican communities, were little more than brotherhoods of individual itinerant preachers who ministered to the poor and lived only from what they were gifted. Their poverty contrasted with that of the monks, especially as the monastic dynasties grew in power and wealth. The friars were seen regularly on the streets of Ipswich and were as much a part of town life as the marketers, merchants and tradesmen, their open-air sermons attracting huge crowds. They took part in the processions of the Corpus Christi Guild and were present at the important civic occasions.

Like the Blackfriars, the Greyfriars had many benefactors, some of whom were buried within the friary confines, including Lord Curson (see Silent Street). However, an inventory made between 1537 and 1538 by Henry VIII shows that while the friars' possessions were contained in a long list of goods and chattels, they were modest in comparison with those found in the monasteries.

A feature of modern Friars Street is the beautifully maintained Unitarian Meeting House, a Grade I listed building built in 1699 and opened in 1700. It is one of the finest surviving Dissenting Meeting Houses in the country and certainly one of the town's most important historic places of religious worship. Purpose-built dissenting chapels of antiquity are rare since the early meeting places for non-conformists were usually private homes and, later, converted houses or cottages.

It was built by the Presbyterians, who had previously met in an 'upper room' at a house in

Silent Street. In 1699 they bought some land in Friars Street and built the new Meeting House, described by Peter Bishop as 'a tiny song-thrush now incongruously sited beneath the sleek raven of the Willis Corroon building.'

The chapel, timber framed with 'Cobweb' windows, has been known by several names in the course of its history. Throughout the 18th and 19th centuries it was designated a church or chapel of various denominations and early in the 20th century it was known as St Nicholas Meeting House. In 1960 the chapel found itself on the edge of a massive road-widening scheme, and although the main buildings survive some of its grounds have been lost and many of the gravestones removed.

Situated between the Meeting House and the Willis building is the Millennium Obelisk, which celebrates the 25th anniversary of the opening of the Willis building, the 300th anniversary of the opening of the Unitarian Meeting House and marks the 800th anniversary of the borough of Ipswich under the charter granted by King John in 1200.

The Willis Corroon building began life in the 1970s, when Willis, Faber & Dumas decided to move all its administrative offices from Southend and London to a new headquarters in Ipswich. Wholesale demolition was required to make space for the new building, including the 'British Lion' public house, the Friars Head public house and other shops and buildings including an old-established leather goods shop called Alfred Clark's. On the parapet of the 'British Lion' was an unusual Coade stone lion, a hard-grained limestone that was fired and became, therefore, stoneware. Most of Cromwell Street went, too, marked by the existing Cromwell Square. This street had been developed in 1892, with sturdy houses on either side of the street being built by the FLS.

The Unitarian Meeting house reflected in the Willis Corroon building.

Daniel Defoe thought the Unitarian Meeting House 'as large and fine a building of that kind as most on this side of England, and the inside the best finished of any I have seen, London not excepted.'

Willis, Faber & Dumas was an insurance company, originally a family firm, who were anxious to restore 'a sense of community to the workplace' and commissioned the architect Norman Foster (born in 1935) to come up with an appropriate design. In what is considered to be a pioneering piece of social architecture, Foster (later Sir Norman, now Lord) created open-plan office floors long before open-plan became normal practice. Since Ipswich was thought to be a town 'not over endowed with public facilities' the company's 1,200 employees benefited from its roof gardens, olympic-sized swimming pool and gymnasium. The building, completed in 1975, is wrapped in a full-height glass façade of Pilkington's toughened 'Antisun' bronze floatglass, which is moulded to fit the street pattern, and 'contributes real drama, subtly shifting from opaque, reflective black to a glowing backlit transparency as the sun sets.' The town guide describes it as a 'dark curvaceous glass drum of an office building' but it appears to have a bronze interior at night.

The design of a glass building at first caused some concern in the town since it is situated not far north of the Ipswich Town football ground and, it was thought, would become a target for hooliganism. Foster, however, allayed fears by arranging for a mock brick-throwing exercise, during which the bricks bounced off the strong glass

surface of what is still called the 'Willis Faber' building.

Some years later, during the 1987 hurricane, it was feared that irreparable damage had been sustained, but after some of the fixings were slackened off the glass was righted without further problems.

Behind the Meeting House is an attractive courtyard with a passageway into St Nicholas Street.

Foster's ground-breaking building won a host of architectural and environmental awards and in 1991 was given a Grade I listing, one of the youngest buildings to be so designated. One of the casualties of the listing was the swimming pool, which closed in 1990 and is now covered by an extra floor with a glass viewing strip so that the old pool can still be seen.

FRIARS BRIDGE ROAD

This is one of the many streets and roads that were mutilated when Princes Street was built and is one of the western boundaries of the Franciscan Friary, which extended south from Friars Street. The Friars Bridge, one of the western approaches to the town, led to the nearby Greyfriars Priory, and the presence in that part of town of the Franciscan Friary is reflected in Franciscan Way and Grey Friars Road running southbound towards the Star Lane

FRIARS BRIDGE ROAD-GRIMWADE STREET

roundabout and eventually to the Stoke crossing. Although the name suggests it was contemporary with the friary, there is likely to have been an older bridge leading to the 'Odenholm' marches, where the town portmen had pasturage.

GREAT COLMAN STREET

This was a new road built in 1821 and takes its name from the Colman family who are shown on Pennington's map as having property there. It was once a driveway off Carr Street and led to a Tudor mansion owned at one time by a man by the name of Sir Harbottle Grymston. A successful Ipswich cloth merchant, John Harbottle, who extended the property northwards and in 1539 described the house as 'lately built', built the mansion, called Harbottle House.

Little Colman Street was incorporated into the Carr Precinct when, in 1887, the 'Carr Street Improvement Company Limited' was formed to purchase for the Corporation much of the property bordering on Carr Street to enable the street to be widened to accommodate the new horse trams. The remainder, called Colman Street for some years, went in 1967 when yet more development took place, taking with it the marquee manufacturers Rands and Jeckell Limited, who moved to Found-ation Street.

Muriel Clegg points out that Great Colman Street is one of the few streets, old or new, that cuts across an existing route. 'Useful it may be' she wrote, 'but the new street created a confusing little pattern by cutting across the double encircling lines of Old Foundry Road and St Margaret's Street.'

One of the casualties of the new road was Harbottle House itself, together with an acre and a half of land, offered for sale at the Great White Horse Hotel in June 1821 by its final owner, Mrs Elizabeth Edge, widow of the Revd John Edge, Vicar of Rushmere.

Colman House now houses Barricella Hughes solicitors and a dental practice, with more development now in progress and the adjacent property lately demolished.

Standing at the top of Great Colman Street, with Colin Girling & Co, Estate Agents and Valuers, on one side and the Salentina Pizzeria on the other, the street is a busy one-way access, but a reminder of its proximity to the centre of ancient town life is a view of the spire of St Mary le Tower seen high above the Northgate Street buildings.

GREY FRIARS ROAD

Here is one of the few street name reminders of the mendicant friars of mediaeval Ipswich as well as a long-lingering memory of the ugly, short-lived experiment in concrete living that was the Greyfriars development scheme, built in the 1960s and refurbished in the late 1990s when the low and dark market area was demolished. There is no small confusion about whether or not Greyfriars should be all one word; the road itself is Grey Friars while the Greyfriars development scheme appears as one and references to the Franciscan friars is commonly spelt as one word (see also Friars Street).

GRIMWADE STREET

The name Grimwade was very well known to generations of Ipswichians throughout the 19th and 20th centuries, 'J H Grimwade & Sons' being written in large lettering on their outfitters shop on Cornhill until its closure in 1996 (now Clinton's Cards). The street was formerly known as Borough Road and formed a link between St Helen's Street and Rope Walk. Laid out early in the 20th century, it formed part of the Ipswich Prison grounds, although the new name was later extended to incorporate St Clement's Street.

A tailor and woollen draper, Richard Grimwade, started business in Westgate Street in 1844, dying 20 years later. His 16-year-old son, John Henry Grimwade, having been left at a very early age to provide for his mother and six siblings, went on to carve out a respectable position in the town and took the family business to new heights. He was elected mayor in 1904–05 and was a council member until his death in 1929.

John's son, Sidney Charles Grimwade, was also

mayor (twice) and his grandson, Edward Charles Grimwade, was elected mayor in 1964–65. Peter Grimwade, John's great grandson, joined the council in 1963, and he was the last of the family to run the shop. Grimwades had always been a family business but when, in the 1990s, there was no heir to carry it on the directors decided to sell.

Opposite the junction with St Clement's Church Lane, prosperous sea captains once lived in the surviving row of houses.

The old premises of Peters Ice Cream are now boarded up and look rather sad, but in its day this was the busy centre for handmade Italian ice cream, which was established in 1897 and is still sold on the streets of Ipswich from mobile handcarts.

HANDFORD ROAD (and Handford Bridge)

The pre-Christian Anglo-Saxons buried their dead close to the right bank of the River Gipping, between the present Hadleigh Road and the London Road where the river crossing was named 'Handford' which, like Stoke, was a crossing as early as the 10th century. A panel of the Charter Hangings shows an Anglo-Saxon brooch that was found at the Hadleigh Road cemetery and is now in Ipswich Museum. The name survives today in Handford Road and Handford Bridge, although the name of the original road, Horsewade, is lost.

Confusion is sometimes caused by 'Handford Mill' being indexed as 'Z' on Speed's 1610 map, which puts it in the Lower Orwell Street area instead of straddling the river to the west of the town.

The Handford Bridge was erected in 1795, at considerable expense, and was carried for some distance across the head of the marshes, which form a small island on the west side of the town. It is encompassed by two channels of the river, which diverge and reunite after a separation of about a mile. The old channel skirts the western side of the town, where it was crossed by a series of small bridges.

Handford Road becomes the London Road as it travels westwards and carries a considerable volume of traffic, particularly on football days, reckoned to

be some 15,000 traffic movements daily. Portman Road now traverses the road, which is a reminder of the days when this was the road out to the grazing marshes used by the town portmen.

Until 1900 Handford Lodge stood at 61 Handford Road, described as 'a genteel family residence', in seven acres beside the Gipping and next door to the Cottage inn. Here lived Peter Bruff, the engineer responsible for the Stoke railway tunnel as well as the new town sewer and numerous other engineering projects (see Burrell Road). Even without his other momentous achievements, the town had much to thank Bruff for in regard to the improved sanitation, since until his improvement there were only a number of shallow (and increasingly inadequate) sewers, which discharged into the river at Common Quay. Work from Bruff's designs began in 1857, but it was not for another 22 years that the plans were finally realised and the new outlet located a mile downstream at Hog Highland – a little unfortunate as this was a popular picnic spot at the time!

However, the matter of waste disposal in the town, though vitally important in terms of health, was not of immediate concern to many residents who saw it as nothing more than an excuse for the borough to raise the rates. There was another gripe, highlighted by Peter Bishop:

'Sewage had a value. It was stored beside the house until there was enough for a farmer to collect. Before the fertiliser of Joseph Fison and his kind, the cost of buying – in 5cwt of either guano or farm manure – enough for an acre – was £1. One adult was reckoned to produce as much per annum, a useful addition to the family budget.'

Ipswich was then an important entrepôt, or bonded warehouse, for sewage which was sent from London by boat for distribution throughout the county.

In the 1880s both professional and working people lived in Handford Road: there were several men who worked at the town barracks, plus railway personnel, as well as gardeners, tradesmen and even a French polisher. The road's public houses included the Elephant and Castle (which seems to have had the same name as that given to Lord Curson's house in Silent Street in its days as a public house) and the Cottage inn.

Between 1846 and 1900 the Bruff family lived at the Lodge and Hugh Moffat recounts a story told to Peter Bruff by a fellow companion when travelling back to Ipswich from London. The stranger asked if he knew Handford Lodge, and without disclosing that he lived there Bruff replied that he did. The man said that when he was stationed at the town barracks he often went to parties at the Lodge where card games were often played. One of the officers accused a lady of cheating and her escort immediately challenged the officer to a duel. Pistols were drawn and each man fired twice, both missing their target but sufficient to satisfy their respective honour. The stranger told Bruff that for years the bullet marks were seen on the dining room wall by the door.

On arriving home Bruff located the bullet holes and decreed that the room was never to be re-papered. The bullet marks were preserved behind two pictures. Handford Lodge was demolished shortly after Bruff's death.

When Bruff died the local newspaper thought he had gone on far too long, saying that the announcement 'might well have been expected years ago, seeing that Mr Bruff had outlived all his contemporaries and passed far beyond the allotted span'.

Mrs Bruff also deserves a mention. Born in Ireland around 1806, Harriett Deborah MacAlpine married Peter Bruff at the St Pancras Old Church, London, in February 1835. She was some six years her husband's senior but nevertheless produced 12 children, including a set of twins. Harriett died about seven years after her husband, aged 102. If the reporter on the newspaper deaths column was still around he might well have thought that Mrs Bruff had passed beyond her 'allotted span'.

HENLEY ROAD

Streets are invariably named for people, occupations or market activity but Henley Road is an example of a town road being named for its destination, in this case Henley. It is a very long road, starting at the Anglesea Road–Fonnereau Road junction (where the Greyhound public house stands) and carrying on north past Castle Hill and out into the Suffolk countryside.

It is easy to forget the sloping nature of the town and why, after walking round Ipswich for the morning, the pedestrian's legs are unaccountably tired. It is because the town is built on a series of hills. It is not noticeable going east to west but try walking up Princes Street, across Cornhill, up Lloyds Avenue, across Crown Street and on up Fonnereau Road to Henley Road; then you have a better idea of how the land rises north of the river.

The development of Henley Road was an extension of the Victorian push northwards, and its most famous landmark is the Ipswich School, moved there in 1851 by Stephen Jordan Rigaud. The main entrance faces the west side of Christchurch Park, the Arboretum in particular, which was an attractive setting for the new school.

The school history is told in Dr John Blatchly's *A Famous Antient Seed-Plot of Learning*, which charts its progress from the 14th century to the present day. Briefly, the school had its roots in the Guild Merchant School of possibly 1200 or earlier followed by the Corpus Christi Guild School in the 14th and 15th century. Early in the 16th century it became part of Cardinal Wolsey's College of St Mary in Ipswich, but after the Cardinal's impeachment in 1529 the king was 'resolved to dissolve the college'. However, the school itself survived, in one guise or another, until the arrival of Stephen Jordan Rigaud who was to oversee the establishment of the new premises on Henley Road. HRH Prince Albert travelled to Ipswich by train on 3 July 1851 to address a meeting of the British Association for the Advancement of Science, and the following day laid the foundation stone for Ipswich School.

'One hundred and twenty boys, all smartly

The Brett Drinking Fountain on the Henley Road approach to the Upper Arboretum with Ipswich School on the other side of the road. John Brett, son of a Carr Street cordwainer, was born in 1801 and was one of those who wanted to provide clean water to the urban poor.

dressed in short Eton packets and white collars, were marched up from Brook Street' writes Dr Blatchly. 'The band of the Queen's Bays was ready to play the National Anthem as the Royal Standard was unfurled above the canopy covering the principal participants.'

There was a fireworks display in the evening, and Prince Albert announced himself pleased at 'assisting at the commencement of works having for their object to give this ancient and valuable Institution extended means of usefulness'.

The Prince visited the Fonnereaus at Christ-church Mansion, then briefly viewed the Ancient House (where Mrs Pawsey famously had only '35 minutes' notice of the Royal visit) and then back to London.

HIGH STREET

The most striking building here is Ipswich Museum and, unusually, the High Street is not the main thoroughfare but part of a 19th-century development. It slopes northwards from the town towards Henley Road where the gradient can be gauged by the steep inclines of the arboretum in Christchurch Park. In November 1866 it was decided that since all other towns had a High Street so should Ipswich. However, the main streets were already possessed of time-honoured names and it was decided that Barley Mow Lane and some of Claude Street should be the new High Street.

In 1878 the Museum Committee agreed that they had outgrown their premises in Museum Street and a site was sought for a new, purpose-built museum. The one adopted was originally acquired by the Corporation and intended for a new church. The Museum complex, which includes an art gallery, the 'Victoria Library' and the School of Art, opened to the public on 27 July 1881. On the same day the new Post Office was opened on Cornhill and the new lock entrance to the Wet Dock was inaugurated; it was a grand day in Ipswich history.

Today it is considered an outstanding example of what a museum should be and has wide ranging natural history exhibits, including a mammoth,

giraffe and rhino, and its collection of birds is one of the best in the country. Historical life-sized displays depict Roman and Anglo-Saxon times, there is a display of Egyptian objects and in the Mankind Gallery is the fork used to eat missionary Revd Baker!

Next door, and opposite the Arboretum public house, is the Suffolk Institute of Technology.

Where the top of Museum Street meets the southern tip of High Street (sliced off from the north part by Crown Street) is a curved building on the corner opposite Tower Ramparts car park (the lower portion occupied by the Carrot Cake shop). It is red brick and has large, rectangular windows with metal frames, in the art deco style very much in vogue in the 1930s and favoured by several town architects at the time, though most of their work has now gone. There are also square and rectangular, light-coloured glazed bricks patterning the doorways and storey divisions. This section of High Street was formerly known as Barley Mow Lane, in honour of the Barley Mow inn that stood on the corner of Westgate Street (now the Ann Summers shop and previously a building society).

KING STREET

One of the oldest buildings left in King Street is the Swan public house, which is situated opposite the entrance to the Corn Exchange and gives a clue to the street's antiquity. It stands on what was once Little King Street when King Street (now north Princes Street) veered northwards to Cornhill. On Joseph Pennington's map it runs south from Cornhill to meet the west end of the Buttermarket. Even in the 1770s it is known as 'Little', but that area between Lion Street and the Buttermarket is all that is left. Its name might be linked with the Wuffinga kings who built St Mildred's Church on Cornhill. Ogilby's 1674 map shows the entire route from Stoke Bridge to Cornhill as King Street so there is no doubt that this was a prime route from the docks to the civic centre of town and for traders at the weekly markets.

Muriel Clegg writes:

'It is tempting to look for a particular royal connection, in which case Edward I, whose visit to the town during the winter of 1296-97 was full of colourful incident, and with whom an otherwise unknown King's Hall is associated, appears to be the likeliest candidate. Regretfully it has to be said that the name King Street is often a mistaken rendering of the familiar 'king's highway' (from the Latin *vicus regius*). It may be so here.'

The Swan was one of the 24 inns that existed in the area in the 17th century and judging by the date (1707) on the front, alterations were made to the structure then (although the original dwelling is much older).

There was also a Crown inn here because the early 16th-century benefactor Edmund Daundy gave his house 'adjoining to the Crown in King Street, for a residence' to Sir James Crowfield, the

first priest at the chantry he founded in St Lawrence.

For modern Ipswichians the most important structure on King Street – apart from the Swan – is the Corn Exchange opened by the Mayor, Frederick Fish, on 26 July 1882. It replaced the earlier Corn Exchange that was built on the Cornhill in 1812 for its original purpose of buying and selling corn and was built on the site of the Sickle inn and King's Head Commercial inn.

Great attention was paid to the design of this new Corn Exchange, due to the unpopular barred windows and open yard of the first. Mayor D.H. Booth laid the foundation stone in October 1880 and two years later 'the hoardings round the new Corn Exchange were cleared away and although the roadway at King Street had not been surfaced the public footpath was open.'

The new building proved successful and in 1888 the Provision Market was moved there from Falcon Street where it remained until it closed in 1970. The

King Street in 1878. Notice that the lot numbers are already on the Sickle inn and King's Head prior to demolition. The Corn Exchange now stands on the site. (W. Vick Photo)

In 1850 the Post Office was in King Street, facing down Queen Street. What is now the Old Post Office (on Cornhill) took its place in 1881. (W. Vick Photo)

22nd SEPTEMBER, 1975
CORN EXCHANGE, IPSWICH

INAUGURAL CONCERT

IN THE PRESENCE OF THEIR ROYAL HIGHNESSES
THE DUKE AND DUCHESS OF GLOUCESTER

ROYAL PHILHARMONIC ORCHESTRA
(Leader: Eric Gruenberg)
Conductor: WALTER SUSSKIND

JUDITH PEARCE (Flute)
GILLIAN WEIR (Organ)
ALLAN SCHILLER (Pianoforte)

IPSWICH CHORAL SOCIETY
(Conductor: John Cooper)

IPSWICH BACH CHOIR
(Conductor: Merlin Channon)

The Duke and Duchess of Gloucester opened the revamped Corn Exchange in September 1975 as an entertainment venue.

THE IPSWICH CHORAL SOCIETY

presents

ORB and SCEPTRE

a Concert of
CORONATION MUSIC with READINGS
to commemorate the
𝔖𝔦𝔩𝔳𝔢𝔯 𝔍𝔲𝔟𝔦𝔩𝔢𝔢
of Queen Elizabeth II's Accession to the Throne

in the

Grand Hall of the
Ipswich Corn Exchange
Sunday February 6th, 1977

at 3.0 pm

RHODA LEWIS and NORMAN FLORENCE
Readers

HARRISON OXLEY - Organ
ST. EDMUNDSBURY CATHEDRAL CHOIR
ST. MARY-LE-TOWER CHURCH CHOIR
THE IPSWICH CHORAL SOCIETY
THE JOSEPH GIBBS ORCHESTRA
Leader: JESSIE RIDLEY

Conductor: JOHN COOPER

The Queen visited the Corn Exchange in 1977 as part of her Silver Jubilee Tour. (Vi Conglaton)

Corn Exchange continued to operate as such for the first half of the 20th century but gradually the changes in the way farmers sold their corn eroded its purpose. For years farmers would bring samples of their crop to the buyers' representatives, standing on their individual 'stands', where it would be examined and 'tested' by the merchant biting the grains or slicing the sample to gauge its quality. Hopeful of a sale, most farmers 'dressed' the sample, sifting out all the shrivelled grains and weed seeds and later, when the moisture content became a component of the buying and selling process, the samples were carefully dried so that the corn fulfilled the requirements of the new 'moisture meters'. The last corn market took place in the Exchange on 29 June 1972 and with it went a tradition of corn trading that had taken place in the centre of Ipswich since time immemorial.

38

THE CORN EXCHANGE
and TOWN HALL,
IPSWICH

Monday 11th July, 1977

SECURITY PASS

.... MRS. V. CONGALTON .... (Holder)
The Holder of this pass may be admitted to the Complex at the notified entrance only on production of this pass.
PTO

VISIT OF H.M. THE QUEEN TO SUFFOLK

A security pass belonging to Vi Congalton, who remembers that security was tight for the Royal visit. 'Once the building had been swept by the sniffer dogs' she says, 'you weren't allowed out. And we all had to be there very early.'

The Exchange began its new use as an entertainment and exhibition venue in 1975. The Grand Hall is used for shows and touring opera companies and the Robert Cross Hall for craft fairs and art exhibitions. In 1977 the Queen visited it on her Silver Jubilee tour and it is currently undergoing renovation and change and its future role is under discussion.

LADY LANE

Halfway along Lady Lane, which links Westgate to the Wolsey car park, is a plaque on the wall of Franklins Needlecraft Stores. It is the only reminder of the Chapel of Our Lady of Grace that stood here for around 300 years and attracted pilgrims from across Europe as well as kings and queens of the realm and played a significant role in Cardinal Wolsey's bid to found his College. In mediaeval East Anglia it was second only to the famous shrine of Our Lady at Walsingham.

The Lane is dwarfed by the Civic Centre, just across the car park, and behind that the police station and the Magistrates Court. To the right is seen the New Wolsey Theatre, and the never-ending stream of traffic is heard whizzing up and down the dual carriageway. It has remained unchanged since the 1960s when this part of Ipswich was dramatically given its modern face.

The Chapel of Our Lady, known also as Our Lady of Ipswich or the Madonna of Ipswich, stood just outside the West Gate and on the north-west side of what was once a much longer Lady Lane, which curved south to Curriers Lane and ran through arable land. It was a shrine of 'Grace', designed primarily to lead men and women to heaven, and housed a representation of Our Lady. A description in an 'old letter', once in the possession of the Revd Francis Haslewood, read:

> 'Our Lady's coat with 2 gorgets of gold to put about her neck, and an Image of Our Lady of gold, in a tabernacle of silver and gold, and a little relic of gold and crystal with Our Lady's milk in it, as they say.'

Stanley Smith, who made a special study of the Madonna of Ipswich, wrote that the original date for the Ipswich shrine is accepted by historians as being probably round about 1152, 'which fits in well with the records that it was well established by 1297'.

Nathaniel Bacon, recorder and town clerk in 1654, thought that 'St Mary's Chapel' was famous for an image of the Blessed Virgin and was held in high regard, 'to which many pilgrimages were wont to be made'.

This Shrine Chapel, or Lady Chapel, was one of five dedications to the Blessed Virgin Mary in the town, the others being St Mary le Tower, St Mary at Elms, St Mary at Quay and St Mary Stoke. As the mother of Jesus, St Mary, or Our Lady, was accorded special honour and devotion and bore a number of titles, localised the world over. Except the chapel, all the Marian churches have survived to the 21st century.

Television and film make it easier for modern audiences to imagine groups of pilgrims arriving at the Shrine Chapel from at least the 13th century onwards. The Catholic religion in mediaeval times was an all-encompassing facet of everyday life and the world has another Ipswich man, Geoffrey Chaucer, to thank for the contemporary 14th-century views of pilgrims in *The Canterbury Tales* (see Tavern Street).

St Thomas More paid a number of visits to the Shrine Chapel. He described a miracle that he witnessed at 'Our Ladye of Ippeswitche' and sent details to both Wolsey and the king.

One of the earliest notable events at the Shrine Chapel came in 1297 when Princess Elizabeth, daughter of Edward I, was married to John Count of Holland. Wodderspoon recorded the events in detail, taking his information from a manuscript that listed 'the entire proceedings down to an exact account of the jewels the royal father bestowed on his fair daughter'. King Edward was 'more than once within the town, and when he married his daughter Elizabeth to the Count of Holland, remained here with a splendid court several days'.

Not only did the king shower the town with gifts 'to the poor people amounting in the total to a considerable sum', but he gave money for the expenses of food for 505 'poor persons' for a week and other sundry alms relating to providing food for thousands of the townspeople. Over 30 local tailors were occupied 'for four days and four nights', making 'linings and canvass' for the countess, while expenses were incurred making robes, curtains and 'other necessaries' for the royal ladies.

The inns were kept busy, accommodating the servants and craftsmen together with the horses and carriages that fetched the entourage from London. Dancers and minstrels were needed to provide entertainment and there was no end to the number of cooks and household servants required. No doubt many found rooms at the Assumption inn, thought to have been in the vicinity of the chapel, though not too near as it was forbidden to build an inn close to a shrine. According to the Revd C. Evelyn White:

'The far-famed Shrine of Our Lady of Ipswich, in particular, and other like religious attractions, were a means of alluring to the town an immense concourse of pilgrims from all parts of the land. The accommodation, afforded by the inns would largely be called into requisition … a well-known Ipswich inn, called the 'Assumption' was doubtless the favourite house, especially among strangers visiting the town.'

In 1517 Queen Catherine of Aragon came to pay homage at the chapel, staying with Lord Curson in Silent Street. This was regarded as an honour, though Lord Curson might not have regarded it quite so benignly as it was the custom then that the host should bear the considerable costs involved in the royal progress. The Queen paid several visits to the chapel, arriving on horseback and escorted by the bailiffs. On her departure from Ipswich, the Queen was presented with a purse of money – £20 for her and 50 marks for the king.

Henry VIII, no doubt keen for a repeat of the Queen's leaving present, came on a pilgrimage in 1522. Lord Curson was again the host. Almost as soon as he had risen, the king 'paid a visit to the chapel of Our Lady, and made his oblations at the shrine. He there heard Mass and had, as a gift from the town, 50 marks in nobles.'

The most important day in the shrine calendar was 8 September, the traditional date of Our Lady's birthday, which was celebrated by processions and commemorative services. It was also the day when the town elders met to elect officials and appoint the burgesses, Members of Parliament, bailiffs and portmen. No wonder, then, that Lady Lane was a hive of activity during the first two weeks of September.

In 1528, soon after Wolsey established his college, he ordered a grand procession to take place on 8 September. Although Wolsey himself would not be present, the town bailiffs and portmen, the prior of Christchurch and 24 'gentlemen of the county' were to join the college staff, together with six priests, eight clerks, nine choristers, and all the servants in procession. It was to be the first of an annual event in the college calendar.

It was decided that a practice run should take place, and on 'Our Ladye's Eve' the participants obediently wound their way along St Peter's Street to St Nicholas Street, across the Buttermarket to Cornhill and then along Westgate Street and through the West Gate to the chapel. But the grand procession itself did not in fact occur. The weather was 'fowl' (sic) and it 'rayned sore, so that we could not go in procession thro the town.'

The following year saw Wolsey's fall from grace and soon afterwards the demise of his college. No one was going to risk implementing the instructions of the disgraced cardinal for fear of regal recrimination.

Although Wolsey was not present for the 1528 procession, he had made pilgrimages to Ipswich, including one in 1517 when he wrote to the King that he was 'so vexed with the sweating fever that I intend to start off for the Shrine of Walsingham and from there to Our Lady of Grace.'

The rapacious and capricious King Henry, so closely associated with Ipswich through not only his visit but also through Wolsey, took an interest in the new college, accepted money from the town and made pilgrimage to Our Lady; but only six years later ordered the shrine's destruction. Following Wolsey's scheme to dissolve the increasingly unpopular friaries and monasteries in order to finance his college, Henry VIII proceeded to 'reform' the nation's religion and remove all monastic assets to the royal coffers. Thomas Cromwell, who had taken Wolsey's place as Chancellor of the Exchequer, was entrusted with the commission to close down the shrines.

In 1534 Cromwell's 'Visitor' inspected the Shrine of Our Lady of Ipswich and found that 'devotion is decayed'. Henry's 'new' Church of England broke with Rome and the realm had a new queen, the king having secretly married Anne Boleyn in 1533.

One fateful night in 1535 the image of Our Lady was smuggled out of the chapel and its ornaments and jewels removed to the king's exchequer. The statue, together with that of Our Lady of Walsingham and Our Lady of Willesden, was sent by ship to London to be held up as an evil example of idolatry. Our Lady had been robbed of all her finery, except her 'half shoes of silver' and some crystal, also set in silver. The statue was to be burned. Sir Charles Wriothesley wrote:

'In the month of July, the images of Our Lady of Wallsingham and Ipswich were brought up to London with all the jewelles that honge about them, at the Kinge's commaundment, and divers others images … and were burnt at Chelsey by my Lord Privie Seal.'

Historians agree that the statue was to have been burned yet there is no precise evidence that it actually happened. Others were, indeed, consigned to the flames and there is contemporary witness to confirm the conflagration. However, the veneration given to St Mary ceased forthwith and the new English church forbade 'acts of idolatry' with severe punishment for disobedience.

Thus the story of the Shrine Chapel passed into history until World War Two when it was discovered that on the west coast of Italy a town called Nettuno had a revered and loved image of the 'Nostra Signora delle Grazie' (Our Lady of Grace). Nettuno and Anzio are twin towns and both suffered badly during the war and came under heavy bombardment in 1944. Allied troops landed in January that year and the Anzio 'beach head' is

famous in the annals of the war. Afterwards the towns were rebuilt, and in the Piazza Mazzino stands the Church of Our Lady of Grace. For 400 years the statue, although damaged in the Anzio bombardment, has been reverently cared for and is known locally as 'The English Lady'. The statue of 'Nostra Signora delle Grazie', it is believed, is Our Lady of Ipswich and was brought to Nettuno by English sailors in the 16th century having rescued it from the fires of the Lord Privy Seal.

The story goes that in 1550 a terrible storm blew up along the Cape of Anzio, which lasted for three long days. A galleon, sailing west to east, ran into trouble and was in danger of being shipwrecked. By a miracle, the captain and all hands, most of which were English, managed to steer the galleon into the relative calm of the bay and succeeded in saving the entire crew and all the merchandise. The captain vowed that in return for their safety they would place their precious statue of Our Lady, kept on the ship's altar as was the custom, on the first piece of

The bronze Ipswich Madonna *above the plaque in Lady Lane is by the Irish sculptor Robert Mellamphy, and was modelled after a study of the statue in Nettuno.*

land they came to. Thus it was that Nettuno received the statue and it has, apart from some perambulations during the war years and occasional moves between churches, been there ever since.

Is the Nettuno statue really that which stood for almost 300 years in Lady Lane? Martin Gillett, the leading expert on Marian shrines worldwide, visited Nettuno in 1938 hoping that 'The English Lady' would turn out to be our Lady of Walsingham, which it was not. However, he did not discount the possibility that the statue had come from Ipswich and gave every indication that it could have. A feature of the Nettuno statue is that the front of the Madonna's shoes are silver. In 1538 the statue of Our Lady sent to London for burning was stripped of her finery and had only her 'half shoes of silver'.

A friendship has grown up between Ipswich and Nettuno and parishioners exchange visits (see Elm Street).

LION STREET

Lion Street is tucked away behind the Golden Lion and was once called St Mildred's Lane as it led to St Mildred's Church (see also Cornhill). Before the 18th century all the lanes that led onto Cornhill would have been narrow but none more so than Lion Street, which was little more than a passageway before the developments on Cornhill. In its days as St Mildred's Lane it led to the stable yard and the 'tap' of the Golden Lion (previously called White Lion, which changed its name sometime between 1571 and 1579 from White to Golden).

There has been an inn or tavern on the site for many hundreds of years, as brisk trade was to be had from the market activity on Cornhill. In 1579, during the reign of Elizabeth I, it appears in the town records:

'The signe of the Golden Lion shall now continue paying therefore yerely to the Towne 1d rent.'

At this time shop and innkeepers were required to hang signs from their shops and the penny rent

was required for the privilege of being allowed to place a signpost on ground belonging to the town, i.e. overhanging the street or passageway. Proprietors took full advantage of the advertising possibilities by placing their signboards as prominently forward as possible but not enough to incur a rental fee.

Around the same time, in 1594, the townspeople were required to put lighted candles in their windows at night, this being the earliest form of street lighting. Dr Taylor wrote:

'Sloppy, filthy streets, no causeway or pavement – how welcome moonlight nights must have been to town-dwellers. One begins to understand the real reason why people went to bed early in those times. The foulness visible in the daytime was a trap then – with night-walkers and thieves thrown in. Consequently, it must have been an advance in public opinion and public measure, when the streets were even but feebly lighted.'

In spite of the relatively high price of candles, it was householders and businesses, rather than the town authorities, who provided this nightly illumination, obligatory between 'five until eight in the evening' from 2 November to 2 February. Defaulters were imprisoned. Nevertheless, as Dr Taylor remarks:

'With narrow, rickety old streets – no two houses alike, no two doorways on the same level – with crowds of traders' signs hanging overhead, must have presented a picturesque appearance when illuminated by hundreds of lanterns and candles.'

In the 20th century, the narrowness of Lion Street remained an issue, since it provided not only access to the Golden Lion but was also the entrance to the Ipswich Constabulary garage when the police station was beneath the town hall. Leslie C. Jacobs records:

'Parking for both police and private motor vehicles presented a problem around the town hall in 1947. Space at the town hall and in the yard of the nearby Golden Lion Hotel became exhausted and prompted the Force to purchase its own garage premises in Lady Lane.'

The Lady Lane garages were always regarded as inadequate and were 'disposed of in 1964 and disappeared with the preparations for the town's Civic Drive project'.

LLOYDS AVENUE

Lloyds Avenue was cut through the ornate Victorian buildings that fronted onto the Cornhill, opposite the town hall, in 1929 and the first traffic passed through it on 5 January 1930. Although the avenue itself was new, there had been an older break in the buildings standing on the north side of Cornhill: Mumford's Passage ran alongside Old Waterloo House and was named for William Mumford, a 19th-century surgeon who owned property thereabouts.

The Lloyds building, which replaced the Old Waterloo House store in 1890 (afterwards Footman & Pretty and now Debenhams), gave the name to the avenue later cut through to allow vehicular access, especially trolleybuses, from Tower Ramparts to Cornhill.

At the top of Lloyds Avenue stands what was once the Odeon cinema but is now the Top Rank bingo club. The original cinema opened in the late 1930s and later became part of the Rank Organisation (as did the Gaumont, now the Regent Theatre). Rank operated both cinemas until the 1970s when the Odeon became a bingo hall. In the late 1980s plans were laid for a multi-screen cinema on Major's Corner and, in 1991, became the new Odeon.

Lloyds Avenue is now closed to through traffic, except for the taxi rank vehicles operating out of the top end, and is fringed by a mixture of small shops and restaurants, building society offices, an estate agency and a bakery.

LONG STREET

Muriel Clegg wrote 'Long Street, once Long Lane, does not seem to deserve its name now, but Ogilby's map (which does not name it) gives the impression that it originally ran right through from Back Hamlet to St Helens' Street, thus justifying its name.'

Lloyds Avenue in the 1950s before it was closed off to traffic. (ITM Collection)

Major's Corner at the junction of Carr Street and Old Foundry Road.

It did not endear itself to *Hunt's Guide*, which said that Long Lane was 'an extraordinary specimen of the horrible places in which some classes of people manage to exist'.

Long Street is now the entrance for the Suffolk College.

MAJOR'S CORNER

This busy junction, where the top of Upper Orwell Street meets St Helen's Street, is opposite the Odeon and is not, as might be thought, named after a military hero but after the Major family, which is mentioned in St Margaret's parish registers from 1586 onwards (and appears as such on Pennington's map). This has, though, done nothing to dent the ongoing and very long-lived legend of 'the old major who lived here'!

Muriel Clegg writes:

'Joshua Major, dyer, bought a tenement in St Margaret's on 27 July 1656: two years later in

June, July and September, the burials of John, Joseph and Benjamin Major, sons of Joshua and Ann are recorded in St Margaret's burial register.'

Joshua Major was appointed one of the surveyors of the North Ward in April 1659 and a month later the Town Assembly agreed that the surveyors 'shall alter the bridge and turne the Water at Maior's Corner that the Water may Runn downe the Lane'.

In 1991 the art deco-style Odeon cinema development swept away many buildings and took its name from the old Odeon in Lloyds Avenue, yet its life as an entertainment venue lasted a mere 14 years. Its appearance was intended to recall the 1930s heyday of the cinema, but in June 2005 it was announced that the cinema was 'no longer commercially viable'.

When the Odeon was built there were fears for the nearby Regent Theatre (formerly the Gaumont) but the borough council did a three-way asset swap whereby they sold the Cox Lane car park to NCP, and NCP sold land it owned next door to the theatre to Rank for the new five-screen Odeon and the borough council took over the theatre. The Odeon now takes its place in history and will soon only live on in the memories of its short existence.

A familiar site that was lost to the Odeon development was the Botwood & Egerton motor garage. The showroom was built in 1923 and had necessitated the demolition of Major's House. In *Early Country Motoring* John F. Bridges writes:

'The new buildings at Majors Corner were completed in 1924 and incorporated showrooms, offices and a garage, but within about three years the adjoining site was purchased and further buildings constructed for the repair and service departments.'

A part of the Botwood building facing onto Woodbridge Road survived the overall demolition for some years. The remnant building was used for a while as a car dealership and furniture shop until June 2005 when it was knocked down for redevelopment.

The Milestone Beer House on the north side is one of the few pre-1960s landmarks. It was known for years as the 'Mulberry', and is still known as such by the locals. It was also been an American theme pub for several years.

Next to the Milestone, at the start of Woodbridge Road, is the Ipswich Caribbean Association International Community Centre.

MARKET ROAD

This tiny remnant of an extension of Friars Bridge Road is the single reminder of the cattle market that, for over 100 years, brought the country to the town on two days a week, Tuesday and Saturday.

When it moved here from the old cattle market in 1856 the Portman Road–Princes Street area saw an explosion of development and to those living nearby the rapid transformation from marshland to

industry must have been extraordinary. No doubt there were many who welcomed the expansion, the coming of the railways and the general sense of activity prevalent in the town, though there would have been some who were sure that it did not augur well for the future.

For the residents of Dogs Head Street, Silent Street and the area round St Stephen's there would have been winners and losers, too. The innkeepers and retailers no doubt mourned the loss of the market trade but the householders breathed a sigh of relief that the commotion, smell and congestion caused by the market had moved elsewhere.

Even at the new premises market days were bedlam, not least because the pens were on the opposite side of the road to the sale yard and the stock had to be driven across and animals invariably escaped at the station end where they were offloaded from the trains. Tuesdays, for those living in nearby streets, meant battening down the hatches; very often stock would escape and householders would find cattle or pigs in their front gardens or even, on occasions, inside the house or business premises. On one occasion a bull broke loose and ran up Museum Street where it jumped through a plate glass shop front. The police in those days carried no firearms but they did have a collection of confiscated rifles and blunderbusses, which they occasionally resorted to in order to dispatch a rampaging animal.

An old guide recalls:

'Past the entrance to Portman Road is the cattle market where a great deal of business is done on a Tuesday. It is a spacious and convenient place for the purpose.'

In the 1930s further changes and improvements were made, including new entrances for cattle from Portman Road instead of Princes Street.

Farming fortunes are now a world away from the time when there were thousands of family farms spread across the county and Tuesday was the day the country came to town, although in 2005 a

Farmers' Market took place on Cornhill for the first time. In the heyday of the post-World War Two market, farmers would bring their wives and children to Ipswich, perhaps having lunch at Footmans, the Queens Hotel or at one of the numerous restaurants and cafes catering for their trade in the Princes Street area. In harvest time arable farmers would bring a crop sample and go onto the Corn Exchange to negotiate its sale and – most importantly – see what other farmers were up to!

MUSEUM STREET

This and the smaller Arcade Street were part of the mid-19th-century development of the western part of the town, and it is named for the museum built there in 1847 by a society founded for the encouragement of the study of 'Natural History among the Working Classes'. There had been a museum room in the old town hall from around 1830 but, with the increasing interest and number of exhibits, larger and more appropriate premises were required.

On 27 October 1846 the *Ipswich Express* announced that it took 'pleasure in announcing that

The old Museum building, now being sold for redevelopment.

some influential gentlemen are taking active steps for the formation of a Museum in this town, which, under proper restrictions, will be accessible to the public'. Leading names of the day, such as Tollemache, Cobbold, Alexander and Ransome, were highly supportive and among the Vice-Presidents were the 7th Astronomer Royal Sir George Biddell Airy and the Reverend Professors Henslow, Sedgwick and Whewell.

The *Suffolk Chronicle* was in broad agreement for the project but wanted assurance that it was not to be run by 'enthusiastic amateurs' and counselled that 'in scientific matters there must be no dabbling'. A reporter from the *Chronicle* attended a meeting of the museum committee and wrote:

'The Spirit of the Age was the presiding genius at the meeting on Monday last, and nothing of party, bigotry nor selfishness for one instant checked the enthusiasm with which the proceedings were watched.'

George Ransome was foremost among the supporters and within days he had raised £121 16s in cash, together with 80 promises of guinea subscriptions. It was proposed that nothing less than a specially-designed building would be adequate, especially as there were murmurings in the press about the lack of 'decent museums' up to that point. It was decided that it should stand in one of the new streets being laid out at that time and both the museum and Museum Street became a reality at the same time. A local architect, Christopher Fleury, was appointed as designer and, for convenience, he took up residence in the street. His design was influenced by the prevailing window tax, which appeared in the annual budget at £5, and explains why the museum was lighted by skylights in the roof rather than by windows. Its shape is triangular and built as such to accommodate the street curve.

The museum attracted support from the Prince Consort, who during his visit to the town in 1851 was said to have spent more time at the museum than anywhere else, and Queen Victoria is reputed to have declared irritably that he spoke of little else for several days afterwards.

Inevitably, not everyone was happy with the new building and a correspondent to the *Ipswich Journal* thought an older building should have been adapted, hinting that some of those 'interesting themselves in getting up the subscriptions are also interested in getting rid of their ground'. George Ransome energetically refuted the suggestion and such was the support for the project that no more such accusations were heard.

To create space, Thomas Seckford's great tudor mansion and gardens on the south side of Westgate Street were sacrificed. Muriel Clegg wrote:

'Museum Street was under construction early in 1847, largely through the efforts of Henry Leverett of Westgate Street. An opening was made in Westgate Street through part of the former Seckford House and its gardens.'

The house had been partially demolished in 1744 and, in common with other Tudor houses at the time, was let go as Ipswich began to feel the effects of the Orwell silting up and commerce drifted away to other ports. Seckford was Member of Parliament for the borough and had amassed a fortune as Surveyor of the Court of Wards and Liveries (see Westgate Street).

The first brick of the museum was laid on 1 March 1847 and, with a few inevitable delays, opened in December that year to great acclaim. The Revd William Kirby, the celebrated entomologist, was president, although he was already nearly 90. At the opening he was unable to give a speech but thanked the Bishop of Norwich for his support and said 'I am a poor old man now. It cannot be long before I shall go, and I trust I shall be happy'. This brief sentiment reduced many to tears.

Initially there were complaints from the curator who was horrified at the behaviour of the visitors. This 'vile and disorderly mob that contaminates our room on public nights' were 'dirty, smelly and noisy' and rushed up and down stairs howling and shrieking. There was also the problem of the piles of peanut shells left behind by the 'lower orders' (peanuts being the prevailing snack of the day and often used as missiles by theatre-goers less than entranced by the performances). However, there were over 10,000 visitors in the first month and the number of exhibits grew rapidly as donations came in from all quarters, including a full-grown lion from Wombwell's Menagerie, which was forwarded to Ipswich in hot weather!

Insufficient income meant that Ipswich Corporation had to take over the museum in 1853 when they increased free opening times. The curator was paid £100 a year and an attendant employed for 10 shillings (50 pence) a week to prevent the 'idle and dissolute' from entering.

By 1878 it was clear that the museum had successfully outgrown its first home. The committee decided to erect a new museum and a School of Art. Presumably by this time the 'vile and disorderly mob' had been tamed and were thought worthy of further education. The collections were moved to the new premises in 1881 (see High Street).

In the 1960s the upper floor, with its iron-railed gallery, was used as a ballroom and said to be haunted by a boa constrictor that was donated to the old museum in its early days. Several different companies and organisations, including a firm of auctioneers and the District Probate Registry Office, have used the old Museum Street building over the years. It is currently on the market again and in a very poor state.

It was in Museum Street in 1912 that a prominent department and furniture store called Fraser's burned down, raising questions about the role of the horse-drawn steam pumps that the fire brigade had to use to put out the fire. The steam pumps had been in service since 1884, but it was to be 1920 before a motorised machine took over. Fraser's had been on the site since 1890, taking the place of the old *Ipswich Journal* offices, which had stood at the corner of Princes and Museum Streets.

Just off Museum Street, near the Methodist Church, is St Mary's Court. Here is found one of several town sculptures, Spirit of Youth, by John Ravera who has public monuments scattered over London and the Home Counties (including Family Group near Battersea Bridge). His second Ipswich sculpture is the bronze Trawlerman in Sainsbury's Hadleigh Road precinct.

The Gothic Methodist Church is by Frederick Barnes and was built as a Wesleyan Chapel. The foundation stone was laid on 20 June 1800. There were complaints at the time that it looked too much like an Anglican church.

Until recently the Inland Revenue had offices at 36 Museum Street, but the premises have been converted to flats and are called The Collectors House. This is seen as an indicator of the move towards repopulating the town. The *East Anglian Daily Times* declared:

'Strange things are happening in the heart of Ipswich. In common with many towns and cities, the centre of the metropolis became less and less populated as the 20th century unfolded. But suddenly, the tide has turned, and buildings and sites that were once offices or factories are being reclaimed for fashionable 21st-century housing.'

Above the doorway is a royal crest, while the insignia of Ipswich Borough adorns the red-brick frontage with its terracotta panels. It was built somewhere between 1885 and 1905 but few details are available since, as a government office, it required no planning permission. The Collectors House is another example of buildings following the curve of the streets created in the 19th century, particularly in the Museum Street–Arcade Street area.

On the opposite corner at the junction with Arcade Street is an interesting fake Norman building, which indicates the widespread Victorian craze for imitation. However, the small cluster of houses on the opposite side of the road, beside the Wesleyan Chapel, is a rare example of genuine Georgian architecture. Very little was built in Ipswich in Georgian times, as this was a low time in the town's fortunes and there were no moneyed gentry or rich merchants to pay for it.

Further down, at the junction with Princes Street, is a stone-built edifice dated 1905 sandwiched between two red-brick buildings, which has several extraordinary gargoyles reminiscent of the mediaeval wooden post carvings that once abounded in the town.

NORTHGATE STREET

This is a reminder of one of the three main gates through which people and traffic passed to gain access to the town. The street was known previously as the northern part of Brook Street and was part of the old town ramparts, sometimes known as St Margaret's Gate. An even older North Gate might have stood here but the one that, ironically, only gave its name to the street a few years before its demolition, on 2 August 1794, was early mediaeval. The *Ipswich Journal* reported:

'The workmen began pulling down the building called St Margaret's Gates. This alteration will not be the least of the numerous improvements in consequences of the Paving Act.'

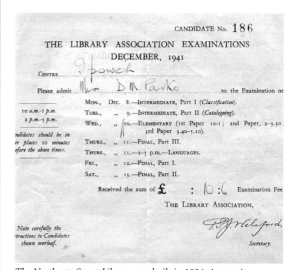

The Northgate Street Library was built in 1924. At one time Ipswich Library ranked high in the country for the number of books issued per head of the population. Miss Doris Parker was for many years the children's librarian.

View up Northgate Street to the Bethesda Chapel in the 1980s.

Remains of the North Gate were incorporated into the cellars of the Halberd inn, which stands on the north side of Tower Ramparts and is, therefore, part of the northernmost arc of the old Saxon town. It had done well to survive until 1794 and lasted 12 years longer than the West Gate.

Known as 'St Margaret's Bargate', 'Bargate' or 'Old Bar', the North Gate straddled the top end of the street between what was the Halberd inn (it keeps the old name on its wall but is now P.J. McGinty's) and the house opposite (once a second hand bookshop and now Alexandria Hair Artistry).

The Halberd stood just outside the North Gate, and although little is known of its very early history it is certain that an inn of some kind has stood on this site for a long time. Gates were the obvious places for inns and taverns to flourish, and the Halberd not only offered accommodation to travellers but its stables were popular and continued to be so right up until the 1920s when local traders used horses and wagons to make deliveries in the town.

In the 1750s the Halberd had a steelyard, which was 'as just and true as any in England'. In 1755 a coachman named William Bennett advertised that he had taken the inn 'adjoining St Margaret's, Bargate, which has a steel yard for weighing hay'. The steelyard was later fitted with a strong new beam, 'made according to the best mechanical principles'.

The Halberd has been renovated and rebuilt several times over the years, and traces of the Victorian stables, where horses and traps were accommodated on market day, can still be seen. It has the dubious distinction of being the first pub in Ipswich to have a colour television installed in the bar.

Oak House, just down the street, was formerly the 15th-century Royal Oak inn. It is much restored with features from other Ipswich buildings and is now used as offices by Jackaman, Smith & Mulley. Oak House began life as a private house but was converted to an inn in the mid-19th century. It was converted back to the appearance of a merchant's house in 1885 and restored again in 1913. One of the corner posts shows a carving of a smith and anvil, which may indicate a one-time occupancy by a blacksmith, entirely logical considering the number of horses that were stabled higher up on St Margaret's Plain and in the streets surrounding the North Gate.

The Assembly Rooms, at the junction with Great Colman Street (now a nightclub), were opened in January 1821 with a lavish ball, attended by almost 200 of the principal personages in the county who partied until four in the morning. A committee was formed in 1818 and nearly £4,000 was raised towards its cost. At the rear of the premises were, in the 19th century, the Judges' lodgings, where their lordships resided during the holding of the summer Assizes. The three-storeyed building with columned façade was initially considered a huge town asset but, in spite of great enthusiasm, the project foundered due to lack of funds. The premises were sold and in 1878 found a new use as the High School for Girls. The school stayed in Northgate Street until 1907 when it moved to Westerfield Road, after which the building became a motor engineering works and then a dry cleaner's.

Ipswich was one of the first towns in the country to adopt the 1852 Public Libraries Act and to open branch libraries to serve outlying parts of the town. The earliest of these were at the junction of Clapgate Lane and Mildmay Road, Norwich Road, Tomline Road and Stoke Street. There were several private and institutional libraries in the town, including that housed in the old Carnegie Building, which was handed to the borough but moved to Ipswich School in the 1980s. The Northgate Street library was built in 1924.

In the pioneering days of public libraries it was thought innovative that tickets were interchangeable and books could be returned to any of these 'service' points. Anyone living in Ipswich, paying rates or being educated in the town could borrow books without charge. Visitors were allowed to take out a subscription for six months and had access to the Reading Room; the Reference library could be used 'without formality of any kind'.

Opposite the town library is one of the town's most photographed features – Pykenham's Gatehouse, named after Archdeacon Pykenham. Until 1914 Ipswich was under the jurisdiction of the Bishop of Norwich, with an Archdeacon of Suffolk as his representative and, in 1471, William Pykenham was appointed to the post. He moved into a house close to the North Gate, rented from the Priory of the Holy Trinity (see Bolton Lane), which owned property thereabouts. However, the Archdeacon considered the house incommensurate with his status and proceeded to build what has been described as a 'palace' on adjoining land. What was really no more than what might be thought of as an enlarged gatehouse it nevertheless had its own brick-built gate known today as Pykenham's Gatehouse.

Not long after completing his gatehouse, the Archdeacon moved on to greater things and began building a massive Deanery gateway in nearby Hadleigh, and although he had further, more elaborate plans for a new and more grand structure in Ipswich they were never realised as Archdeacon Pykenham died in 1497.

The main part of the building, which backs onto Tower Street, is now the Ipswich & Suffolk Club and was previously a Farmers' Club where farmers and agriculturists could meet on market days as both a social and business venue.

A timber-framed building, with its wattle-and-daub studwork exposed, stands above the entrance arch and was once occupied by the gatekeeper. On the spandrels of the inner arch is a shield bearing a fish, possibly a pike, an heraldic pun on the name Pykenham. The Ipswich Building Preservation Trust now occupies the gatehouse. Since it was formed in 1978 the Trust has come to the aid of not only Pykenham's Gatehouse but also the former Half Moon and Star in St Matthew's Street and a 17th-century house in Bolton Lane.

On the corner of Northgate Street and Old Foundry Road, next to the library entrance and in what is now a private residence, was, in the 1960s, the 'Mikado' coffee bar in the glorious 'era' of coffee

Drawing by Percy E. Stimpson in 1888 of the view up Northgate to St Margaret's Plain, with the Pykenham Gateway on the left and the Halberd on the corner.

bars, with their 'coke', 'frothy coffee' and juke boxes. Ipswich was well provided with coffee bars and each had a group of patrons who considered it their own 'turf'. Coffee bars were usually dimly lit and invariably the haunt of disaffected or rebellious youth, but certainly a place where, in those days, young women could safely go on their own. The choice of record on the juke box often had a message in the title or lyrics intended to attract someone's attention.

The noisy hiss of the 'espresso' machine and air thick with smoke, combined with the dulcet tones of Elvis Presley and the like, sum up the 'Swinging Sixties' for many. 'Teddy boys' would 'hang out', usually in different coffee bars to the 'Mods', which later gave rise to street confrontations between the 'Mods' and 'Rockers'.

OLD CATTLE MARKET

Except for the recent advent of Farmers' Markets, Ipswich is almost devoid of any activity that brings the country to the town, as the weekly markets had done for thousands of years. Only the names of the streets are left as reminders, and the old cattle market could hardly be more explicit. The open square in front of the Eastern Counties bus station was, for over 40 years, the cattle market.

The cattle and Provision Market first opened in what is known as the old cattle market in 1810. It was brought to the notice of the bailiffs that holding markets in public streets was both dangerous and inconvenient, exposing the townspeople to 'mischiefs so likely to ensue from persons riding or driving carriages through [the streets] on Market Day.'

Although the cattle market adjoined the Provision Market, it was not actually part of it but took place in front of the Blue Coat Boy public house, now a row of offices incorporating the Coachmans Yard. It formed a rectangle from Dogs Head Street to Silent Street and up to Falcon Street and was enclosed by a low wall surmounted by an iron fence.

By the 1850s the cattle market had long since outgrown its confined space. Following complaints from the market proprietors, a committee was appointed in 1851 'to consider the desirableness and practicability of removing the cattle market from its present site'. The committee reported in January 1852 that, in their opinion, 'the present site is much too small, it is in the centre of the Town with no access to it except through narrow and intricate streets and is therefore obviously but ill adapted to the purpose.' Several alternative sites were suggested, including a piece of land called Chenery's Meadow to the north of Tower Ditches or a portion of the Corporation Marshes next to Friars Bridge. The latter was chosen since it was cheaper and had the added advantage of being Corporation land and its development would increase the value of the adjoining land.

In 1856 the new cattle market opened on a site on the marshland off Portman Road, in what was the up and coming part of town. The marshes were raised by almost two feet to allow for a solid and dry platform on which to build the cattle pens (see Market Road).

Since the 1930s the old cattle market has been used as the terminus, depot and office for the Eastern Counties Road Car Company, which was amalgamated with four local bus companies to form Eastern Counties Omnibus Company.

OLD FOUNDRY ROAD (formerly St Margaret's Ditches)

From the earliest times until the 19th century this was known as St Margaret's Ditches, a reminder that it was on the route of the town's northern boundary ditches (or ramparts). The road still leads eastwards

from Tower Ramparts and curves down to Carr Street, thus marking out the ancient town defences employed since the seventh century. Until the 1930s there were still houses here, perching along the top of the old rampart, accessed by steps from the street. It was at premises in St Margaret's Ditches that Robert Ransome (1753–1830) opened a foundry, triggering the 19th-century expansion that established the town on the national and international industrial map. The foundry grew to occupy an area from Great Colman Street to Carr Street before moving to a new, 11-acre dockside site in 1849 – the famous Orwell Works.

The son of a Quaker schoolteacher, Robert Ransome (1753–1830), had started a small foundry in Norwich where he carried out various progressive experiments in iron working. In 1785 he took out a patent for tempering cast-iron plough shares and in 1789 moved to Ipswich. An announcement appeared in the *Ipswich Journal* that 'Robert Ransome (late of Norwich), Iron and Brass Founder', had set up business in an old foundry 'opposite St Mary at the Key Church, Ipswich'. Mr Ransome wished to inform the farmers that he had a large assortment of cast-iron shares 'which he sells on the lowest terms, for ready money'.

Ransome set up shop with a single workman but success was almost instantaneous. He moved to larger premises on St Margaret's Ditches in a disused maltings, beside an old skittle alley, the alley having been closed down in 1785. Being a Nonconformist, he would have had a certain satisfaction in taking over a skittle alley, which was considered by some to be both frivolous and a dangerous temptation to gamble and indulge in loose living. Along with 30 other skittle, or ten pin, alleys, it had been closed by the town authorities who claimed to be anxious that working people might be tempted to bet on the outcome of such amusement, and the alleys were, therefore, banned. They did 'inconceivable mischief to the lower ranks of this town, by enticing them to spend their money, whilst their numerous families are in want of the common necessities of life.' It is interesting that a painting executed in 1810 shows

Ransome employees playing in the skittle alley, so the town ban must have been lifted and the 'mischief' tamed.

The fact that Robert Ransome came to Ipswich was no coincidence. There had been a Quaker Meeting House in College Street since 1700, and among those who worshipped there were the Alexanders, one of the town's most influential families, who were bankers, ship owners and merchants. They practiced their business in accordance with Quaker principles, which required ethical use of resources, famously demonstrated by such well-known manufacturers and social reformers as the Fry, Cadbury and Rowntree families. In Ipswich this sense of commercial brotherhood attracted men like Ransome, and in due course Charles May (see Bolton Lane) and the Sims family who were to form Ransomes, Sims and

Ransomes mowers still tend the lawns of Buckingham Palace, the courts at Wimbledon, Twickenham rugby ground and the Old (golf) Course at St Andrews in Scotland. [Cox's County Who's Who, 1912]

May. The big names in banking such as Barclay, Lloyd, Gurney and Alexander were all Quakers.

The key to the success of the Quakers in 18th-century England lay in their reputation for excellence in both making and selling products that were useful to society. Manufacturing, science, doctoring, botany and banking all benefited from their enquiring and experimental approach. Ransomes, Sims and May all worked with William Penn's maxim, 'True Godliness don't turn men out of the world, but enables them to live better in it, and excites their endeavours to mend it.'

In 1803 Robert Ransome made a technological breakthrough, which was to revolutionise production and compound his already hugely successful enterprise. Some molten iron burst out of a mould and spilled onto the foundry floor. Where the iron had touched the cold floor, this rapid cooling of the iron had meant it acquired extra hardness. Using this discovery, he took out a new patent for 'chilled cast iron' and launched a new range of products to add to the revolutionary self-sharpening plough share.

Robert's two sons, Robert and James, both joined the family business in due course, as did James's son, James Allen Ransome, who became a partner in 1830. Over the years the firm acquired different titles and diversified as and when necessary to sustain the business. Following the agricultural depression of the 19th century, Ransomes turned to bridge building, mills and lawnmowers. They also became pioneers in the development of the agricultural steam engine and exhibited a portable steam engine at the Royal Agricultural Society's show in 1841.

In 1836 the firm joined the railway building boom and patents were taken out in 1841 for railway components, especially chilled iron crossings, switches and sleeper fastenings. This coincided with the arrival in Ipswich of Charles May, a pharmacist from Ampthill in Bedfordshire, who hailed from another Quaker family with formidable connections. It was Charles's brother, Francis, who started the match manufacturers Bryant and May, and the May family were renowned surgeons and chemists (see also Bolton Lane).

The firm became Ransome & May and Charles began applying his scientific mind to engineering. He invented the 'compressed wooden trenail', a fail-safe device for fixing rails to the sleepers, and by 1866 12,000 miles of track had been laid using the trenail principle across England, parts of Europe, India and Australia. They had to set up a separate company, Ransome and Rapier, to deal with the volume of trade demanded by 'railway mania'.

In addition to his foundry work, Charles was an amateur astronomer and a consulting engineer for three of the principal instruments for the Royal Observatory at Greenwich, which brought him into contact with Sir George Biddell Airy, 7th Astronomer Royal. In 1849 Charles's father wrote to one of his nieces:

'Thy Uncle Charles is having an Observatory built, it is nearly finished, it is placed not far from the greenhouse and is seen both from the dining and drawing room and is rather a pretty object'.

Unfortunately the Mays left Ipswich in 1851 so had little time to enjoy the fine observatory, and it is not clear that it was ever fitted out with instruments.

Sir George had had his astronomical interest sparked during a visit to Ransomes where Robert Ransome showed the young Airy the ringed planet Saturn through a telescope of his own making. After his appointment to the Royal Observatory, Sir George commissioned Ransomes to replace all the observational instruments with new telescopes including, in 1851, a new generation of telescope called the Airy Transit Circle. This was a huge device fixed to rotate vertically between north and south and used to accurately time and measure stars passing through its exact centre and so define the exact position of the Greenwich meridian. Sir George was responsible for the world standard Greenwich Meantime, and the Greenwich signal

began as a series of pulses sent to the railway companies to regulate their clocks.

Kenneth Goward of the Orwell Astronomical Society writes:

'Airy certainly was influenced as a child in astronomy by Ransome and he spoke of this in his first (of six) lectures in Ipswich to the Mechanics Institute in 1848.'

The lectures were later turned into a book, *Popular Astronomy*, which became a standard work on the subject for the remainder of the 19th century, running to nine editions.

Through his scientific friendships, Charles was aware of photography, and Ransomes trade catalogue was one of the first to use photographs for publicity purposes.

After Charles May's departure in 1851, Ransomes took on William Dillwyn Sims (related to the banker and philanthropist Richard Dykes Alexander), who became a partner in the company. By 1848 Ransomes needed larger premises and began the task of moving closer to the docks, to a purpose-built site named the Orwell Works. *The Victoria County History* of Suffolk recorded in 1907:

'[The Orwell Works] begun in 1849 and have been continually extended, with an immense foundry, a smith's shop with (more than) a hundred forges, a plough shop, several engine-erecting and boiler shops, a turnery, a grinding department, a threshing-machine department, and a lawn mower department. They have a dock frontage of over 800 feet, alongside which steamers of 1,500 tons can load, and there is direct rail communication along the quay'.

The new works provided employment for upwards of 2,200 men and boys.

During the two world wars, Ransomes was central to the war effort. Several bombs were dropped on the dock area and on the night of 9

ORWELL PLACE

April 1941 13 high explosive bombs were dropped in an attempt to destroy the factories.

Ransomes continued in various forms until 1989 when the whole of the agricultural implement business was sold to Electrolux. The company retained the lawnmower business until 1998 when they accepted a takeover offer from the American industrial group Textron Inc. Ransomes had manufactured the first lawnmowers in 1832 and their machines were considered the 'Rolls-Royce' of mowers.

Robert Ransome died in 1830 having retired five years earlier. In his retirement he took up copperplate engraving and the construction of a telescope. He was buried in the Quaker burial ground in College Street, close to the Friends' Meeting House that he had attended on his arrival in Ipswich over 40 years earlier. Regrettably, the Meeting House was demolished in 1995 and with it the grave of Robert Ransome.

Soon after Ransomes left St Margaret's Ditches, already renamed Foundry Road, it became Old Foundry Road.

When the St Margaret's area was developed in the 1960s the highway lost a swathe of buildings to the Carr Precinct (now Eastgate Shopping Centre) and the DHSS offices (which were subsequently demolished in 1999). The plaque marking the site of the Ransome premises is on the wall of the QD stores that now occupies a large area of the south half of Old Foundry Road.

Along Old Foundry Road is the Orbit Housing Association, formerly Phillips & Piper's Clothing factory. During World War Two, the factory moved over to making parachutes before reverting to its original purpose, including the manufacture of cheap suits, which it had done since as early as 1851. In 1983 it was converted to flats by Barratt Homes but later taken on by Orbit, who now run the 104-flat complex. Beside it is Pipers Court.

ORWELL PLACE

The street between Tacket Street (of which Orwell Place was once a part) and the junction of Upper Orwell Street with Eagle Street is named Orwell Place and is one of the suggested sites for the lost East Gate. Muriel Clegg writes:

Orwell Place in 1898. The house on the right was the birthplace of the actress Mary Anne Keeley, née Goward, (1805–1899), whose father was a brazier and tinman. The house to the left was then the residence of Dr Stebbings. (ITM Collection)

111

'When, in 1923, two massive piers approximately 4 feet thick and 17 feet apart were found when clearing ground near the Fore Street junction with Orwell Place, the site of the East Gate seemed to have been confirmed.'

Why Orwell Place was the name chosen, or 'inflicted' says Muriel Clegg, to replace Tacket Street, or its older name Stepples Street (from its raised stepping stones), is unknown, but it dates from early in the 19th-century and shows a certain lack of imagination in taking the 'Orwell' from nearby Upper Orwell Street. Orwell Place could apply to anywhere in Ipswich but Stepples Street would feed the imagination so much better!

Something else to feed the imagination is the fact that Orwell Place was once the site of one of the town's several dunghills and cesspits, the one in the Buttermarket called the 'Colehill' and that to the east of Orwell Place was 'Colehill' (sometimes called 'Coldunghill') or the Warwick Pits. It was at Warwick Pits that the street sweepers were given leave to dump 'any manner of muck or filthe', but in 1570 two men, Henry Ashley and George Wilds, were granted permission to set up 'tainters' near to Warwick Pits. These tainters were wooden frames with tenterhooks, built to hold woollen cloth under strain after fulling, not perhaps the ideal site given the proximity of the cloth to the steaming, fly-ridden piles of dung.

The Martin & Newby buildings attest to an ironmongery business that was patronised by townspeople from its establishment in 1873 until 2004 when it closed due to the prevailing economic climate of competition that affects family shops. In July 2005 a fire broke out as the buildings were undergoing conversion into flats and retail outlets. It took six pumps and a turntable ladder to bring the fire under control and, happily, save the building from complete devastation.

ORWELL STREET

The street marks the route of the stream that once flowed down from the higher ground to the north of the town towards the Orwell River and, even as late as the 1970s, was referred to locally as the 'Wash'. It runs south from St Helen's Street and stretches down to Star Lane. Upper and Lower Orwell Street is now divided by part of Fore Street.

Hunt's Guide highlighted the street's association with the docks:

'It is a street of the dingy and doubtful character which belongs to old and poor localities running down to the water in large sea towns.'

Lower Orwell Street

At the junction of Lower Orwell Street and Fore Street is another of Ipswich's quirky wedge-shaped buildings, now the Absolute Thai Restaurant and Take Away. Just across the road is Blackfriars Court, on the east side of which is a small hump of grass. This is the only remaining part of the ancient town rampart.

Blackfriars Court is the visible boundary of the old friary and the extant foundation masonry is all that is left of the Dominican friars whose house occupied a large extent of ground between Foundation Street and Lower Orwell Street.

Wodderspoon records that considerable portions of the building still existed until 1849 and that a chapel, 'which stood in a space of ground above the new Almshouses', was standing when Kirby published his *Twelve Prints* of *Antiquities in the County of Suffolk* in 1748. This has, of course, long since been destroyed, though by a considerable miracle a small reminder of the friary is left to us, cowering under 'low rises' and tucked away in Blackfriars Court.

The Dominicans were called the Black Friars (or Blackfriars) as they wore black cloaks over white habits and came to Ipswich in 1263. Although their original house was in Foundation Street, it gradually extended so as to cover a large part of Lower Orwell Street and Orwell Place. The Black Friars were preaching friars and sometimes referred to as the Friars Preachers. Their relentless preaching methods often attracted ridicule and the other religious communities frequently resented their uncompromising (some might say 'holier than thou') stance. Nevertheless, the Black Friars had attracted many friends and local benefactors, including the Bigod family, and benefited greatly from the wills of the great and the good of the town.

After the Dissolution the site of Black Friars was granted in 1541 to William Sabyn but later purchased by the Corporation. Part of the old Refectory was adapted for use as a Grammar School, while other sections were divided off to form an establishment 'for the reclamation of beggars'.

Upper Orwell Street

St Michael's Church stands on Upper Orwell Street and is the only 19th-century foundation to stand in the town centre. One of East Anglia's leading church enthusiasts, Roy Tricker, writes:

'Its foundation stone was laid in 1880 and it is interesting to note that buried in the wall with it is a bottle, containing a copy of *The Times*, a description of the church, some coins and a list of the Building Committee.'

St Michael's is a witness to the thriving and populous 19th-century town, when the central parishes had to be sub divided. In the 1870s the new parish of St Michael's was formed and a site acquired in Upper Orwell Street for the new church as the result of slum clearance. Its grimy exterior, somewhat softened by the wild Buddleia that grows there in summer, belies its once cheerful interior. It was built in the 19th-century Evangelical tradition and contains interesting contemporary glass, including a panel of St George with his foot on a scarlet dragon.

It is no longer used for services and its future is undecided.

Between the church and the Ipswich Cab Company is a small garden offering shade and rest, which was opened on 30 March 1977 by the Mayor, councillor H.R. Davis. Crane Limited, manufac-

Anglo-Saxon Silver Penny minted at Ipswich between 1024–1030 AD. The moneyer's name was Lifinc. It depicts King Cnut of England & Denmark (1016–1035 AD). The obverse reads 'CNVT REX ANGL' and the reverse 'LIFINC ON GIPESPI'. (Lockdales)

turers of malleable iron pipe fittings and bronze and steel valves, presented the garden to mark the 50th anniversary of the first metal poured in the malleable foundry of their Ipswich factory.

Among the shops and restaurants along the street is Lockdales of Ipswich, dealers in coins, stamps, banknotes, postcards, cigarette cards, ephemera, jewellery, medals and militaria. They organise regular auctions, often held at the Novotel hotel near St Peter's Church, and Ipswich is the auction headquarters as well as being the centre of their Ebay operation. Lockdales have been on Upper Orwell Street for 10 years and the staff maintains a special interest in the possible site of the Anglo-Saxon mint, which many think is under the NCP car park. This site has been christened the Mint Quarter and development proposals are imminent.

Whatever its location, it is certain that during its lifetime the mint played an important role in the town's prosperity and reputation. Following the Conquest, the Normans demanded extra taxes from the town's moneyers, in whose mint the royal money had been made since the time of King Edgar (959–975). Until the Conquest the moneyer's names were Anglo-Saxon – Alfwold, Aldgar and Ethelberght – and in the time of King Edward the Confessor there were names such as Brunic, Leofwine, and Leofsi using the abbreviation 'Gipe', 'Gipes' and 'Gipesi'. Another in the early 11th century was named Wulsie, possibly an ancestor of Cardinal Wolsey.

'Gipeswic' appears in various forms; it is abbreviated to 'Gep' on the reverse of Edgar's pennies and, in the reign of Cnut, appears as 'Gipespi'.

The mint continued in operation until the reign of Henry III (1216) and its coins continue to surface at sales and auctions. In March 2004 a penny made in Ipswich during the reign of William the Conqueror by the moneyer Aegelwine, was sold at auction. It depicted a crowned bust holding a sceptre and was sold for £391.

The Ipswich & Norwich Co-operative Society has its Education Centre in Upper Orwell Street in what was previously a doctor's surgery.

PORTMAN ROAD

Portman Road was built in the mid-19th century and is arguably the best known of any Ipswich thoroughfare both nationally and internationally. Originally known as Portman's Walks, it led originally to the marshland granted to the 12 portmen of the town following the Charter of King John to Ipswich in 1200. As part of their 'perks of the job' the portmen had pasturage for their horses on 'Oldenholm Medow' (later 'Portman's Meadow'), marsh and meadow land west of the river.

It began life as Portman's Street (running between Birds Garden and Priory Street on White's 1867 map), and is now known the world over as the home of Ipswich Town Football Club. Portman's Walk is now called Sir Alf Ramsey Way. The northern end of Portman Road was previously known as Mill Street, or 'The Way', leading from Barrack Corner to Handford Road and thereafter to the Corporation Marshes.

In addition to the charter election of borough hierarchy, 'good and lawful men', the Common Council ordained that 12 capital portmen should be sworn in and entrusted with full power to govern the borough and maintain its liberties, 'in manner as they are in other free boroughs of England'. Arrangements were made for the first elections of 12 portmen, which took place at St Mary le Tower on 1 July 1200. Townspeople witnessed the swearing in of the 12 who undertook to tend, consult and aid the town officials in all matters and, with their persons and belongings, preserve and maintain the town of Ipswich, its charter and the honour and liberties of the people. Perhaps the brass horn, reputedly presented by the king, was sounded to herald the new era. (The Moot Horn, as it is called, is

Churchman's and Ipswich Town FC grew up alongside each other on Portman Road.

represented in panel two of the Charter Hangings 2000 and is now in the Museum in High Street.)

Portmen continued to play a full part in town life until 1835, by which time there was much discussion as to the fate of the marshes. At considerable expense to the town, attempts had been made to improve drainage and the council discussed selling off the marshes, especially since the demand for building land was increasing and there were mumblings about the 'out dated' exclusive rights of the portmen. With the town rapidly encroaching on the area thoughts were turning to their future. The coming of the railways decided matters and once the new station was built off Burrell Road better access to the town was immediately required. Plans were soon under way to build Princes Street and it became necessary to upgrade Portman's Walks from a track to a road.

Portman Road links the bottom of Princes Street with Handford Road and extends as far north as St Matthew's Street and so out of town on the Norwich Road. Its name is now synonymous with football, but during the second half of the 19th century and much of the early 20th century it had a life of its own. Among the many business that opened premises there were the Alderman Printing & Bookbinding Company, Churchman's and the clothing factory J. Harvey Limited.

The town's football line-up in 1906. (ITM Collection)

On 2 June 1888 crowds witnessed the ascent of Captain Dale's scarlet and yellow balloon 'Eclipse', heralding the opening of the new recreation grounds off Portman Road to mark Queen Victoria's birthday. A few years later, in 1911, Lord Kitchener (who was appointed High Steward of Ipswich in 1909) attended a Boy Scouts' rally at Portman Road.

It was also a place to worship, as the Presbyterians opened a church at the northern apex of Portman Road and Burlington Road to accommodate the large influx of Scots who moved to Suffolk in the 1860s. It is currently an Ipswich International Church (an Elim Pentecostal Church) and the Oasis Centre.

On the opposite side of the road is the British Telecom building, opened in 1955. Its featureless walls are in stark contrast to St Matthew's Church (see St Matthew's Street).

The Empress Skating Rink, which stood at the junction of Portman Road and Portman Walk, was opened in July 1919 and was a welcome distraction after four years of war. The Rink later became Harvey's clothing factory, which was demolished in the 1960s, but during its lifetime characterised

Portman Road as a place beyond the town centre where people could work, play and socialise in open surroundings. Space was certainly needed, since between 1851 and 1881 the town's population rose from 33,000 to 50,000.

Close to the 15-acre Portman Walk Recreation Ground was the East Suffolk Cricket Club ground, first used as a football club in 1884 when it became dual purpose, cricket in the summer and football in the winter. It is now an Astroturf training pitch behind the Britannia stand and the football club is now Ipswich Town FC whose home ground is the stadium with the all-seater capacity of 30,300.

The Ipswich Associated Football Club (AFC) was formed in 1878, although it was not until 1936 that the club turned professional. Ipswich AFC became one of the first teams to use goal nets and there were boards around the ground as no stands were allowed. In those early days fields and trees edged three sides of the ground and the fourth was overshadowed, in 1901, by the construction of Churchman's tobacco processing plant (see Westgate Street).

In 1905 the Ipswich Cricket, Football and

Athletics Ground Company was formed, and although there was still no distinction between the cricket square and the football pitch there was a stand and some fencing. Good natural drainage gave the pitch an enviable reputation for its high quality, retained to this day. During World War One, however, the army requisitioned the ground and the pitch suffered accordingly. When peace came the club needed to generate some income and opened its doors to whippet racing and a groundsman, brought in to repair the damaged pitch, kept chickens, goats and sheep in the stand.

At the beginning of 1936 the newly formed AFC applied to turn professional. Pressure to alter its amateur status mounted when a rival team, named Ipswich United, was formed and threatened to stage alternative matches at the Greyhound Stadium. On 29 August the same year the two teams turned out as one in the new royal blue and white strip. Tony Garnett of the *EADT* writes:

'Everybody involved in bringing professional football to Ipswich attended a pre-match luncheon at the Great White Horse, the most fashionable hotel in town in those days. A toast was proposed by Stanley Rous [later to become Sir Stanley] who was secretary of the Football Association and a Suffolk man, Captain 'Ivan' Cobbold, the Town chairman, responded. The band of the Scots Guards [Cobbold's regiment] paraded and Ipswich Town Football Club was launched.'

Captain John 'Ivan' Murray Cobbold (1897–1944) was the first chairman of the new football team, succeeded in time by his son, Patrick, after he was killed in London in 1944 by a flying bomb. Although the club competed in the 1939–40 season, World War Two cut short activities and the club closed for the duration. Only a few months before he died, Captain Cobbold had wiped out a heavy debt and the club started the 1945 season with healthy finances.

Once the club turned professional the pitch was

rotated 90 degrees so that games were played north to south, rather than east to west, and railings erected. Terracing was built on the North and South ends and a small wooden seating area, with a capacity of 650, was purchased from Arsenal and placed on the East Side. (This stand was later sold to Ipswich Witches speedway for their Foxhall Stadium.)

A club badge was required and after a competition, which brought hundreds of entries, the winning design was by John Gammage, a former Postmaster and Treasurer of the Supporters' Club. Mr Gammage drew on the fact that buildings and animals dominate most heraldic designs and immediately thought of the Suffolk Punch horse:

'I regarded the Suffolk Punch as a noble animal, well suited to dominate our design and represent the club. And to complete the badge I thought of the town of Ipswich which contains many historical buildings, including the Wolsey Gate, and is close to the sea with a large dock area.'

The design remained the club badge unchanged until 1995 when the badge was given a slight facelift. The turrets of the Wolsey Gate were moved to the top, the Suffolk Punch made bolder and the words Football Club replaced FC.

The new professional Ipswich Town FC won the Southern League Championship at its first attempt and in 1938 was elected to the Third Division South.

In 1978 more history was made. The team beat Millwall 6–1 to get them into the Final of the Football Association Cup and, against all the odds, went on to beat Arsenal by one goal to nil to take the Cup. The team toured through the streets in an open-top bus and 100,000 fans crowded onto Cornhill to unite in a triumphant roar as captain Mick Mills, amid a sea of blue and white banners and scarves, held aloft the FA Cup won in what had been the 50th FA Cup Final at Wembley. Shop

The statue of Sir Bobby Robson, created by sculptor Sean Hedges-Quinn, stands beside the Ipswich Town FC stadium and was unveiled on 16 July 2002.

PRINCES STREET

There is some debate as to whether this should be Princes Street or Prince's Street and is typical of instances where an original apostrophe is dropped for ease of use. The street is generally accepted as having been named for Prince Albert and was initially written Prince's Street.

Princes Street runs south from Cornhill to the bridge opposite the railway station, which makes it one of the longest streets in the town. Its southern end once ran across the marshes and shortly after the railway arrived was known for a short time as Railway Station Road.

In September 1845 the Eastern Union Railway Company had issued a report, proposing a new bridge immediately in front of the station to take the increased traffic and improved road leading from the station to the town. Prince's Street and Commercial Road were the result. The bridge was built in 1849.

In July 1860 the *Ipswich Journal* reported that Princes Street was still 'rugged and aboriginal in

windows were decorated and the euphoria in the town made a deep and lasting impression, even on those who had little interest in the game, the *EADT* headline declaring 'In Our Blue Heaven'.

On the 25th anniversary of their victory over Arsenal Tony Garnett wrote in the *EADT*:

'I can still recall those emotional hours before and after Roger Osborne knocked in the 77th-minute winner and then became drained by heat, humidity and the sheer excitement of the Wembley experience.'

In 1981, with Bobby Robson still at the helm, the Town won the UEFA Cup with a 5–4 aggregate victory over the Dutch side AZ Alkmaar.

The club is fortunate in having some of the most loyal fans in British football and the Supporters' Association has funded almost every improvement at the ground since World War Two.

Princes Street bridge across the Orwell, opposite the station, with Ipswich Town Football Club in the background.

In the early days of the mid-19th century market, stock was frequently driven across Princes Street to the sale pens on the other side. (ITM Collection)

Removing tram poles at the top of Princes Street. (ITM Collection)

appearance' though the new railway station was opened on 7 July.

Princes Street was developed in two halves and, as *Hunt's Guide* said, the town end was 'a street bored through a mass of houses, gardens, streets and lanes diagonally, leaving corners and angles of old buildings, dead walls with the marks upon them of table ends dislodged, and bits of lanes running off at curious tangents'.

The Railway Station Road end, which went up as far as the Queen Street junction, made better progress than the top end, where there were more streets and numerous properties that needed demolishing. Negotiations with property owners were often long and drawn out, while the southern half had fewer impediments.

Originally the road was to be 30 to 35 feet wide but was later altered to 'at least 35 feet', which meant much of the negotiation had to begin again, and many owners were understandably anxious that they should be duly recompensed for the loss of their habitat. Although the railway station was the prime reason for its construction, the name Prince's Street was soon applied to the entire street, the top half of which has always been home to banks, insurance companies and building societies.

An important feature of Princes Street from 1856 onwards was the new cattle market (see Market Road). As late as the 1950s, animals were loaded from pens at sidings near the bridge and animals herded along Princes Street to the market. There was a proliferation of auctioneers, surveyors and estate agents at that end of the street.

Northern Princes Street is packed with insurance offices, reflecting the Victorian expansion of commercial activity, and at the Cornhill tip stands Barclays Bank, in what were the old offices of Alexanders & Company (originally in Bank Street) who amalgamated with Gurneys & Co in 1878.

Surprisingly, Nikolaus Pevsner found the 1960s Fisons building 'an excellent modern office block of interesting concrete construction (by F. Samuely), with curtain walling all round and a pretty inner courtyard'. It is now a Berkeley Business Centre.

QUADLING STREET

This street names owes its origin to an Ipswich coachbuilder, Edwin Quadling, whose premises stood at the junction of what is now Quadling Street and its continuation, Wolsey Street. Quadling Street has been altered several times over the last few years and was at one time the boundary for Cardinal Park East. In earlier times there was a footpath connecting with Commercial Road, which ran along the path of the railway sidings thus linking the works to the railway. The modern Quadling Street runs alongside the Royal Mail Sorting Office parallel with Commercial Way (now Road).

Quadling's business straddled the dying days of the old coachbuilders and the emerging railway era. Hugh Moffat in *East Anglia's First Railways* writes:

'The firm of Catt and Quadling had a brief but not uneventful life. In February 1847 one of their carriage-building shops, a brick building, collapsed during a gale. Inside fifteen men were at work on eight carriages for the EUR, five of which, with gleaming paint and varnish, were all but ready for delivery.'

Luckily only two of the men were injured, but the damage was estimated at £700 and the loss fell on the partners. William Catt decided to write off his losses and on New Year's Day 1848 the partnership was dissolved. Catt took over the coach works, leaving Edwin Quadling to concentrate on construction and engineering connected to the new railway industry. The Eastern Union Railway (EUR) was at the time struggling to make the new Ipswich rail link viable, and Quadling was anxious to capitalise on the new business (see also Burrell Road). In 1847 Quadling made a deal with The Little Company, an alliance of local businessmen including John Chevallier Cobbold and John Footman, to set up business at the corner of the street which now bears his name and to build himself 'good substantial' premises. He and The Little Company agreed to lay a siding from the EUR dock tramway, and Quadling was contracted not only to connect a line but also build 50 coal wagons. This time he took out fire insurance for his buildings, called the Greyfriars Works.

However, only three years later poor Edwin Quadling suffered another setback when a gale 'swept with prodigious power' and carried off the roof of one of the sheds and blew down the walls causing the bricks and rafters to fall onto the carriages under manufacture. Unfortunately his insurance did not extend to storm damage and a few months later he was declared bankrupt. At the hearing the commissioner thought it strange that Mr Quadling had suffered two such misfortunes and said 'either he must have been a very odd kind of builder, or Ipswich must be a very stormy place', which was greeted with laughter from all those present, except Edwin Quadling.

Following Quadling's departure, the premises were converted into a flaxworks but the commissioner could have been on to something because in 1860 the works roofing was blown off in yet another storm and 'workers had to fling themselves down spreadeagled upon the flax to prevent it following'.

Shortly afterwards the Corporation came under pressure to do something about the stench of rotting flax that pervaded the area thereabouts and the flaxworks moved on.

Quadling's Greyfriars Works were later taken over by E.R. & F. Turner and then by Kent Blaxill. Parts of the old Quadling works were still visible in Quadling Street in the 1980s.

QUEEN STREET

Unusually, suggests Muriel Clegg, the Queens' Hotel in Queen Street (demolished in about 1970) may have taken its name from the street, a reversal of normal practice. The precise age of the name Queen Street is unclear, as is the queen for which it was named.

The 17-roomed Queen's Hotel and Restaurant was a very popular establishment, especially during the 1950s when it was patronised by farmers bringing their families to town for lunch on market day. It

closed on Christmas Eve 1971 and was demolished to make way for the Britannia Building Society.

Queen Street marks the eastern boundary of the Carmelite Friary, which extended from Queen Street to St Stephen's Lane, south of the Buttermarket on the site of the Buttermarket Shopping Centre. The Carmelites ranked as one of the mendicant orders after a revised rule from Pope Innocent IV allowed the friars to switch from a contemplative order to one of active life. They could find houses and support themselves by begging, though they were permitted to hold property in common, and, judging by the size of their complex, had considerable patronage.

The Carmelites, with their white cloaks over a brown habit, gained the name White Friars and first came to 'Gipeswic' in 1278. They were the poorest of the friars but had a reputation for learning.

In the 1520s the Whitefriars house fell into the hands of Cardinal Wolsey, but he never realised its assets and it was left to Henry VIII, at the Dissolution of the Monasteries, to give it to John Egar (or Edgar). Some of the land had already been sold off by the impoverished friary and parts subsequently appropriated for a county goal, giving rise to Gaol Lane, which led from the Buttermarket to the Provision Market, later Old Gaol Lane. The gaol was later sold to a carpenter, William Wollaston, and in 1727 to William Churchill. Mr Churchill effected many changes including the eradication of the name Old Gaol Lane.

On the corner of the Buttermarket stands East Anglia House, where the cartoonist Carl Giles (1916–1995) worked for 50 years on some 7,500 cartoons for *The Daily Express* and *Sunday Express*. Just in front of the Giles Tavern, on the island at the Princes Street junction, stands Grandma with Rush the Dog, the Terrible Twins, Lawrence and Ralph, and poor, sickly Vera. The statue has become an icon of the town, and the indomitable, behatted battle-axe of Giles's fictional family delights and amuses visitors and locals as they traverse the junction of King Street, Cornhill, Buttermarket, Princes Street and Queen Street.

The junction of Queen Street and the Buttermarket in 1830 showing brick and plaster houses with upper rooms overhanging the pathway. The corner shop was once 'Batley's, the Hatters' with Fraser's opposite. (W. Vick Photo)

The statue is placed on the same spot as one to the fallen of World War One, erected there in 1918 but now in Christchurch Park. This part of town was formerly known as Cheapside and was an extension of the Buttermarket ('Chepe' being an Old English word for market).

Giles was an artist, musician, horseman, yachtsman, film maker, racing driver, draughts champion, engineer, craftsman and, above all, cartoonist. He was born in London where his father was a shopkeeper and his grandfather a jockey who rode for Edward VII. His first name was Ronald but as a young man he had a hairstyle reminiscent of Boris Karloff, who had made his name playing Frankenstein's monster, so he became known as 'Karlo' and then Carl, and so became known as Carl Giles, later shortened to Giles.

In 1942 Giles married his cousin, Joan Clarke, and the couple spent their honeymoon in the Dickens Suite of the Great White Horse. During World War Two they rented a cottage just north of

Ipswich. By then a cartoonist on *Reynold's News*, Giles became friendly with some of the thousands of American servicemen of the 'Mighty Eighth' based in Suffolk, and the men themselves especially appreciated his humorous depiction of cigar-chomping 'Yanks'.

When war ended the couple moved to a farm just outside Ipswich and Giles rented a studio in East Anglia House, overlooking Queen Street. By then he was working for the *Sunday Express* and used to send his work off to Fleet Street each day by train. He was notorious for being late with his copy, and editors sent their men to wait anxiously on Liverpool Street Station for the next episode in the life of the Giles family. Inevitably many local scenes featured in his cartoons, and he often used the 'Tolly Cobbold' trade name. He was a close friend of the Cobbold family, and an enthusiastic imbiber of their beer. Various members of the family occasionally recognised themselves in the published cartoons.

Ill health forced Giles's retirement in the early

The Giles statue is a town icon and the indomitable, be-hatted battle-axe of Giles' fictional family delights and amuses visitors and locals as they traverse the junction of King Street, Buttermarket, Princes Street and Queen Street.

1990s, but in 1993 he was well enough to attend the unveiling of the statue by his friend Warren Mitchell (of 'Til Death Us Do Part) together with Johnny Speight. Warren Mitchell said:

'A lot of cartoons are caricatures, but Giles's cartoons are of real people, although he is a great artist. Most statues are ignored, but, with this one, children will stop and say "What is that?" and their parents will have to explain.'

The sculptor, Miles Robinson, studied at Ipswich School of Art and was approached by the Ipswich Promotion Bureau to design and make the Giles's Family sculpture.

The Chelsea Building Society building near the sculpture started life as a bank and was designed by the same 19th-century architect who built the Crown & Anchor Hotel in Westgate Street, Thomas W. Cotman.

ROPE WALK

It goes without saying that in a town that has long-standing associations with merchant shipping and boat building, and one that is the central town for a large rural population, rope making was a primary occupation, especially in the 15th century. Rope Walk has been known as Ropers Lane and Rope Lane, and although there might have been other such walks this is the only one to survive in name. On Pennington's map Rope Walk is clearly shown as a long, rectangular space with trees either side running north of open land belonging to 'Gravener'. Rope Lane runs from St Clement's in the west to an area of Glebe Land to the east.

Muriel Clegg writes:

'Rope making was carried on in the Rope Walk until well into the nineteenth century. In 1650 Frauncis Searle was permitted to use "Roaperes' Lane for rope-making" as Iatelie Gallant had the same under the same yearly rental.'

From the 13th to the 18th century ropes were made using a 'rope walk' method (sometimes called the 'band walk') to enable rope makers to produce long ropes up to 300 yards long or longer with an even diameter for use on tall ships, which required long and very strong ropes. It was no good splicing several short ropes together as it would double the rope diameter at the joins causing problems in the rigging.

Rope made in a continuous process was, therefore, stronger and its overall evenness essential to the pulleys in the ship's rigging. The 'walk' principal was that the yarns (spun from hemp) were strung out and twisted into strands and then stretched out between revolving hooks that twisted the strands together to make rope. In mediaeval times rope works were usually family businesses. Ropes were made in the lanes and alleys off the main streets, children helping to turn the wheels which revolved the hooks while someone walked back down the rope walk, feeding out additional fibres as necessary. The long, narrow lanes and streets of 'Gipeswic' were ideal for the process and many of them might well have come about as a result of rope-making operations.

Modern rope is made from oil-based synthetic fibres such as nylon or polypropylene, but those made in Rope Walk would have been made from natural fibres such as sisal, cotton, jute or hemp – all brought in by ship and stored in sheds strung along the quaysides.

Rope Walk is now indelibly associated with the Suffolk County Council offices and the Civic College, now Suffolk College. The College was opened by the Queen in 1961 and was built where streets of small terraced houses stood before being demolished in the 1950s. This area of the town was then known as 'The Potteries' and wholesale clearance meant that many streets were lost, including Pottery Street, Dorkin Street, New Street (though a small fraction survives) and Arthur Street.

Its place in town history is of enduring interest, especially as it is now seen as a lost community that still lingers in folk memory. The name is said to originate from the Rope Walk Pottery, occupied in the 1860s by George Schulen, who manufactured 'glazed pipes and every description of brown earthenware'.

The first change to The Potteries came during the 1930s as a result of 'slum clearance', but the death knell was sounded in the 1960s when the concept of 'development' began to take hold. This is, even now, transforming almost the entire parish of St Clement's into a wall of apartment blocks fronted by the marina. In his study of The Potteries, which was the largest working-class district in the town, historian Frank Grace has explored the lives and experiences of the inhabitants in an attempt to rediscover this 'lost' community. Local memory of the area is still strong and Frank has gathered recollections of old Ipswichians who lived in the area in the inter-war years in what became familiarly called 'The Potteries' or 'The Rope Walk Area'.

The Seventh Day Adventists have a church here.

ST GEORGE'S STREET

Known also as Globe Lane, St George's Street takes its name from St George's Chapel that stood here until 1810. Wodderspoon writes:

> 'St George's Chapel stood in Globe Lane, upon the site of a line of houses now called St George's terrace.'

The chapel, mentioned in Domesday, was still being used when John Blosse left 3s 4d in his will in 1448 for the 'reparation of the church of St George'. G.R. Clarke mentions that it was still in use as 'late as the middle of the sixteenth century, in the time of Henry VIII'. Post Reformation, it fell into ruin and, in a will of 1610, is described as being 'now used as a barn'.

The barn, however, was damaged in a fire in 1764, which 'consumed all the hay and corn on the premises'. It was caused by a boy who was attending a funeral but knocked his lighted torch against some palings adjoining the barn (it was customary, at this time, to bury the dead by torchlight). The custom was afterwards abolished and the remainder of the chapel was finally pulled down in 1810.

'S Georgs chap.' is marked on Speed's map with a line of trees to the west and a few dwelling houses along the street to the south. It also appears on a plan of Christchurch Estate, made by John Kirby in 1755, as 'George Lane', where it is seen connecting with the east end of Pedders Way (now Anglesea Road) and continuing north as Akenham Road (now Henley Road).

Dr Taylor recorded the site of St George's churchyard:

> 'In 1882, when Bedford Street was cut from the more ancient Globe Lane, and the foundations for the houses excavated, numerous well-preserved skeletons were unearthed. Nothing remains of this ancient state of things now except the name on a row of modern houses, 'St George's Terrace', and on the green gate of a house opposite, Bilney Cottage.'

It was from the pulpit of this round-towered chapel that the wandering preacher, Thomas Bilney, disputed church doctrine with Friar Bruisyard before his arrest in 1527. An account of Thomas Bilney is found in John Foxe's *Book of Martyrs* and the original has a wood cut depicting the preacher being dragged by the monks out of the pulpit of St George's Chapel. Bilney was an early promoter of the Protestant doctrines of Wycliffe and Luther. In 1527, however, the town was still dominated by the Roman Catholic Church, and the local friars were unused to having their authority flouted. Bilney eventually shared the fate of other Protestant martyrs by being burned to death.

In the 16th century, and probably long before, the Globe inn stood in St George's Street and for a time the street became known as Globe Lane. In 1579 it was still known as St George's Lane but shortly afterwards became Globe Lane.

The inn name has a confused history. For a time it became the Hat and Feather, then back to the Globe and, for a short time, was called the Bricklayers Arms. At the beginning of the 19th century a retired passenger coach driver named John Cope became licensee and renamed it the 'Shannon' in honour of one of his coaches, causing further confusion as there was already a Shannon inn immediately opposite.

The old Globe inn is now Globe House. Restored in 1987 by the Ipswich Building Preservation Trust, it is now a hairdresser's. The Shannon inn continued as a pub until 1923 when it was bought and converted into a dwelling house, eventually being turned into garages.

In the second half of the 18th century there were plans to open a Spa on St George's Street when it became all the rage to 'take the waters'. An 'Ipswich Spaw Waters' was opened on St Margaret's Green, and when a spring was found on the west side of St George's Street there was a proposal to erect warm and cold baths. It was, however, resisted locally and nothing came of it.

The Old Salem Chapel, which was built in 1812 for the Particular Baptists, went out of religious use at the end of the 19th century. The New Wolsey Theatre now uses it as their rehearsal studio. It is also used for performances of the annual Pulse Festival and an alternative venue for the Children's Christmas Show.

ST HELEN'S STREET (and St Helen's Church Lane) Both the street and the lane take their name from the church that has stood on that site since Norman times and has now bestowed its name on St Helen's Primary School (off Jefferies Road). Its older name, St Helen's Wash, is a reference to its once being the path of one of the many town streams and a part of St Helen's Street was also once called Great Wash Lane. Dr Taylor wrote:

'In 1521, there was a fine stream of water running by St Helen's Church – the natural drainage of the springs, which formerly issued from the junction of the light sands with the impervious London clay, cut through in the valley of Spring Road.'

G.R. Clarke recorded:

'On the high grounds adjoining to Caldwell Hall, near where the old Woodbridge road used to pass through St Helen's-street, then called Great Wash-lane, are several never-failing springs, belonging to the corporation, from which a great part of the town is supplied with water. The various streams are collected into about a dozen different brick buildings, most of them arched over; from where they are carried into two main pipes, one running on the left-hand side of Car-street, and another on the right-hand side of the same street.'

There is an entry in Nathaniel Bacon's *Annals* to the effect that John Mann was allowed to 'stopp the water' on payment of the yearly sum of sixteenpence, 'from nine in the morning till two in the afternoon, and from eight in the evening till ten in the same.'

St Helen's was known as The Wash and was once the path of a town spring that was prone to flooding. (ITM Collection)

Next to the church is Wells Court Flats, the name referring to the old wells that stood thereabouts.

St Helen's Street (which has its apostrophe on maps but not on all the street plates) now begins to the right of the Odeon Cinema complex and continues past the Regent Theatre, County Hall and eastwards toward Grove Lane. During the day there is an almost constant stream of traffic heading westwards into town and beyond, although, like so many Ipswich streets, it has always been a busy thoroughfare, funnelling traffic of all descriptions in from outlying districts. It is difficult to imagine that *White's Directory* of 1844 shows Robert Clarke as 'farmer, St Helen's Street' at a site approximate to Argyle Street.

Although the present flint and stone Church of St Helen is mediaeval in origin, it was much restored between 1835 and 1837 and almost completely rebuilt a year later. The old tower was replaced by the present one in 1875 and the nave extended westwards in such a way that the congregation faces north instead of the traditional easterly direction. The porch is one of the oldest surviving parts of the

building and has a worn niche above the entrance and a sundial set on the apex of the gable. St Helen's, nearly half a mile east of the old County Hall, is one of the furthest from the town and the only one of Ipswich's mediaeval churches to be built outside the town walls. Houses crowd up to the east end, with only a narrow passage way to the north side, but there is a small oasis of green in the remaining portion of the roadside churchyard.

Inside are a few surviving memorials, two of them to Richard Canning but commemorating two different men. The first is to Richard Canning who was the minister at St Lawrence's until his death in 1775 and proclaimed 'a man of unblemished honour and integrity, and of taste and erudition'.

The second is a plaque with scrollwork, dated 1726, for another Richard Canning, Commander of the Royal Navy, which reads:

'Having served his country with unexceptional courage and conduct during the wars of K William and Q Anne retired to this town and through the resentment of Party, founded on misreported Facts died a private Captain.'

At least one author of the church's history has 'itched' to know what caused the downfall of Richard Canning and what the 'misreported facts' were.

Other memorials attest to diverse parishioners across the years: Lieutenant General Richard Phillipson, of the Dragoon Guards and MP for Eye (died 1792); George Cole, FRCS and a surgeon in the Bengal Medical Services, who died on the Red Sea during a passage from India in 1858; Jane Charlotte Shillito (whose husband was also in the Bengal Medical Services), who died at sea off the Azores in 1854, and the Revd Stephen Cole, who died in Madeira in 1854.

St Helen's was once linked to the Leper Hospital of St James, which stood nearly opposite and well away from the town. The Fair of James the Apostle took place hereabouts, held by the 'lepers of St Mary Magdalen', and first recorded on 27 April 1200.

Gaumont staff, 1929. (Ipswich Borough Council)

Where the Regent Theatre stands, to the west of Orchard Street and the north side of St Helen's, there was once a silk factory. The theatre, and nearby Regent Street, just off St Helen's, refers to George IV when, as Prince Regent, he came to review the troops at Ipswich Barracks. The Prince Regent was accompanied by Baron Linsingen (later of Birkfield Lodge, Stoke) of the 3rd Hussars, who had been sent to Ipswich to rest after the Peninsular Wars. The Prince rode through the town to St Matthew's and breakfasted in the mess house of the barracks, the Baron providing 'an elegant breakfast'.

The Prince made a second visit to Ipswich to attend a concert in the new Assembly Rooms, where he was 'wined and dined'. On his accession to the throne as George IV, the bailiffs for the borough, James Thorndike and J.E. Sparrow, issued a proclamation that was read on Cornhill and the Common Quay. At the bailiffs' expense, a 'sumptuous collation' was prepared at the town hall in celebration.

The Regent Theatre opened to great enthusiasm in 1929 as a cine-variety hall. Almost 2,000 people turned up for the opening and crowded into the foyer, a long queue forming as far as Botwood & Egerton's garage and beyond to Major's Corner. The Mayor, Dr Hossack, performed the opening ceremony with resident organist Frank Newman on the new Wurlitzer organ. The opening film was 'The Last of Mrs Cheyney' starring Norma Shearer and Basil Rathbone, an 'all talking' picture with front circle seats costing 2s 4d.

David Lowe, manager of the Regent from 1958 to 1989, recalls the 'luxurious Regent restaurant' that enhanced a visit to the theatre and, if desired, 'tea could be served in any of the fourteen boxes at the rear of the stalls'. The boxes, together with the manager's cottage at the rear of the theatre, made the Ipswich Regent unique.

The restaurant later closed to make way for the Victor Sylvester Dance Studio and people flocked to learn the fox trot, the quick step or the waltz. Victor started his career as a world champion exhibition dancer who also taught ballroom dancing, but a lack of suitable dance music for his own classes led to his recording a selection of dance tempo numbers. The Victor Sylvester Ballroom Orchestra was one of the leading dance bands of the 1940s. Very quickly dancing instructors were using his music at studios that sprung up all over the country. However, it was not entirely the desire to learn ballroom dancing that brought many young men and women to the Ipswich dance studios, but rather the injunction to 'hold each other close' with a handkerchief pressed between the two bodies to ensure the couple were dancing 'in unison'. Many decided that 'forward, side, together ... back, side together', while keeping the handkerchief from falling, was not as boring as it first sounded!

In the 1950s and 1960s the Regent – then known as the Gaumont – moved with the times and the big names of rock 'n' roll came to play at Ipswich, including Buddy Holly and the Crickets, Little Richard and the Everly Brothers. Later came the Rolling Stones, the Beatles, Tina Turner, Tom Jones and Status Quo, with numerous other pop and rock bands and solo artists following in their wake to the present day.

In 1965 the then owners, The Rank Organisation, spent £50,000 on a major renovation of the Regent and continued to run it as an entertainment venue until 1991 when the borough council assumed ownership. Grade II listed, the theatre is a good surviving example of a pre-war entertainment house and retains many original art deco features

Local musicians and dramatic societies have also been encouraged to perform at the Regent, including the Ipswich Operatic Society, The Gilbert and Sullivan Society and, for thirteen years, the Co-

The Gaumont on St Helen's, now the Regent Theatre. (Ipswich Borough Council)

op Juniors played their Christmas show there. However, in 2004 it was decided to bring a four-week professional pantomime back to Ipswich, and in association with Duo Entertainment Limited the first Regent Pantomime was J.M. Barrie's *Peter Pan* starring Brian Blessed and Kirsten O'Brien.

Further along St Helen's is the old County Hall and what was for many years the County Gaol, the first stone of which was laid by P.B. Broke on 22 September 1786. When the foundations for the gaol were dug a great number of human bones were discovered as well as some sepulchral urns, indicating that the land might once have been part of the churchyard of St Helen's or St James' Hospital. The boundary wall enclosed about an acre and a half of ground and in front stood the turnkey's lodge, on top of which executions took place.

Prisoners were separated into debtors and felons, and in 1821 the treadmill, invented by William Cubitt, was introduced into the prison. In addition to the gaoler there was a chaplain and a surgeon, who was given an allowance for whatever attendance he was required to give.

One of the oldest names on St Helen's is Elmy Cycles, established in 1922, and since the demise of Martin & Newby, Croydons and Grimwades (all of which have disappeared in the last few years) it is now the town's oldest surviving shop. It is a reminder of the 1930s and 1940s when bicycles were used through necessity, and were often the only means of independent travel, and the 1950s and 1960s when the bicycle was still a highly popular mode of transport but had developed a leisure and recreation aspect.

Elmy Cycles was one of the few shops to sustain damage in World War Two. A bomb in Cemetery Road blew all the windows out and the shop was boarded up. At the time people used to take their accumulators in to be charged up for use in their radios, one of the few means of keeping up with the war news and listening in to the very necessary morale boosting programmes, which were starting to bring entertainment into people's homes for the first time.

ST LAWRENCE STREET

This street is in the heart of the old town and was in the thick of the markets that clustered around the Buttermarket. In the 18th century it was known as St Lawrence Lane, or just Lawrence Lane, a description more suitable than 'street', perhaps, as it is very narrow and short in length.

In the 14th century it was the cloth market site and in 1343 was described as 'the highway called the Clothemarket'. In around 1447, however, the cloth market moved to the Cornhill and the fruit market took over.

G.R. Clarke recorded that in Elizabethan times there were great oyster beds in the river and 'a regular fish market was then held opposite to St Lawrence's Church, in what is now called St Lawrence-street'. It was, he thought, strange that such 'desirable articles of consumption' as oysters had been neglected for so long. The fishermen took spat from the oyster beds and various sorts of fish were found on the market – sole ('well known to be of the finest quality'), mullet, turbot, smelt, skate, whiting, haddock and lobster were all caught in abundance.

The church from which it takes its name is on Dial Lane. The tower is seen from Westgate Street, and both St Lawrence and St Stephen are clearly visible from the south end of St Lawrence Lane. *Hunt's Guide* said:

'St Lawrence Church steeple peers at you over the houses on the south side of the street, as you stand upon the Cornhill: in the old pictures of the Cornhill, that steeple was a more conspicuous object in the scene, but since the corner shop of Mr Schulen has been made loftier, only the parapet and flagstaff are to be seen from the hill.'

The benched area in front of the west window of St Lawrence, opposite the entrance to Craft Market, is a popular resting place, as are the shady walks either side of the church. On one side is an eating area that runs off the back of Pickwicks on Dial

Lane. On the church wall behind the bench is a reminder of the mediaeval clothiers. A pair of shears is depicted in an array of 19th-century flushwork. Dr John Blatchly writes that although the flushwork is commonly assumed to be mediaeval, it was designed by Howard Gaye and built to encase the crumbling 15th-century tower by Frederick Barnes in 1882.

ST MARGARET'S GREEN

The small slip road that links St Margaret's Plain with Bolton Lane is still called 'Green' but bears no resemblance now to the square green of old where the parishioners of the old Wicklaw hundred met, where the Holy Rood (or Cross) Fair was held, and which in the 17th and 18th century was overlooked by the houses of the gentry. Dr Taylor wrote:

'A few old houses (formerly the mansions of the wealthy, and some of which still contain beautifully-carved woodworks, within and without), show that St Margaret's Green was once an important and fashionable locality. Before Trinity Priory was disestablished, and when the two churches stood close together, St Margaret's Green was a lively place.'

The Fair was held on 14 September and for the following two days from the 12th century until 1751. The Crown originally granted the Fair to the Priory of the Holy Trinity in the 12th century but after the Dissolution the right passed to the Crown, then to the Withipoll (or Wythypoll) family at Christchurch Mansion. A charter granted to the Corporation in 1665 by Charles II confirmed the town's control over the fair. After 1751, with the introduction of the new Gregorian calendar, it was held on what was called Old Holy Rood Day, 25 September. An advertisement appeared in the *Ipswich Journal* in September 1769:

'Butter and Cheese Fair commonly called Holy Rood or St Margaret's Fair, will be held as usual upon St Margaret's Green in Ipswich aforesaid upon Monday the 25th instant and

that the boarded warehouses erected for the reception of Butter and Cheese are now ready.'

Vendors who intended to erect stalls were supplied with 'proper stuff of all sorts at the usual prices' and were required to apply to Robert Fancett 'at the Blue Posts on the Green'.

In White's 1844 Directory its nature had changed somewhat:

'St Margaret's Fair, held on September 25th, was formerly a large cheese and butter mart, but is now only noted for sausages and sweetmeats.'

Hunt's Guide said:

'It was a great cheese and butter market, and was kept up as a pleasure fair until lately; indeed less than twenty years ago, theatrical shows and gingerbread stalls continued to visit the spot. The Fair was regarded in later times at least, as a feast of fried sausages; and there was a general understanding in the town, till very recently, that the sausage season came in with St Margaret's Fair.'

At one time there was a ban on selling 'imported' goods at markets, so fairs attracted a different, and often larger, attendance than those held weekly. It is no surprise, therefore, to find that there were once several inns and taverns in the area, chief among them the Pack Horse inn (see St Margaret's Plain), The Saracen's Head and the Running Buck, called the Buck (now The Key Bethesda Community Charitable Trust offices).

The Saracen's Head was closed in 1960 and auctioned for sale shortly afterwards. It was bought by Revett's for £10,000 and used for a car and motorbike shop. It then became an electrical shop for a while but is now the Saracen's Head Business Centre. Today there are a few square feet of grass and two benches beside a plaque that marks the site of the Holy Rood Fair.

The 'Buck' was particularly popular with those from outside the town who brought their produce to the annual fairs. Carriers stabled their horses there and both blacksmiths and farriers set up business on the opposite side of the road, next to another inn called the Dog and Partridge. When the old forge belonging to George Cook was demolished in the 1930s it was believed that it had been a working site for over 400 years. G.T. Cook's farriery was used in World War One to house and shoe horses, which were requisitioned off the farms for service in France.

Others inns included the Dog and Partridge, which closed in 1914, and the George and Dragon. The latter was the scene of an incident reported in the *Ipswich Journal* in 1857, as recalled by Trevor James:

'A certain George Robinson was charged with causing wilful damage there to the amount of four pence. The defendant was one of a number of people who were quarrelling on the Plain after closing time on a Saturday night. The landlady of the George and Dragon asked them to go away quietly and the defendant then threw an oyster shell at her, which missed but broke a window.'

On Manor House, St Margaret's Green, an Ipswich Society Blue Plaque denotes that Nathaniel Bacon (1593–1660), a 'pious, prudent learned' man, lived here from 1593 to his death in 1660. Nathaniel was Member of Parliament for Ipswich from 1646 to 1660 and the author, in 1654, of *Annalls of Ipswiche, The Lawes Customes and Government of the same*. Bacon's *Annalls* are a compilation of the Corporation records, which finish in 1649, the year in which Charles I was executed. The book was not, however, printed for some years as the work was thought to contain 'many gross mistakes and strong political prejudices'.

During the Civil War Ipswich was primarily Puritan, but Bacon was shocked by the execution of the king and ended his record:

'The last daye, of Januarie puts a sad period to my penn. And thus, by the goodness of Allmightie God, I have summed up the affaires of the government of this town of Ippswiche under bayliffes whoe are happie in this, that God hathe established their seate more sure than the throne of kings'.

However, being a good administrator with a clear sense of duty, he was chairman of the Eastern Association Committee during the Civil War and a strong supporter of the Puritan cause. William H. Richardson eventually edited the *Annalls* in 1884.

Although no longer occupied by A.C. Harding, as in the 1960s, the house still overlooks St Margaret's Green.

In the 1790s the Cobbold family lived on the Green, until their move to Holywells mansion in 1814. They had in their employ a household servant named Margaret Catchpole. Margaret was to lead an eventful if tragic life and become Suffolk's leading heroine, while the Cobbolds were one of Suffolk's foremost families throughout the 18th and 19th centuries; the two stories came together in the fictional life of Margaret Catchpole written by the Revd Richard Cobbold. He describes the garden of his parent's house:

'In the garden belonging to the mansion at St Margaret's Green was a very deep pond, with turfed sides, which were sloping and steep, so that the gardener had to descend to the water by a flight of six steps. Formerly it had been a handsome square pond, with edges neatly kept, and surrounded by alpine strawberry beds.'

Two stately weeping willow trees dipped their leaves into the pond. To make a sketch of the Woodbridge Road without including the willows would, wrote Cobbold, 'have robbed the town of Ipswich of one of its most prominent and pleasing features of landscape beauty'.

At this idyllic spot an incident occurred that would ingratiate Margaret indelibly with the Cobbold family and give rise to Richard Cobbold's eventual novel. In June 1794 Margaret went into the garden to gather some herbs for the kitchen when she heard a distressed shriek. She ran down the path to the pond where the Cobbold children stood, screaming. Young Henry Cobbold had fallen into the deepest part of the water where he was flailing helplessly. Margaret instantly sent the nursery maid to fetch a ladder and rope and swung up into the strongest bough of the weeping willow 'that spread itself over the centre of the pond'. She caught the child's collar and held him above the water until help arrived in the form of the coachman and gardener who then rescued both Henry and Margaret.

'Margaret' wrote Richard Cobbold in his novel, 'was the providential instrument in preserving the life of a member of Mr Cobbold's family. It will not, then, be a matter of surprise, that the records of her life should have been so strictly preserved among them.'

St Margaret's Green is affectionately remembered as the home of the Grey Green Coach Company Ewers. Started in 1928 by George Ewers, it ran express services from Ipswich and Felixstowe to London, as well as offering coach outings on the famous 'Grey Greens'. The art deco-style building was converted into an estate agents and auctioneers in 2005. Seven lorry loads of ready-mixed cement were required to level the floor, which originally sloped so that when the coaches were washed the water would run away.

ST MARGARET'S PLAIN

This is a continuation of St Margaret's Street and was, like the Street and the Green, just outside the ancient defence ditches, or rampart, and within sight of the North Gate. It begins east of the imposing Bethesda Baptist Church, built in 1913 by F.G. Faunch, its polished granite columns facing down Northgate Street.

During the hundreds of years that the Augustinian Priory of the Holy Trinity stood approximately where Christchurch Mansion does now, the Priory Canons regularly crossed St Margaret's Plain, and it is now the route for visitors who enter Christchurch Park through the Soane Street Gate. The most significant alteration to its shape came in 1936 when several shops and houses were demolished for redevelopment. Remarkably, a building thought to date from the mid-16th century was saved though it was mutilated to accommodate the road widening in the 1930s. Formerly known as the Old Pack Horse inn, the building at the junction of Soane Street and St Margaret's Plain once had its three gables side by side facing Crown Street. In what was an early attempt at conservation, the building was reconstructed, parts in reproduction, rather than destroyed. An Ipswich architect, John Sherman, turned the three gables to face St Margaret's Street, so forming the building seen today.

As its name suggests, the Pack Horse inn is a reminder of the days when pedlars travelled the country, carrying their merchandise strapped either side of a packsaddle. From their baskets, they sold ribbons, gloves, lace, pins, thread, looking glasses, necklaces, bracelets, brooches, hats and 'chapbooks' (cheaply produced books containing ballads and moral or religious tales). The itinerant pedlars also made the Old Pack Horse a hot bed of news and gossip with their travellers' tales. With so many horses in and around the inn it is no wonder that part of Bolton Lane was once known as Stablers Lane.

Spring and summer were the usual times for the pedlars to arrive and sometimes there were trains of packhorses travelling together, their approach announced by the sound of the bells attached to the collars of the lead horses. They were particularly attracted to ports like Ipswich where they could not only sell but also buy silks, precious metals, oils,

Although the Old Pack Horse inn is much restored it retains a corner post bearing a shield that bears a Tau, or St Anthony's, cross with a sun and two moons for the Holy Trinity and was once a pilgrim's rest for the Priory. (ITM Collection)

spices and other luxuries coming in from abroad. Some pedlars grew prosperous and themselves became dealers and merchants, employing other pedlars to carry their goods along a network of trade routes.

Before the Dissolution, pilgrims and Priory visitors also used the inn, but this trade ceased after 1538, although servants and followers of visitors to Christchurch Mansion took their place. For centuries, news from home and abroad would be swiftly spread throughout the town, though it would invariably be heard first at the Old Pack Horse.

In the 1960s it became the Café Blanchfleur, its name commemorating a connection with the Blanchfleur family. It once served as a guesthouse for the Priory of the Holy Trinity but is now an estate agents and a guitar shop.

Close to the junction with Northgate Street was, for many years, Green and Hatfield's antique shop, made famous on 19 June 1938 when Queen Mary stopped off on a visit to the town. Green and

Hatfield's was one of the few buildings to survive among the houses and shops that lined the south side of St Margaret's; the rest were demolished in 1936 to make way for redevelopment.

ST MARGARET'S STREET (or Thingstead)

The three roadways to the south of St Margaret's Church – St Margaret's Street, St Margaret's Green and St Margaret's Plain – were known as Thingstead, a Danish name for a meeting place. Muriel Clegg wrote of the Danish connection but said 'the site must have had an earlier origin'. Roads radiated from that ancient meeting place, 'northwards, the way was Thingstead Way, as Ogilby recorded it in 1674'.

Dr Taylor wrote that 'hardly a house stood beyond the North Gate as late as the time of James I' and that from entries in the records of the early 17th century 'it is clear the town wall was still standing'.

For at least three centuries St Margaret's Street was known as 'Raton Row' and, like its London counterpart, became Rotten Row. 'Raton' refers to

St Matthew's Street, around 1900. (ITM Collection)

rats so it is likely that at one time St Margaret's Street was rat infested.

In common with the plain and green, the street was known for the inns and taverns that serviced the pilgrims, traders and farmers that frequented the markets and fairs. There was the White Lion, which survived into the 19th century and, in later times, the Admiral's Head, named for Admiral Vernon (see Vernon Street). In the 1800s both pubs were nominated points for the carriers to attend and pick up or deliver goods. They arrived on Tuesday and Saturday mornings (market days) and departed about four in the afternoon.

ST MATTHEW'S STREET

Named for the Church of St Matthew, part of it was formerly known as Westbar Lane due to its proximity to the West Gate and being west of the town walls. It is now cut in to two equal halves by the Civic Drive roundabout and is a continuation of Crown Street.

In 1830 G.R. Clarke recorded that this was one of the first streets 'M'Adamised':

'Several of the streets have been M'Adamised, and answer exceedingly well, particularly St Matthew's, from the entrance of the town to the Suffolk Hotel, and we wish that the same system had been extended across the Cornhill, along Tavern-street, through Car-street, into the Woodbridge road, for if this were done, travellers in the way from London to Yarmouth would not have the inducement which they now have to avoid the town, in order to escape the inconvenience of passing over the stones.'

St Matthew's Church, its east end now crouching beside the busy sweep of Civic Drive on one side and

In 2004 BBC Radio Suffolk won Station of the Year and was represented at the Sony awards by Charlotte Spackman (Assistant Editor), Andrea Davidson, Gerald Main (Managing Editor), Emily Fellows and Jim Bowman. (photo: BBC)

the BT building on another, has its entrance on Portman Road. Being the closest church to the Town Barracks, it was known in the 19th century as the town's Garrison Church. G.R. Clarke wrote that it occupied 'one of the most commanding positions in the town … and the view of the country outside is very striking', though the view now is of the Civic Centre across Civic Drive. St Matthew's became the centre of activity each Sunday when the resident troops paraded to church, especially if there were officers present or some ceremonial event occasioned the use of the regimental band.

The church is mediaeval, thought to have been on this site since the 11th century, but was considerably changed and renovated during the 19th century, some of the work being carried out under the direction of the prolific English Gothic Revival architect Sir George Gilbert Scott (1811–1878). Sir George did a great deal of work in East Anglia and specialised in the restoration of ecclesiastical buildings, although many of his designs were described as 'florid'. Although his proclaimed aim was for sensitivity in dealing with ancient fabric, he

rarely showed it in practice and much of his work is considered destructive. Nevertheless, his hand is seen here in the widening and extension of the north aisle that took place in 1876 shortly before his death.

The adjoining St Matthews CE Primary School is built on the church cemetery.

ST NICHOLAS STREET

In a town so closely associated with the sea it is no surprise to find a street and church named for the patron saint of sailors, St Nicholas, one of the most popular saints in Christendom. This 14th-century church was built on the site of an older Saxon church (dedicated to St Michael) with some materials salvaged from the older structure.

In 1830 G.R. Clarke recorded speaking to an eyewitness about work done in St Nicholas some 12 years previously:

'Workmen, in taking down an old monument of the Eisdale family, for the purpose of erecting a gallery, discovered on the north aisle of the church a painting extending for

The Wolsey Pharmacy, seen here in the 1920s, was for many years thought to be the birthplace of Cardinal Wolsey. During the 1930s to 1950s the pharmacist was George Nelson Edwards, a member of the Nelson family.

several feet, of which they informed some of the neighbouring residents; and this [eye witness], who with many others, saw it at the time, says that it was of considerable extent and size – supposed to be the figure of St Michael, rudely executed on the wall itself, and coloured in distemper.'

Carved stonework can still be seen, bearing an Anglo-Saxon inscription that translates as 'Here St Michael fights against the Dragon'.

The church is now an island of 14th-century ecclesiastical witness, surrounded by the brash, noisy trappings of 20th-century town life, epitomised by the roar of traffic on Franciscan Way. Yet inside it is still possible to recall how it might have been in the days when the Wolsey family came here to worship, from their family home just down the street. It was to this church that young Thomas, born around 1471 or 1472, was brought and where his parents are buried. He was to become the most powerful man in the realm after the king, and his effect on the progress of British history is of

It is said that Wolsey's last words were 'If I had served God as diligently as I have done the King, he would not have given me over in my grey hairs' and were used in Shakespeare's play Henry VIII.

Lately a graffiti cartoon has appeared on the boarded up window of the old Pharmacy, depicting Wolsey on one side of his college entrance porch and Henry VIII on the other, both looking rather pleased with life and themselves!

profound and deep importance. His ambition knew no bounds and he was as much loathed as he was powerful, poets and ballad writers having fun rhyming the two words 'fat' and 'hat', referring to the Cardinal's red hat, and gave rise to such doggerel as:

'Begot by Butchers, but by Bishops bred
How high his honour holds his haughty head!'

Thomas's father, Robert, is reputed to have been one of the town butchers, though it is probable he had other business interests, possibly as a grazier rearing cattle on the town's outlying marshlands. Robert Wolsey (Wulcy or Wulcie) was one of those who operated in the Shambles and evidence of his trade is found in the borough court rolls. R.L. Cross points to his many court appearances including one in 1467 before the famed notary Robert Wymbyll:

'Robert Wulcy, the Cardinal's father, was brought from prison and released on bail to stand trial for selling 24 halfpenny pies containing corrupt meat (*de Carnibus infectis*) to the public.'

On another occasion he was fined for not exhibiting the skins of the animals he had slaughtered (this being regarded as evidence that the meat was both local and fresh). It is also believed that he is the same Robert Wulcy who ran a pub, which again brought him before the courts, accused of illegal brewing. He invariably failed to maintain the gutter in front of his house and left his pigs to wander the highways, allowing them to defile the streets. However, he was successful enough in business to marry into one of the town's leading families, the Daundys, who provided several generations of bailiffs and town officials. The great town benefactor Edmund Daundy was Thomas's cousin.

Much was made of Wolsey's relatively humble beginnings in the large volume of words that have been written about him. The poet John Skelton wrote:

'So bold and so bragging and was so basely
    born,
So lordly in his looks and so disdainsly,
So fat a maggot, bred of a flesh fly,
Was never such a filthy gorgon, nor such an
    epicure.'

More than once Skelton wrote of Wolsey's 'greasy genealogy,' and that he came out of a 'butcher's stall'.

This, though, was all in the future for the young Thomas, who applied himself diligently to his studies. His father sent him to Oxford where he became a fellow of Magdalen College and took up a post as chaplain to the Archbishop of Canterbury. By 1507 he was a royal chaplain and the new King Henry VIII's almoner not long afterwards. In 1515 Pope Leo X made him a Cardinal and in the same year the king named him Lord Chancellor of England. Since the king would rather be hunting and pursuing women than attending to the affairs of state, this meant that Wolsey had effective control of the realm.

The whispers about his provincial background irritated Thomas, constantly reminding him of his humble upbringing. Not long after he founded his Cardinal College in Oxford in 1525, he turned his attention back to Ipswich. It might silence the critics if Ipswich were made as great as Oxford. He had plans to establish 'feeder' colleges in various parts of the country and, perhaps in a move intended to see him return triumphantly to his native town, decided that one of them should be in Ipswich.

Thomas knew the priories and friaries of Ipswich intimately, and he decided that the best site for the new college would be the Augustinian Priory of St Peter and Paul, which was accordingly 'appropriated' in 1527, with St Peter's as the College Chapel. To help finance the project he obtained the suppression of seven other monasteries in Suffolk and Norfolk and initiated plans to appropriate St Matthew's Church and the Shrine Chapel of Our Lady, incorporating both into the new college complex. Elaborate plans were drawn up for an inaugural pilgrimage to the Shrine Chapel, which

The Wolsey Pharmacy building. In 2005 the Ipswich Buildings Preservation Trust bought the building from the borough council for a nominal fee with a view to restoring it as two shops.

would pass along St Nicholas Street, so that his peers would reappraise the importance of Ipswich.

It was to be expected that the townspeople were generally pleased that they were to share in Wolsey's good fortune and that the new college would put the town on the national map, as no doubt many were. Unfortunately, the king decided that Wolsey should be charged with the impossible task of obtaining the annulment of his marriage to Queen Catherine of Aragon so that he could marry Anne Boleyn. Destined as he was to fail in his mission, Wolsey began a rapid fall from royal grace, and by 1529 the most powerful man in England was stripped of his offices. He was arrested and denounced as a traitor. His possessions passed to the king, though Wolsey pleaded that he take care of his colleges at Oxford and Ipswich. He died in November 1530 while on his way, under armed guard, to the Tower of London.

Wolsey's college did not survive. It operated for just three years and was seized by the king shortly after the cardinal's death. Only the red-brick gateway on College Street remains. It is useless to speculate on what Ipswich might have become had the college been better established at the time of Wolsey's fall or what heights the town could have aspired to had Henry VIII attended to his marital affairs in an alternative fashion. All that can be said is that Wolsey's intended Ipswich college, had it been established and flourished, would have brought changes in the town's fortunes and character.

At the junction with Silent Street stands what was once the Wolsey Pharmacy and traditionally held to be the birthplace of Thomas Wolsey. A plaque on 47 St Nicholas Street, however, commemorates the birthplace as being on the opposite side of the road in a house now demolished.

Wodderspoon wrote:

'Tradition says the house in which Wolsey was born stood on the site occupied by a residence on the left hand side of the alley leading from St Nicholas street to the church-yard of St Nicholas, and in this year [1846] tenanted by Mr G. Cowell, surgeon.'

St Nicholas' Church was redundant for 20 years but in 2001 was re-acquired by the Church of England and linked to the nearby St Edmundsbury & Ipswich diocesan office (on Franciscan Way) by a glass 'hub' close by the Cromwell Square car park. Inside the hub is a café, next to a shop, and in the church itself is a library. A feature of the modernisation is the installation of new underfloor heating and careful renovations, which will allow it to be converted back into use as a church should the need arise.

South wall of St Nicholas', the church to which the young Thomas Wolsey was brought and where his parents are buried. Carved stonework can still be seen inside, bearing an Anglo-Saxon inscription that translates as 'Here St Michael fights against the Dragon'. (Photo: St Nicholas Centre)

Next to the St Nicholas Centre, on Cromwell Square, Saxon House is being constructed for use as a call centre.

A second commemorative plaque at 41 St Nicholas Street marks an Ipswich man of letters, V.S. Pritchett (1900–1997), who was born there, his parents lodging above a toy shop. He was not simply a 'writer' since he was also a renowned short story writer, as well as novelist, travel writer, review and literary critic. His much-acclaimed autobiography *A Cab at the Door* told of his family's frequent moves which gave him a lifelong love of travel.

They subsequently left but returned to Ipswich in 1910 and lived for a while in the Cauldwell Hall Road area. Victor was knighted in 1975 and made Companion of Honour in 1993. He died in 1997. However, the plaque records him as 'V S Pritchett' as this is how the reading public knew him best. The lower part of the house is occupied by a clothing shop and a health and beauty centre.

St Nicholas Street was, for 80 years, the home of the much-attended Hippodrome, built in 1905 by E.H. Bostock (of Bostock and Wombwell's Menagerie). The theatre's construction required ingenuity as it had to be fitted in between Cutler Street, St Nicholas Street and St Nicholas Church Lane. Its designer was Frank Matcham (1854–1920), one of the country's leading theatre and music hall architect, whose designs were 'festive, often elephantine, and have distorted Orders and ornament'.

The Theatre opened on 28 March 1905 and offered a mix of music hall and pantomime shows. Its plaster decorations were lavish and typical of music halls of the day. By the end of the 1920s the era of the hippodromes was coming to a close and it became a cinema. During World War Two it reverted to live entertainment, putting on highly successful revues. In the rock 'n' roll era, pop bands played there on Monday nights, but in the late 1950s it became a ballroom and eventually a bingo hall. The Hippodrome was demolished in the 1980s and replaced by Cardinal House (Ensors). In February 1985 the *EADT* said:

'The ghosts of Max Miller and Phyllis Dixey, Old Mother Riley (Arthur Duncan) and Rob Wilton, Sandy Powell and Billy Cotton could well haunt the stage. But in more recent years the need to pack a thousand bingo fans at a time in to it had brought adaptations that all but disguised its roots as a theatre. Clusters of benches around cafeteria-style formica-topped tables remain instead of theatre seats.'

ST PETER'S STREET

A small piece of St Peter's Street survives though most of its southern half has been taken up with the Star Lane traffic scheme. Originally it led from St Nicholas Street down to Stoke Bridge, past the Church of St Peter (now on College Street). It is thought to have been part of King Street at one time, in what was a very long roadway from the Cornhill to Stoke Bridge.

Even today the north side of St Peter's Street and the southern portion of St Nicholas Street retains the feel of 'old Ipswich' and is inhabited by cafes, restaurants and small shops, which invoke a 'villagy' feel, especially on Sundays when people are out and about enjoying the town.

Opposite Saints Winebar Café is The Sailors' Rest, a unique William and Mary house built around 1700 and used by British and foreign sailors' societies between 1925 and 1957.

ST STEPHEN'S LANE

The Church of St Stephen, which gives this lane its name, was here at Domesday but is now barely in the lane and better described as being in Arras Square. The lane once extended from the church right down to the houses and gardens in the Turret Lane area. However, the much-shortened length still bears the name of the church to which it has led for hundreds of years. An alleyway through to Upper Brook Street, which comes out beside Wilkinsons, is there named St Stephen's Church Lane.

The lane was not merely a pathway to the church as excavations have revealed that houses and shops once crowded along both sides and it may have led to or through a first-century cemetery.

Some small evidence remains as witness to the 15th century at 17 St Stephen's Lane, a timber-framed building that juts out over the lane opposite the high, blank walls of the Buttermarket Shopping Centre. Here was once a row of shops and private residences and 17 was formerly a merchant's house but was converted to an inn in around 1560. Refurbished in 1720, it stood next to a gabled rectory (long since demolished), and when the cattle market was moved to the old cattle market site in 1810 it became the Sun inn. It was frequented by drovers and dealers visiting the market and would have been a busy and noisy pub on Tuesdays and Saturdays. After the market moved to Princes Street business fell away and it closed in 1901.

In 1795 the 'Ancient and most Venerable Order of the Druids' held a meeting there, 'at the house of Brother William Phillips at the sign of the Sun inn'.

During the 1960s it became a well-known antiques and specialist book shop, inspiring many young women in the town with its unusual name Atfield and Daughter. Although it closed as a shop in 1998, it is still under restoration by the Atfield family who have discovered pottery dating from 650 AD and a skeleton, possibly linked to the churchyard of St Stephen's.

On the pavement outside is a large brass 'bell', which replaces a bollard put there by Douglas Atfield who became tired of having his shop knocked about by lorries turning into the supermarket yard. After protracted negotiations with the council the bollard was removed but the bell put in its place. The bell shape (there is another at the Carr Street end of Old Foundry Road) impedes large vehicle wheels in time to warn drivers that they are close to a building but the gradual angle of the bell prevents the vehicles from tipping; a bollard would be constantly knocked over.

SHIRE HALL YARD

More a short street than a yard, the name commemorates the Shire Hall that once stood there 'in an open, airy space of ground'. It was a large and nearly square brick building, erected in 1699 by voluntary subscription. Sir Samuel Barnardiston, the Parliamentary Member for the borough at the time, made a large contribution towards it. The exterior was plain and unadorned, and it was divided into two distinct courts, 'spacious, lofty, and commodiously fitted up for the purpose'. An adjoining apartment was provided for the use of the Grand Jury.

SILENT STREET

How does a street become named Silent? As might be guessed, it was not always so called but was part of a complicated evolution of streets and lanes surrounding what is now the old cattle market. Before the establishment of the market in 1810 it ran across part of that area which had been, in pre-Reformation times, the Carmelite Friary. The Provision Market had its main entrance opposite Silent Street and the planners named it New Market Street. But this was one of those occasions, however, when people did not take to the change and it was neither liked nor used. Silent Street was widened northward in 1812 to accommodate the cattle market (now the old cattle market).

Its ancient name, as seen on Ogilby's map, was 'Cole Hill alias Half Moon Street', the former being the older name, the latter a popular landmark pub that stood at the St Nicholas end. There is much discussion to be had about the precise location or nature of 'Cole Hill', otherwise known as 'le Colhel', which might have referred to an area rather than a specific street or lane. It is probable that the Colehill was the mediaeval town's dunghill, or rubbish tip, a large mass of stinking refuse and sewage left to rot with all the inevitable consequences and stench. Whether Silent Street was the site of the Colehill or the name is a confusion with the 'Cold Dunghills' of Rope Walk remains uncertain.

The name Silent Street came into use around the 1760s and has continued up to the present day. Two possible explanations emerge. The first relates to the plague, a recurring and endemic disease throughout the 16th and 17th centuries, and possibly to the epidemic that hit Ipswich in the wake of the Great London Plague in 1665. If Silent Street were indeed the area of the Colehill then there would be no better place for the plague to incubate and thrive and was, therefore, silent due to the death toll of its inhabitants?

The second explanation belongs to the 1650s when Curson House, built at the south-east corner of Silent Street, was used as a hospital for casualties in the Dutch wars. The volume of noise was such that the patients got little rest so to silence the continuous racket of horses hooves and wagons' wheels, straw was laid down to 'silence' the street.

Lilian Redstone writes:

'Curson House with spacious parlours and hall built round a courtyard at the south-east corner of the present Silent Street and Rose Lane (then Curson Lane) was the home of a count of the Holy Roman Empire, Robert styled 'Lord' Curson, who lived here in state with his yeomen and servants, his wife, Dame Margery, and her three gentlewomen, and two chaplains to serve the chapel within the large garden.'

Sir Robert Curson (*c.*1460–1535) built the house on Silent Street in 1500. A great adventurer, he was born around 1460 and prospered so well that he was knighted in 1489 and appointed Sheriff of Norfolk and Suffolk. In 1499 he obtained permission from Henry VII to join the army of the Holy Roman Emperor, Maximilian I, in order to fight the Turks. However, he and five others were accused of treachery against the king and brought back to England to face trial. However, while two of the five were beheaded and two sent to the Tower of London, Curson not only escaped with his life but was also pardoned. It seems he might have been a double agent as three more times he was brought to book as a traitor and three times he escaped with a pardon.

In 1513 he served in France under Charles Brandon (see Brook Street), by which time he was known as 'Lord' Curson. The Emperor Maximilian made him a Count of the Holy Roman Empire and the title 'Lord' stuck.

In 1520 Curson was among Henry VIII's retinue at the 'Field of the Cloth of Gold' when Henry attempted to ally himself with Francis I of France, each trying to outdo the other by their ostentatious display of conspicuous wealth and power. Perhaps inspired by Curson's attendance, Jean Ingelow (see Arcade Street) wrote in one of her poems:

'And O the Buttercups! That field O' the cloth
    of gold, when pennons swam -
Where France set up his lilied shield, His
    oriflamb,
And Henry's lion-standard rolled:
What was it to their matchless sheen,
Their million million drops of gold
    Among the green!'

Both Henry VIII and Queen Catherine visited Curson in Ipswich, though on separate occasions (see Lady Lane). Curson House must have been a splendid and extraordinary place in its day. Dr Taylor describes the house as 'noble', with a portico standing far out into the street.

Lord Curson died in 1535 and was buried in the Greyfriars where a 'magnificent tomb' was erected in his memory. At the Dissolution the tomb was removed to St Peter's but has since disappeared. In Edward VI's time Curson House passed to the Bishop of Norwich and became known as The Bishop's House.

After its service as an army hospital it became known as the King's Hospital but later became first a brewery and then a public house, the Elephant and Castle. The 'strong and stately brick porch', which projected into Westgate Street, was demolished in 1760.

In 1910 the women of the Women's Social and Political Union (WSPU) had their headquarters at 19 Silent Street, run by a leading suffragette, Miss Grace Roe. Many contemporary unions and groups supporting women's rights had representation in the town from 1866 until the outbreak of war in 1914, when their crusade was overtaken by events.

A petition for women to be included in the 1866 Reform Bill was sent to Parliament and contained 15 Ipswich signatures, two of whom were school mistresses – Miss Susan Appleton, who ran a boarding school for 'young ladies' at 6 Burlington Road, and Elizabeth Butler, who, with her sisters, also ran an establishment 'for young ladies' at Anglesea House, 90 Berners Street. Elizabeth Crawford, author of *The Women's Suffrage Movement*, wrote:

'Miss Butler was preparing her pupils for the Cambridge Local Examination, an indication that she was likely to have come within Emily Davies' sphere of influence. Another of the Ipswich signatories was Matilda Betham Edwards, close friend of Bessie Rayner Parkes.'

In 1871 a suffrage meeting was held in the lecture hall where the speaker was Rhoda Garrett. Rhoda's cousin, Millicent Fawcett, was present and the proceedings were chaired by Edward Grimwade. As a result, says Elizabeth Crawford, 'an Ipswich committee of the National Society for Women's Suffrage was formed, with Harriet Grimwade, Edward's daughter, as secretary.'

The preponderance of non-conformists among the leading citizens and politicians of the day went a long way to boosting the morale of the suffragists. Support also came from the Revd Goodrich Langley, vicar of St Mary Elm Church, who attended a meeting in the council chamber of the town hall, called to hear two London speakers lecture on women's suffrage (see also Arcade Street).

As the movement gathered pace, more groups opened offices in Ipswich. In 1906 a branch of the London Society for Women's Suffrage was formed, and in 1909 the Women's Freedom League was set up in Ipswich and Hadleigh. By 1913 there was also a branch of the Church League for Women's Suffrage. To boost fundraising, the WSPU opened a shop on Dial Lane in 1913, managed by Miss King, and many of the famous names of suffrage history visited Ipswich, including members of the Pankhurst family, Mrs Fawcett and Charlotte Despard.

SIR ALF RAMSEY WAY

On 30 July 1966, before a capacity attendance of 96,924, England beat Germany 4–2 in extra time to win the World Cup. The men on the pitch became national heroes overnight, and the legend of the 1966 World Cup began, but for Ipswich Town Football Club supporters there was icing on the cake. England's manager that day was Alf Ramsey

(1920–1999), who had gone from Ipswich in 1963 after an eight-year reign at Portman Road to be the full-time manager of the national team

One of the club's first great triumphs came in 1962, when Alf Ramsey took them from the Third Division South to First Division Champions. Appointed manager in August 1955, Ramsey immediately began to reshape the side that was to put them on the football map, the press dubbing them 'Ramsey's Rustics'. In the 1956–57 season the club gained Third Division South status, the Second Division Championship in 1960–61 and the First Division Championship in 1961–62.

Under Sir Alf, England lost only 17 out of 113 games and won 69. Town supporters celebrated with particular satisfaction at the triumphant outcome of the 1966 World Cup.

When Sir Alf died in 1999 the town's MP, Jamie Cann, said:

'Sir Alf didn't come from Ipswich originally but he made it his home. He has lived here ever since, always just an ordinary, un-assuming man of the people, always helping charitable causes. He was well-loved and respected in the town and will be sadly missed.'

Alf Ramsey was the only England manager, before or since, to score a World Cup Final victory, and when Bobby More lifted the Jules Rimet cup 'the General' broke into an uncharacteristic grin. The accolade from Ipswich came late in the day, but when Sir Alf died in 1999 a statue was commissioned and the previously named Portman Walk was renamed Sir Alf Ramsey Way.

A life-size bronze statue of Sir Alf was unveiled by former Town star Ray Crawford in August 2000, and among those present were Lady Ramsey, several players from the Ipswich team during Sir Alf's reign as manager and members of the 1966 World Cup-winning team, including Sir Bobby Charlton.

The sculptor, Sean Hedges-Quinn, was an Ipswich Town supporter and the unveiling was the culmination of an 18-month project organised by the Supporters' Club. In 2002 he was to sculpt another hero of Suffolk football, the much-admired Sir Bobby Robson. Ipswich manager from 1969 to 1982, Bobby Robson led the team to its memorable FA victory over Arsenal at Wembley in 1978. Bobby was knighted in the 2002 Queen's Birthday Honours. He had followed in Alf Ramsey's footsteps by taking on the England manager's job in 1982 and staying there for a gruelling eight years.

SMART STREET

This is in the vicinity of Foundation Street and commemorates one of the benefactors of the charities, William Smart, who added to Henry Tooley's bequests in 1599 (see Foundation Street).

A reminder of the Victorian expansion of educational establishments is still seen on Smart Street where the old school remains, with 'Boys' inscribed over the doorway.

SOANE STREET

This was likely to have been an extension of Old Bar Gate (see Northgate Street) and formed the entrance to the Holy Trinity Priory and St Margaret's Church.

It no doubt had an older name but in the 19th century was named Soane Street for Sir John Soane (1753–1837), a prominent and prolific architect of his time whose career took off after patronage from friends in Ipswich.

Numbers 4–8 Soane Street is the Freemasons Hall and is on the borough's list of Ipswich Buildings of Special Architectural or Historic Interest. Soane was a convinced Freemason and had a hand in designing the hall.

STAR LANE

The great traffic gash that is Star Lane extends eastwards from Grey Friars Road to Grimwade Street, and the Star Lane traffic scheme of 1973 wiped out many roads, streets and lanes of old Ipswich. Muriel Clegg thought it derived its name from its nearness to the Church of St Mary at Quay, sometimes called 'Stella Maris' ('Our Lady, Star of the Sea'). One part of Star Lane, close to St Clement's Church, still bears a rare sign offering the information 'Star Lane (Previously part of Waterworks Street)'.

A building, thought to be the old Drapers' Hall, stood in Star Lane and is mentioned in a will of 1598. In 1830 G.R. Clarke deplored its bad state of repair and hoped 'that some spirited lover of the arts would purchase the property and rescue this really elegant structure from oblivion'. Alas, there was no lover of the arts available at the time.

In the 19th century there was a narrow passage called Pleasant Row, which led from Star Lane to Shire Hall Yard 'by a little gate at the south-east corner'. In the 1830s it was used to access a malt office, the business premises of which were in Pleasant Row. It is thought that the malt office had once been the Draper's Hall and gave every sign of being a very grand edifice, with walls of stone, two feet thick, with similar carvings and shields that might be found in a church, though it did not stand due east and west, but north and south, and was not, therefore, designed as a church or chapel.

STOKE HAMLET

The hamlet of Stoke, on the south side of the river, has been an integral part of Ipswich since the earliest times when the first river crossing was made where Stoke Bridge still stands (see also Bridge Street). The fact that Saxon Ipswich ware has been found at Stoke, and the Church of St Mary at Stoke (called St Mary Stoke) is mentioned in Domesday, makes Stoke as ancient as 'Gipeswic' itself. Consisting mostly of farmland, with a mill at the river crossing (Bridge Street), Stoke could be considered the bread basket of the old town. In the 1440s there were two mills, one for grain and the second for fulling, and it is likely there was more than one bridge from the earliest times.

The name Stoke is taken to mean 'the place

St Mary Stoke Church.

The Old Bell inn at the Stoke Crossing.

protected by a wooden stockade' and is one of the places of original Saxon settlement and was, until the turn of the 20th century, still relatively rural. At the end of the 19th century William Budden wrote:

'Then came the railway; at first only to Stoke, where remnants of the early station [opened in 1846] still remain. The heart of the Stoke Hills had not been cut into. Stoke Hills was a favourite rambling place for Ipswich boys.'

When, eventually, the railway was taken through to Ipswich, one of its champions was Peter Burrell, after whom Burrell Road was named. The Burrells lived at Stoke Park Mansion and contributed much towards not only restoring the church but also towards the establishment of Stoke's church schools. Burrell (afterwards Lord Gwydyr) had a special interest in the church, as he was married there in 1849 to Sophia, daughter of Frederick Campbell of Birkfield Lodge, and initiated the design of the north transept, which was added in 1864.

An Over Stoke History Group has recently been formed and in their booklet, *From Bridge to Brook*, Alan Best and Jill Freestone write:

'Stoke Park Mansion was approached by two driveways from Belstead Road, the first at Fountains Road and the second opposite Balmoral Close. A third carriageway led from Wherstead Road to the house, going through an imposing railway bridge and the present-day Bourne Park.'

Burrell's father, Merrik Lindsey Burrell, bought Stoke Park Mansion in 1837, at the death of its previous owner, Ambrose Harbord Steward. Merrik died the following year and his son Peter, having married, decided to build a new mansion on the site of the old one. It was to stand for just over 80 years, before being demolished in the 1920s. Stoke Park was developed in the 1960s, although the local residents fought to keep the tree-lined walkway along Belstead Road (which name commemorates what was then part of Lord Belstead's forest).

Birkfield Lodge, which belonged to Burrell's

View of Stoke from the Wherry inn, c.1800. Notice St Mary Stoke Church and the Stoke windmill. (Ipswich Borough Council Museums and Galleries)

father-in-law, was built by Baron Linsingen, who had served with the Duke of Wellington in the Peninsular War. As a member of the 3rd Hussars he was sent to Ipswich Barracks and later accompanied the Prince Regent, who came to inspect the troops at the cavalry barracks in St Matthew's.

TACKET STREET

There seems no definitive reason for this street name but its origins are likely to lie in 'tack' or 'tackle' maker, which describes those who worked in shipyards or as maintenance man on ships. Certainly it, and the adjoining Orwell Place, has always been a popular 'watering hole' for sailors.

Between 1700 and 1780 it was known as Tankard Street, which gave its name to the Tankard inn, but reverted to Tacket Street through pressure from members of the Tacket Street Congregational Church, who thought that the Tankard Street Congregational Church gave out the wrong message.

'Tacket Street' wrote Dr Taylor, 'is now almost a plain street, but here were formerly situated, perhaps, the grandest mansions in the town. The merchant princes of Ipswich lived near their warehouses and shipping; they built their houses where they conducted their businesses; perhaps blended work with pleasure – smoked pipes, drank wine or Hollands, Nantz or Cognac with their customers whilst having a deal together.'

Unfortunately Tacket Street continues to be a plain street and, as elsewhere, is plagued by almost constant traffic using it very much as untold generations have always done, to get from one part of town to another. This does not mean, however, that its history is plain, for here once stood a theatre where the famous actor David Garrick (1716–1779) made his first public appearance in what had been the house of Sir Anthony Wingfield, whose family name is commemorated in nearby Wingfield Street.

There is a long tradition of theatre and the arts in Ipswich so it is no surprise to find that in 1736 an entrepreneur merchant and brewer, Henry Betts, acquired the Wingfield house and converted it into a tavern, naming it The Tankard (as the street was then named). Adjacent he built the Playhouse, or New Theatre, which opened on 12 November 1736.

It was to the Tankard Street Playhouse that a young David Garrick (1717–1779) came in 1741. He had quit his job in his uncle's wine shop to join a company of comedians in London and was eager to try his hand at acting. Garrick, a raw and nervous tyro with no confidence in his own ability, was cast as Aboan, the African slave in Thomas Southerne's tragedy *Oroonoko*. This gave him the opportunity to appear before the audience 'under the disguise of a black countenance' so that should his performance fail he would escape being recognised. Garrick did not fail. Instead the Ipswich audience gave him some confidence-boosting applause and his career on the stage was assured. He returned to London and by the end of the year was the talk of the theatrical world for his performance in Shakespeare's *Richard III*.

He went on to enjoy a 30-year career at the top of the acting tree and was one of the most influential and popular figures in British theatre history.

The Playhouse was at its most successful during the Napoleonic Wars, when some 8,000 soldiers were garrisoned in the town and their officers developed a taste for the theatre. In return the Playhouse held charity nights to buy extra clothing for those fighting in Europe. The National Anthem was played at every performance and such were its fortunes that it was rebuilt in 1803 with a larger stage and more lavish décor.

The decline of the Playhouse began when the European wars ceased and its end was hastened by the new Lyceum Theatre on Carr Street, built 'in the Italian style' in 1890 by a London Architect, Walter Emden, and offering grander and more spacious premises. The Playhouse was acquired in 1892 by the Salvation Army for use as a citadel.

TAVERN STREET

If ever there was a suitable name for a street that best describes its past and conjures up the spirit of the late 18th and 19th century town, it has to be Tavern Street. Nothing sums it up better than *Hunt's Guide*:

'In the present day this street is, at times, the scene of immense traffic. On a fine Saturday evening, from seven o'clock till about ten, the length of the street from the White Horse, past the Cornhill, and for some distance up Westgate Street and St Matthews, is often literally filled from side to side with throngs of people passing to and fro, on business and on pleasure, gossiping and enjoying themselves, while at every few yards you will generally come upon a crowd surrounding a band of musicians or street singers.'

Hunt himself saw plenty of such comings and goings, since he lived at 28 Tavern Street, and had a commendable liking for the town as well as possessing the required talent for observation and sense to record it for posterity.

From at least the 18th century until the mid-20th century the numerous alehouses, wine shops and nearby inns that lined Tavern Street were frequented by townspeople and visitors alike, for Dr Clarke observed 'the life of the nobility and aristocracy of a county is associated with historical castles and mansions, whilst that of the people is associated with its inns.'

There were once precise differences between inns and taverns, as explained by Trevor James in *Ipswich Inns, Taverns and Pubs*:

'Innkeepers were required to provide accommodation and refreshment for genuine travellers, but not for casual callers who lived nearby. Tavern keepers could supply food and drink to all who required it but were not allowed to offer overnight accommodation. Ale or beer houses were only allowed to supply drink. These were the terms of the three types of licence.'

Taverns and inns have always been the subject of

The Great White Horse in the 1950s.

statutory observation. For example, in 1291 no taverner was allowed to keep his establishment open after the Curfew bell had sounded and fines were levied on those trading without a licence. Brewers had to be specially licensed and were forbidden to sell beer under price or to brew beer for sale 'in other than the ancient brew-houses'. In Henry VIII's time, ale had to be sold in pots which were measure marked and sealed by the Corporation.

There were also two kinds of inn – hostelries and herbages – the former where servants and beasts found accommodation, the latter for guests only. The early mediaeval inns were affiliated to the religious houses and catered for pilgrims and strangers needing shelter.

In Charles I's day there was an attempt to reduce the large number of taverns, which were declared to be 'unnecessary' and 'a source of great evil to the county'. Great evil or not, at the beginning of the 18th century there were over 30 inns and taverns in the town, many of them in the Tavern Street area.

'For years its old pubs kept the spirit of the town very much to the fore' wrote Julian Tennyson in *Suffolk Scene*, 'there were so many of them that Ipswich became known as the Town of Taverns – and grand old taverns they were, too, timbered and crooked, full of hidden, musty corners, with the shadowy histories of smugglers lurking on the landlord's lips.'

As a result of the 1830 Beer Act yet another drinking establishment was added to the list, that of Beer House. Any householder who paid rates could apply for an excise license to sell beer and brew it on the premises. The precise governmental reasoning behind the Act remains unclear, though it might have been to promote beer to the detriment of gin. Within eight years of the new Act 46,000 beer houses opened nationally, and in White's 1844 Ipswich Directory there are 62 Beer House entries, one in almost every street in town. By the 1880s drunkenness was a serious social problem as Beer House numbers multiplied.

The best-known and most prominent reminder of the conviviality and sociability of Tavern Street is the Great White Horse, situated at the junction with Northgate Street and Upper

Brook Street. Its Georgian façade hides a timber-framed structure dating back to the 16th century. An inn has flourished there since at least 1518 when it was the Whit Hors inn and one of the many pilgrims' inns. Made famous by Charles Dickens, and the lodging place for kings and famous personages, the White Horse (the 'Great' is invariably dropped) has also been the first and last sight of the town for passengers using the coaches from its courtyard.

The building was completely refronted between 1815 and 1818 and almost immediately narrowly missed demolition. In 1818 the borough council acquired a block of properties between Tower Street and Northgate Street, including the Great White Horse, intended for redevelopment.

The White Horse came into its own at the dawn of the Coaching Age in the early 18th century, which lasted until the coming of the railways. After the introduction of steel springs in 1754, coaches became comparatively comfortable and many new stagecoach routes were opened up and by the 1760s the Great White Horse had stabling for 46 horses. In 1736 George II stopped off on his way from Lowestoft to London. He held 'court' in the dining room where he received town dignitaries and members of the clergy who 'all had the honour of kissing the King's hand'.

In the early years of the 19th century the Great White Horse was the stop for London, Norwich and Great Yarmouth and at one time there were nine regular coach services running to and from London, through Ipswich, daily. Just round the corner, in Upper Brook Street, the Coach and Horses was also immensely popular with travellers and from there were daily departures of such famous coaches as the Quicksilver, Retaliation and the Shannon.

The most famous character to visit the Great White Horse immortalised it, and the town of Ipswich, as no mere monarch could. Through the works and visits of Charles Dickens, not least the *The Pickwick Papers*, an indelible image of the town as it was in the 1830s emerges. Mr Pickwick describes his arrival:

'In the main street of Ipswich, on the left-hand side of the way, a short distance after you have passed through the open space fronting the town hall, stands an inn known far and wide by the appellation of The Great White Horse, rendered the more conspicuous by a stone statue of some rampacious [sic] animals with flowing mane and tail, distantly resembling an insane cart horse, which is elevated above the principal door.'

Dickens appears to have liked Ipswich but apparently not the inn, which he says is famous in the neighbourhood for its size, 'in the same degree as a prize ox, or county paper-chronicled turnip, or unwieldy pig'. He criticised its 'labyrinths of uncarpeted passages' and 'clusters of mouldy, ill-lighted rooms' and used the layout to advantage in the now infamous scene where Pickwick is unable to find his way back to his own room:

'The more stairs Mr Pickwick went down, the more stairs there seemed to be to descend, and again and again, when Mr Pickwick got into some narrow passage, and began to congratulate himself on having gained the ground floor, did another flight of stairs appear before his astonished eyes.'

Eventually he dives into what he thought was his room only to be confronted by a 'middle-aged lady, in yellow curl-papers, busy engaged in brushing what ladies call their "back-hair"', and Sam Weller has to rescue him and return him to his own bedroom.

As well as the 'ill lighted rooms', Dickens also referred to a 'badly-furnished apartment with a dirty grate, in which a small fire was making a wretched attempt to be cheerful' and called it an 'overgrown tavern' with a 'dispiriting' atmosphere. Not surprising, then, that when Dickens made a return trip to Ipswich to give a reading of his work he did not stay at the White Horse and the landlord, William Brooks, did not attend the readings!

The Pickwick Room postcard.

It was at 'this overgrown tavern' that the London coach stopped at the same hour every evening. 'Tony Weller', father to the fictional 'Sam', was a coachman. He wore a 'wide-skirted' green coat over a long waistcoat, ornamented with large brass buttons and his legs 'encased in knee-cord breeches, and painted top-boots'. He had a large silver watch that hung at the end of a copper chain, which he consulted frequently. He says to his son:

'Now it's time I was up at the office to get my vay-bill, and see the coach loaded; for coaches, Sammy is like guns – they require to be loaded with wery great care, afore they go off.'

Mr Weller Senior, like his son, mixed his v's and w's!

In 1966 the White Horse was bought by Trust House Forte, who wanted to demolish it, but local opinion, backed up by a protest from the Pickwick Society, saved it. However, it has now been modernised to death inside and it has lost much of its character.

Halfway up Tavern Street is a site now occupied by Superdrug (but for many years British Home Stores) which is connected with the family of Geoffrey Chaucer (*c.*1340–1400), the father of English literature and author of *The Canterbury Tales*, who ran a tavern thereabouts. (The plaque is on Tower Street.)

The Malyn family owned and occupied an establishment in Tavern Street during the 13th and 14th century. Robert Malyn, who had vintner

outlets in Tavern Street and Brook Street (now Northgate Street), died young. His Ipswich property, and his son, John, became the subject of a complicated family dispute, as a result of which his sister Agnes, accompanied by the Ipswich bailiff, went to London and abducted her nephew, John, in order to regain their interest in the property. Agnes and the bailiff were tried for the abduction and sentenced to pay damages of £250, though after a term of imprisonment they returned to Ipswich where they managed to buy back some of Robert's business.

Meanwhile, John set up a new business in London, calling himself John 'le Chaucer', taking his surname from the traffic in 'chausses', the footwear carried as deck cargo on early mediaeval wine ships. John's son took the name Geoffrey Chaucer.

There is no record of Chaucer ever visiting Ipswich, but it is clear he knew the area. In *The Canterbury Tales* he refers to the 'forked beard' merchants who sailed the seas 'betwixe Middelburgh and Orewelles' and the 'Flandrish beaver hat' that were so familiar in the port of Ipswich. The mendicant friars, again so familiar on the town's street, play a part in the Canterbury pilgrimage, not unlike those which visited the Shrine of Our Lady of Ipswich.

The Malyn tavern became a Coffee House and by 1767 offered coffee and tea plus card and dining rooms. Francois de la Rochefoucauld visited it in 1784:

'Ipswich is very well inhabited, many gentlefolk living there, and besides that, tradespeople. All gather every evening in a coffee-house, where one can play cards and eat, which is very convenient for strangers.'

The Old Coffee House, as it became known, was rebuilt in the late 1600s and acquired some wonderful wood carvings, including Faith, Hope and Charity on the corner post. Alas, the fabulous and ornate frontage was destroyed in 1817 to provide a few more inches of pavement. John

Shewell Corder wrote in *Ye Olde Corner Postes of Ipswiche*:

'In the year 1815, or thereabouts, the Corporation of Ipswich conceived a plan for widening Tavern Street, and though no doubt the reform was urgently needed one can but deplore that whilst so much that was really picturesque was destroyed, and a little more ingenuity was not expended in the rebuilding.'

This corner of Tavern Street and Tower Street was also the site of the New Assembly House, which stood adjacent to the Coffee House and opened in 1753 with a large reception ball and concert attended by over 300 townspeople. It superseded the old Assembly House in St Peter's Street and was, in its turn, replaced by the Assembly Rooms on Northgate Street in 1821.

The shop that attracts much attention from visitors is that which for many years was occupied by Croydon & Sons, at 50 to 52 Tavern Street. The group of 1930s timber-framed buildings of Tudor-like appearance were designed by the same Ipswich architect, John Sherman, who was responsible for the three gables on the side of the Old Pack Horse inn on St Margaret's Plain.

Croydons went into receivership in 1994 and the business was taken over by the long-established High Street jewellers Preston & Duckworth. In 2004 Preston & Duckworth moved to the former Lawleys store in the Buttermarket but the following year they too went into administration and the store has become part of the Robert Gatward chain. The old Croydons' shop was taken over by Blacks, the 'Outdoor Experts'.

The Ipswich Institute has occupied premises in Tavern Street since 1834. It began as the Mechanics' Institute in 1824 with the aim of instructing members in the principles of the arts and sciences, ensuring 'the diffusion of knowledge and sound information amongst the middle and industrious classes' and imparting other 'useful knowledge'. During the 1800s mechanics' institutes were founded in many towns and represented the first serious effort at 'self improvement' for the adult working classes. Usually they were sponsored by 'enlightened' middle-class philanthropists who had to assure local businesses that there was no danger of increasing knowledge liable to 'cause those who possess it to show want of respect to their superiors or to disobey their masters.' Later it dropped the 'Mechanics' and became the Ipswich Institute.

The Ransome and Alexander families were supporters of the Ipswich Mechanics' Institute, which began life in St Matthew's Church Lane before moving to the Buttermarket, finally making a permanent home in a former chemists shop in Tavern Street. Further along the street was the Working Men's College, started some 30 years later, in the Old Assembly Rooms, and a lecture hall was acquired in Tower Street

So much has happened on Tavern Street over the centuries that, even in modern times, the buildings have passed through many hands, often changing use as they go. In 1906, for example, the River Island clothing shop was a Boots store and before that a popular department store called Frederick Fish & Son. As Mayor, Frederick Fish presided over the opening of the Corn Exchange in 1882.

The annual Race Ball was held in the Tavern Street Assembly Rooms during Race Week. From around 1720 until 1911 (though the last steeplechase was run in 1895) Ipswich Races brought race goers from near and far. During the Napoleonic Wars the officers garrisoned at Ipswich were enthusiastic attenders.

The bank of Messrs Bacon, Cobbold & Co once stood on the north side of Tavern Street, and nearby John King (1776–1831) founded the *Suffolk Chronicle* in 1810. With his partner, Robert Garrod, he edited, printed and published the newspaper from his Tavern Street offices. There were other hotels here, too, including the Victoria and the Homeleigh (Commercial).

The HMV outlet occupies what was once one of Ipswich's premier stores, Frederick Corder & Son Limited, a large department shop with a second

The Old Coffee House, etched by H. Davy. John Shewell Corder lamented that the Old Coffee House was 'ruthlessly sacrificed' and in its place came a 'dreary wall of white brick'.

entrance on the Buttermarket. However, when, in the 1970s, Footmans rebuilt their store in Westgate, Footmans and Corders were united under the Debenhams banner.

THINGSTEAD (see St Margaret's Green)

Thingstead is a Danish name for a meeting place, in this case on St Margaret's Plain just outside the northern town rampart. Although the name is no longer employed, it has a long association with civic and judicial events, fairs and was a general meeting place for the hundreds of Wicklaw, under the jurisdiction of Ely Abbey and known as the Liberty of St Etheldreda.

THOROUGHFARE, The

The Thoroughfare is just that, a passageway from the south-east corner of Cornhill, behind the Old Post Office, leading to The Walk or the Buttermarket. In the 1960s the building now part of Barclay's Bank was once Hutton's Costumiers.

Although The Thoroughfare is shown on both Ogilby and Pennington's map, it is not named and it is likely the name was not in use until the late 19th century.

TOWER RAMPARTS

One of the oldest names in Ipswich, it describes the fortifications that fringed the northern and eastern limits of the town. The ramparts were mounds of heaped earth with a palisade, or fence, on the top and certainly date from the late 12th century and possibly earlier. It is possible that at one time parts of the ditches were flooded as in 1291 there is mention of a watercourse called 'Botflood'. A 1975 report on the archaeological features of Ipswich showed that although stretches of the rampart were still visible at the beginning of the 20th century, north of Old Foundry Road, Tower Ramparts and St Margaret's Ditches, the last surviving fragment was in Shire Hall Yard adjacent to Lower Orwell Street. However, this remaining mediaeval fortification was levelled in the late 1950s.

Although King John's rampart is gone it gave its name to Tower Ditches, on the north side of St Mary le Tower. Tower Ditches, known as one time as Tower Terrace, is now called Tower Ramparts and is a reminder of one of the most ancient parts of the Saxon town.

It is uncertain what form the ramparts took before 1200 but, following the granting of the Charter in 1200, 'Gipeswic' began to bustle with increased civic activity. The continuing prosperity of the ports and the burgeoning trade attracted the attention of King John and it is, perhaps, typical that Ipswich should have surrounding it not grandiose walls but ditches with wooden fencing. King John's coffers were bare and anxious that his protégé borough was properly defended, thus securing his 'investment', in 1203 he ordered that the town ditches and walls be made good. There was little chance that anything more grand would be built.

The Tower Ramparts shopping precinct was opened on 7 November 1986 and built in the 1980s on the site of the Tower Ramparts School (formerly

Entrance to Tower Ramparts shopping centre. Corporation buses started using what was then Tower Ditches in the 1930s.

Tower Ramparts by John Moore (1821–1902). (Ipswich Museums & Galleries)

the Municipal Secondary School for Boys), which was dismantled, along with the old Footman Pretty's stay factory. The school first opened in September 1899 as a Higher Grade school and served many generations of Ipswich school children until its demolition.

The Corporation's bus station operates from Tower Ramparts and in the 1960s was known as 'Electric House', in honour of the offices of the Eastern Electricity Board that for many years occupied the building now trading, among other things, as a futon outlet, offices and an art gallery.

In the 1980s Radio Orwell, with its indisputable slogan 'the station with the nicest listeners', operated from Electric House.

TOWER STREET

It is often presumed that Tower Street takes its name from the Church of St Mary le Tower, but it is by no means certain that the church was not named 'le Tower' to distinguish it from other churches dedicated to St Mary and that it took its name from a nearby tower. There might have been another tower then existing in close proximity to the church, perhaps as part of the rampart, though there is no record of any such lookout or defensive tower. Historians over the years have discounted thoughts of 'le Tower' being that of the Norman Castle, which was more likely to have been at St Mary Elms (see Elm Street).

In the days of the mediaeval markets the junction of Tower and Tavern Streets was known as the Hen Market. Documentary evidence places it there in 1327.

Whatever its origins it is certain that Tower Street has been witness to momentous civic occasions down the ages, most important of which was the gathering of the townspeople in the churchyard in 1200 to hear the declaration of the town's first Charter. The men of Ipswich had started negotiations for a Charter during Richard I's reign (1189–1199) but its grant was left to the new King John.

In only the second year of John's reign, on 25 May 1200, the Charter was granted to 'S'comunitatis

ville Gypewicic', the fellowship (or community) of Ipswich. Between June and October that year the burgesses convened a series of meetings to hear the various tenets of the Charter read aloud. They met, together with large numbers of townspeople, in the church and churchyard of St Mary le Tower to hear the Charter read aloud. A copy was placed in the hands of John Fitz-Norman and William de Belines, two men who swore faithfully to uphold the Charter and keep it safe for the townspeople. A Common Seal was ordered to be made and be kept by the burgesses.

These were momentous days: the town burgesses and their heirs were thenceforth and forever 'quit of toll, lastage, stallage, passage, pontage, and all other customs throughout our land and seaports' forever and were allowed to have a Merchants' Guild. They were permitted to have their own lands and, in short, Ipswich became a free town. Free, that is, so long as they paid the king the dues they had undertaken as part of the negotiations for the privileges granted. The Charter was to be renegotiated many times with other monarchs over the years.

King John's interest in Ipswich says something for its importance in 12th-century England, although his motives were not entirely altruistic since the king was, to say the least, impecunious and eager to boost his income from tolls and taxes from centres of industry within his grasp. 'Gipeswic's' mint and trading capabilities, therefore, afforded the town special attention. Roger Bigod (see Cranfields Yard), a descendant of the original Norman bailiff, attended King John and was one of those sent to summon the King of Scotland to do homage to him at the Lincoln Parliament. (The Bigods later became disillusioned with the King and joined the rebel Barons who met at the High Altar in Bury Abbey in 1214 to demand a charter of liberty, the Magna Carta.)

The location of Tower Street made it a convenient place for the newly-appointed town dignitaries to meet and conduct business and was easily reached by numerous streets, including a lane that once lead

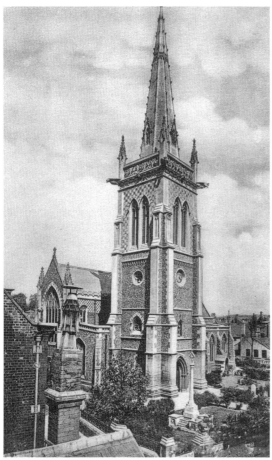

The tower of St Mary's can be seen from many vantage points in the town and the church is mentioned in the Little Domesday Book as having already been in existence since the reign of Edward the Confessor (1005-1066), its Latin name being Sancta Maria ad Turrim *(St Mary at the Tower).*

from Brook Street to St Mary's churchyard. This was always known as Tower Church Lane and part of it is known as Tower Church Yard. It runs along the edge of the churchyard and eventually leads to Oak Lane and so to Northgate. Just along Tower Church Yard is Hatton Court, which perpetuates the name of Sir Christopher Hatton who lived in the court and was considered 'a liberal patron of learning and eminent for his piety, charity and integrity'. Sir Christopher ingratiated himself, by his elegant and graceful dancing, into the favour of Queen Elizabeth and became Lord Chancellor in 1587.

St Mary's was the church of the Corpus Christi Guild and from here the Guild set out in procession on the Feast of the Holy Sacrament. They went in the following order: first the Carmelites, followed by

the Greyfriars, Blackfriars, clerks in surplices and the tabernacle, containing the Host, together with plate and ornaments. Next came the secular priests, the Canons of the Holy Trinity, Canons of St Peter and St Paul, the bailiffs, the portmen, Aldermen of the Guild and lastly the brethren of the guild. This must have caused something of a stir in the town.

A plaque on 13 Tower Street commemorates the Ipswich-born Admiral Benjamin Page (1765–1845) who as a child lived in Northgate Street but retired to Tower Street after a distinguished naval career. It was here that the Duke of Wellington 'paid a visit to Admiral and Mrs Page, with whom he had returned from India,' on 20 January 1820.

Page joined the Navy at the age of 13 and in 1803 was appointed Captain of HMS *Caroline* and served on her in the East Indies. In 1835 he was made an honourary freeman of the borough and his portrait,

The 'Charter' Hanging depicting three seals – that of King John (left), The Corporation seal of 1200 (raised centre) and the seal of King Richard (right). An Ipswich 'cat' (with the first ever movable rudder) is seen in the centre on the river (Isabel Clover & Ipswich Arts Association).

together with paintings of six naval actions in which he took part and a model of the *Caroline* were donated to the town.

Perhaps as a result of his adventurous and hectic life at sea, Admiral Page was a lover of peace and quiet. In 1830 Thomas Hearne, a street hawker nicknamed Must-Go, sold watercress around the town, and he must have been particularly good at attracting the attention of his customers because he was granted a small pension from Admiral Page on the condition that he did not shout his wares near the Admiral's Tower Street home.

The Admiral's House was for many years the centre of operations for the Diocese of St Edmundsbury and Ipswich but is now under the auspices of The Ipswich Institute.

The Rep public house occupies the old Ipswich Arts Theatre, converted into a lecture theatre for the Mechanics Institute in 1849, after which it became Poole's Picture Palace. It was here that Charles Dickens gave several readings during his visit to the town. The Picture Palace closed in 1940 and the building was used as a club for Allied Forces during World War Two. It reopened in 1947 as the Ipswich Arts Theatre, which lasted until 1979 when the Wolsey Theatre (see Civic Drive) replaced it. The final show was *Happy End*, performed to an audience seated in restaurant style with the usual seating removed. The building was then converted to a theme pub, 'The Old Rep'.

TURRET LANE

People have been using Turret Lane for at least 1,000 years. A hollowed-out tree trunk well, discovered at Turret Lane in the northern limit of the area, was dated by dendrochronology to approximately 670 AD. Although originally nothing more than a lane, there were undoubtedly industries flourishing at the time, many to do with the functions of the port and shipbuilding in particular. The archaeologists unearthed several clench bolts and roves, and fish bones indicating both freshwater and marine fishing.

It takes its name from Turret House that once

stood close by, though in 1582 the northern part linking to Lower Brook Street was named Orford Lane. Since Turret House has long since disappeared it is impossible to know when it was built, but on Joseph Pennington's map it is shown to be occupied by Mrs Sparrow and was surrounded by gardens. By 1844 the house had given its name to the lane, although both house and garden were built over by 1867.

WALK (The)

The Walk is an intriguing, bustling byway winding narrowly from Tavern Street down towards the Buttermarket and is a pedestrian-only shopping thoroughfare. It was designed by Cautley and Barefoot between 1932 and 1933 and in January 2005 was granted special conservation status. The buildings are half-timbered reproductions and many of the narrow fronted shops, jostling for position under the covered walkway, have ornate carved details.

Protected status is also extended to the Yorkstone paving and further powers are retained so that additional planning controls can be introduced in order to protect the appearance of The Walk. This is an example of how reproduction architecture takes on its own character and becomes, in its turn, a town treasure.

WATERWORKS STREET

The old name for Waterworks Street is Dunghill Pound Lane and it appears as such on Ogilby's map. It was probably used as a mediaeval 'pound' or enclosure for stray or escaped animals as well as being one of the town's dunghills. In Tudor times there was a particular problem with keeping the street free of wandering pigs, which were impounded by the town authorities and only returned to their owners on payment of a fine. The more recent name Back Street was changed to Waterworks Street after the waterworks were built on the ruins of the extensive paper mills which burnt down in 1848. For many years the chimney of the waterworks was visible for miles.

Hunt's Guide said of the waterworks:

'By means of powerful machinery, the water from the various springs round Ipswich is conveyed to a reservoir, at a great height at these works, and thence the town is supplied. In the streets, at intervals, are hydrants at which water is to be obtained.'

In case of a fire the hose was kept at the police station and could quickly be fixed to the hydrants. The lack of fire-fighting equipment was one reason for the new waterworks. In 1848 a fire broke out at the offices of the *Ipswich Express* in the Buttermarket but the water pipes used for fire fighting proved useless, there being no pressure and insufficient water. Thus, when Ransons paper mill in Back Street burned down it was decided the time had come for the town to have a more modern water system. In addition, the Metropolitan

Commissioner of Sewers had submitted an alarming report about possible water contamination and found the supply 'sadly fragmented'. Water had previously been supplied to various public pumps by wooden pipes direct from springs.

Graphic accounts of the destruction of the paper mills appeared in the *Ipswich Journal*:

'It is almost impossible to describe the consternation which prevailed in the populous neighbourhood, from the tumbling down of ruins, the hasty removal of so much furniture, the hissing of the flames, the shrieks of the women, the shouts of the firemen, and the crashing of walls.'

In 1875 it was decided to form a publicly funded fire brigade, instead of relying on those maintained by private companies, and the Fire Engine Station

Fire officers in 1919. The fire service operated out of Bond Street, just up the road from Waterworks Street, from 1899. Horses were used until 1918 when the first motor fire engine, a Model T Ford, was purchased. (ITM Collection)

was in Waterworks Street. Horses for the fire appliances were kept at the Sea Horse Hotel in Key Street, although on occasions horses were provided from the Royal Horse Artillery at Ipswich Barracks.

A building still seen on Waterworks Street, opposite St Clement's, is yet another reminder of the 18th and 19th-century influence of the Quakers, or Society of Friends, on the town (see also Old Foundry Road and Bolton Lane). Richard Dykes Alexander founded the Ipswich Ragged School in 1849, and the schoolroom (dated 1857) recalls the days when philanthropic men and women provided the 'poor and needy', as indeed had been the case throughout the centuries before the advent of the welfare state.

WESTGATE STREET

Until 1781 the West Gate to the town stood at the St Matthew's end of what is now Westgate Street (where Bretts is now) and, in the 17th century, served as the borough gaol. It was known as Gaol Gate Street (or, sometimes, St Matthew's Bar Gate) and the eastern section, leading onto the Cornhill, was called Bargate Street (as it appears on Speed's 1610 map) or West Gate Street. The West Gate is at a more northerly point in the town layout than might be expected, but an entrance gate at a more westerly point was neither required nor possible as the land to the west of the town was marsh (see also Portman Road). A fragment of the West Gate was uncovered in 1967 and was found to be well constructed and incorporated finely dressed Caen stone imported from Normandy. Unfortunately this fragment was destroyed in the 1960s swath of development.

West Gate was a solidly-built structure of brick and stone with an archway that had a headroom of some 15ft (4.5m), enough room to allow a man to enter on horseback. On the outside there were two towers with connecting houses and inns running off either side and along the line of the ramparts. Although the precise date of the original building is unknown, the lower part was known in 1332 as 'New Gaol'. Burgess John de Caldwell rebuilt the upper

The West Gate in 1825.

part in 1448 and it served as a gaol, as well as a town entrance, until the 18th century.

When it ceased to be a gaol the structure was used as a gunpowder magazine with the lower rooms used as a guardroom for the army. Local residents, though, were unhappy living so close to the gunpowder and in 1780 the powers that be bowed to public opinion. Also, the narrow entrance of the gate was proving inconvenient for the increasing volume of traffic that passed through it and thus, in 1781, it was decided to sell the gate 'to the best bidder' so that it could be pulled down. It sold for £32.

It had guarded the western approaches for about 400 years but was no longer required. However, its memory lingered for a while as in 1887 the town built a replica of the gate, in its original position, as part of the Golden Jubilee celebrations.

Excavations made in Westgate Street for the laying of the sewer in 1881 revealed an Anglo-Saxon 'corduroy' road, made of logs, across marshy ground. A similar road, made of oak logs laid over heather and alder branches, was found a few years later on Norwich Road.

Westgate Street and Tavern Street together formed what was once the main road to London so, as might be expected, both have always had a goodly share of taverns and inns. Cockfighting with gamecocks went on at the Bear and Crown in the 18th century when it was one of the town's principal inns. It was the headquarters of the Liberal Party,

Westgate Street from Cornhill, 1859. (W. Vick Photo)

who were known as the 'yellows' or 'buffs', in the same way that the Great White Horse was known as the 'blue' house of the Tories. At the beginning of the 19th century it was damaged by fire and part of the site was rebuilt as The Suffolk Hotel, the first hostelry in the town to use the new term 'hotel'. In Queen Victoria's coronation year a civic reception and banquet was held at the Suffolk amid much noise 'from the firing of cannon'. Mail coaches left from the hotel for London, Norwich and Great Yarmouth, the 'Original Blue' leaving daily at 1.15pm. When it closed, the hotel was used as a wine and spirit merchants and for a while was called The Suffolk Stores, but it was demolished in 1838.

The Crown and Anchor Hotel, which also flourished in the 19th century, was described by Dr Taylor as 'the most imposing hotel in the town … the inside of the house is archaeological – the outside, architectural'. Fred Russell, an architectural artist whose work was much in demand locally, designed the highly-ornamental front. It was rebuilt

and enlarged in 1897 by Thomas W. Cotman (nephew of the famous watercolourist John Sell Cotman), in a Venetian-Gothic style, incorporating two older inns, the Chequers (at one time known as the Rampant Horse) and the 16th-century Griffin. The rear of the premises once backed up onto Tower Ramparts and is now taken up by Select Hair Design and the All Fired Up Ceramics Café. Its boundary was roughly in line with Providence Street (onto which the side bar opened), which runs alongside Marks & Spencer and opens onto the Tower Ramparts car park. The Gothic lettering on a stone furled banner still reads The Crown & Anchor Hotel. It stands sandwiched between Debenhams and Clarks shoe shop and operates as a branch of W H Smith and The Link.

The Griffin was renowned for its role as one of the town's first theatres, and in the early 1700s the Duke of Grafton's players performed there regularly. At one time the inn was kept by Mr Selby, a legatee under the will of the eccentric Lord Chelsworth (the

WILLIAM MILLS,
ICE AND YEAST IMPORTER,
44, WESTGATE STREET, IPSWICH.

W.M. only sells the Finest Brands of Yeast.　Call or send for Samples.
Bakers and Householders should buy their YEAST at above Address.

Norwegian Lake Block Ice supplied all the year round.

UNCLE TOM'S CABIN, Vernon Street & Austin Street.	The "IVY LEAF," Hyde Park Corner.
STEWARD & PATERSON'S STOUT & PORTER. NORWICH ALES.	If you want a Splendid Glass of **BASS'S BURTON,** ALSO Charrington Nicholl and Co.'s Brillant Ales, Drawn from the Wood, call at the above.
Don't forget to drop in the Cabin when passing by.	
W. T. JUBY, Proprietor.	GEORGE MARTIN, Proprietor.

ESTABLISHED 1839.
WILLIAM POOLEY'S NATIVE OYSTER ROOMS,
44, Westgate-street, Ipswich.

MY NATIVE OYSTERS ARE INCOMPARABLE.

☞ Please Note Address—44, Westgate Street.

Advertisement for William Mills, who shared number 44 with the Native Oyster Rooms, from a Chronology Book of Dates, 1897.

A group of women workers from William Mills of Westgate Street, c.1900.

Rt Hon John Howe), who died in 1804 and was buried in an altar tomb in St Matthew's churchyard. Lord Chelsworth had a 'strong predilection for the drama'; several actors and supporters benefited under his will and so began the tradition of the Griffin Yard theatre.

All the inns and pubs along Westgate Street have long since closed but when, in the words of the Revd C. Evelyn White, they 'passed away', a rhyme was composed:

'The 'Rampant Horse' shall kick the Bear,
And make the Griffin fly.
Turn the Bell upside down,
And drink the Three Tuns dry.'

The Bell was on the corner of Westgate Street and Cornhill (and later became Grimwades) and the Three Tuns once stood on Cornhill.

At the Museum Street junction was the 'Barley Mow' with the familiar slogan 'Tolly for Quality' emblazed on its end. In 1878 it was the subject of controversy after complaints were made before the borough Magistrates that the house was a source of trouble in the town and that the 'adjoining urinal was a nuisance'. By coincidence, Edward Grimwade was on the bench, which gave rise to some indignation since he was chairman of the Paving and Lighting Committee that was responsible for another urinal in the old cattle market.

When, in 1846, the site for the new town museum was chosen, work had just begun on Museum Street. This necessitated an opening being made in Westgate Street, cutting through part of the dilapidated Tudor 'Seckford House', once the home of Thomas Seckford (1515–1587), Member of Parliament for the borough, founder of Woodbridge School and courtier of Elizabeth I. The house and gardens are clearly marked on Ogilby's map and show a turreted mansion with a stand of trees to the south of the property, extending about two thirds of the way along the south side of Westgate Street. Among his other interests and achievements, Seckford is remembered for what Arthur Mee describes as his 'notable service' to the first book on rivers and streams of England, compiled by William Harrison with Seckford's financial assistance. He also financed Christopher Saxton, dubbed 'the father of English cartography', to make the first serious attempt at mapping the country.

Westgate Street is now a busy shopping

THE BARLEY MOW TAVERN,

36, WESTGATE STREET, & 1, HIGH STREET, IPSWICH.

Wines & Spirits. Catchpole's Ales & Stout.

LONDON AND LOCAL PAPERS TAKEN.

Head Quarters for Local Sports.

W. ELLISS,
Proprietor.

GENERAL CATERER.

1897 advertisement for The Barley Mow Tavern in The Diamond Jubilee Chronology.

concourse containing Debenhams and H. Samuel at its east end, together with WHSmith, Marks & Spencer, NEXT, Virgin Megastore, Clarks Shoes and numerous other smaller shops, charity shops and a health food store. Where Primark now stands, opposite Marks & Spencer, was the site of the public hall, built in 1868 and the first public building to be lighted by electricity. Here audiences were entertained by such novelties as the Phantoscope, the first motion picture projector, brought to the public hall by Poole and Young's in 1872. Charles Jenkins from Indiana, who revolutionised the motion picture industry, invented the Phantoscope. Jenkins used a box with a light in it to project the image outside the box and people flocked to the town hall to see the latest public entertainment.

Charles Poole also brought the Myriorama to the public hall in 1900, it being a continuous cloth bearing pictures on two rollers that was unrolled as a narrator told the story. Poole also brought cinematograph shows to the Mechanics' Institute (in Tower Street) where he later opened the first 'cinema', known later as Poole's Picture Palace.

No doubt many of those who attended these new innovative forms of public entertainment bought their tobacco and cigarettes at William Churchman's shop at the junction of Westgate Street and Crown Street, known as Hyde Park Corner. The name Churchman is synonymous with Ipswich and serves as a reminder of the days when smoking was considered a fashionable and harmless pastime, and Churchmans was a major employer in the town. William Churchman, a tallow-chandler, started selling tobacco and snuff in 1790 and, in the words

Westgate Street in 1909. Waterloo House (right) later became Footman's and is now Debenham's.

The old Crown and Anchor building on Westgate, now WHSmith.

of Peter Bishop, 'hit the big time after the naughty nineties had launched the cigarette on an innocent world.'

By 1897 Churchmans had outgrown the Hyde Park Corner premises and moved to a factory in Portman Road. Its original site, not far from the Ipswich Barracks area, had no doubt been a factor in its success since it was eminently more desirable for the officer classes to be seen smoking the fashionable cigarette than the cigars and pipe tobacco it replaced. The Churchman name was added to those that began to appear in civic undertakings, and Arthur Churchman (later Lord Woodbridge) donated large tracts of lands to the borough.

Only a few years after the new factory was operational, competition from American tobacco firms threatened to become so acute that the Imperial Tobacco Company (of Great Britain and Ireland) was formed and the Ipswich firm of Churchman's was absorbed into it. Churchman's 'Tenners' – 'the cigarette that satisfied' – became popular in the 1920s, as did their later 'No 1 filter', manufactured to cater for the new filter cigarette market.

After the Great War, a bonded warehouse was built to ensure that an adequate stock of tobacco was available in times of emergency and even more expansion took place in the 1920s and 1930s. By the 1970s it was part of the John Player group and eventually passed into the W D & H O Wills empire, which finally closed Churchman's in 1990.

The Churchman name lives on in the annals of those cartophilists whose hobby is collecting cigarette cards. These cards started as blank cards put into paper cigarette packets in the mid to late 19th century to act as strengtheners but evolved into advertising cards. It became popular to collect sets of cards and keep them in specially manufactured collectors' albums. Churchman's produced around 150 sets from 1897 to 1939 and subjects range from 'A Tour Round the World' and 'Curious Dwellings' to sporting personalities, 'Empire Railways', 'Rivers and Broads' and 'The Navy at Work'. In 1940 the wartime government banned cigarette cards as being a waste of 'vital raw materials'.

For many years the South Stand of the Portman Road football ground was known as 'Churchman's End', or Stand, after the Churchmans cigarette factory, which bordered on one side of the ground. The stand was originally erected in the 1940s, and although it has often been rebuilt since then there are still parts of the lower level of the stand that date back to the original structure. It is now known as the Greene King Stand, although spectators no longer stand.

WINGFIELD STREET

This street is now elbow shaped and most of it is taken up with the entrance to the NCP Foundation Street car park. Sir Anthony Wingfield, KG (c.1485–1552), friend and executor to Henry VIII, had a house in nearby Tacket Street which he inherited from his uncle, Sir Humphrey Wingfield, who was a great friend to Henry Tooley and his family. Although a little smaller than Lord Curson's house in Silent Street, the Wingfield residence was nevertheless grand, the great parlour measuring 27ft by 17 (see also Tacket Street). Panelling from Wing-

View along Westgate to Cornhill with the Crown and Anchor on the left. (ITM Collection)

field's house is now at Christchurch Mansion, it having been removed firstly in 1870 and taken to a private house and then acquired by the museum in 1929. It was during Sir Humphrey's occupation that the fabulous carved panelling was executed (the initials H and A appear intertwined and were the initials of Sir Humphrey and his wife, Anne). Contrary to the usual Ipswich tale of destruction and demolition of all things old, the panelling survives in Christchurch Mansion where the Wingfield Room was built in 1931 for the display of the panelling and overmantel.

Dramatic redevelopment overcame Wingfield Street, packed with tiny houses and 'The Phoenix' public house, when the bulldozers arrived at the end of 1962.

PORT AND DOCKLANDS

Trade within the British Isles and with the rest of Europe is the foundation on which Ipswich established its position as a major port from the seventh until the 17th century. As remarked by R.A.N. Dixon, 'Ipswich was a flourishing port when Liverpool was still a swamp and Hull an insignificant village'. It was this contact with the outside world that kept the town lively and stopped it becoming moribund. Early in the 18th century, Defoe found Ipswich to have 'a great deal of very good company' and further observed:

'The company you meet with here are generally persons well informed of the world and who have something very solid and entertaining in their society; this may happen, perhaps, by their frequent conversing with those who have been abroad, and by their having a remnant of gentlemen and masters of ships among them, who have seen more of the world than the people of an island town are likely to have seen.'

Because of the lie of the land, it is possible to be in the town and not be aware of what is virtually a second entity, the port. Lilian Redstone wrote:

'Mediaeval Ipswich had two business centres, the one upon rising ground where country produce was marketed on the open Corn Hill and along the main streets, the other at the river level where a flourishing overseas traffic, stimulated by proximity to the Netherlands, was handled at the Common Quay and other small wharves.'

The *Anglo-Saxon Chronicle* records the days when Vikings regularly plundered 'Gipeswic',

possibly in search of such riches as belonged to the rich and prosperous Wuffingas. The townspeople might have been living in simple wooden houses and eating off unglazed pottery, but an inspection of the fabulous contents of the Sutton Hoo burial chamber, close to the Deben River, gives a glimpse of the beautiful and sophisticated objects available to those able to afford them. In 991 'Gipeswic' was viciously attacked and only four years later the town was 'laid all waste'. One guidebook says:

'The Vikings used [the river] to carry them in that direction. Centuries of men, standing on the Gipping valley slope where Ipswich now is, and looking along the shining salt-water reaches of the Orwell, must have caught the glint of weapons and seen the dipping oars of war vessels stealing in.'

Town and port have grown alongside each other, the one influencing the other as prosperity peaked and troughed. As a 1938 guide put it:

'If you are coming south, it is the first estuary on the East Anglian coast that takes you far inland. If you are sailing north from the Thames, it is the first river that carries you into the heart of East Anglia.'

The great mercantile prosperity of the 16th century, when Ipswich was a Mecca for rich traders and merchants, was followed by a period of decline, not regained until the end of the 18th century. In 1698 Celia Fiennes recorded:

'The town looks a little disregarded, and by enquiry found it to be thro' pride and sloth, for tho' the sea would bear a ship of 300 tun up quite to the key and the ships of the first rate can ride within two mile of the town, yet they make no advantage thereof by any sort of manufacture, which they might do as well as Colchester and Norwich, so that the shipps that brings their coales goes light away'.

She also criticised their lack of enterprise in not providing ships' supplies:

'They have a little dock where formerly they built ships of 2 or 300 ton but now little or nothing is minded save a little fishing for the supply of the town.'

During the first half of the 18th century the Orwell began to silt up rapidly so that by 1744 only small vessels could reach the quays and had to load and unload below the town. In 1711 Sir James Thornhill described Ipswich as having a 'river without water'.

The story of the modern port began in 1805 when the River Commissioners were empowered to carry out 'deepening, widening, cleansing, altering and otherwise improving' the stretch of the River Orwell between Stoke Bridge and Levington Creek.

In the years that followed, the traffic of the Port of Ipswich reached such proportions that the population of the town doubled and the new prosperity spawned yet more development of the riverside and an ambitious plan to create a 'wet dock and contiguous channel'.

A clue to the historic importance of the docklands is found firstly on the Common Seal of Ipswich, which dates from the year of the Charter (1200) and bears the earliest known depiction of a ship with a rudder fixed to the stern post by pintles and gudgeons in place of the earlier steering oak on the starboard quarter. Defoe, in his history of the plague, wrote that the 'dreadful malady' was carried to Ipswich by the large vessels called 'the Ipswich Cats'.

G.R. Clarke wrote in 1830:

'These cats were of large tonnage, standing very high above the water; we remember to have seen one or two of them in our early days, they were wider in proportion than other vessels of similar burthen; their hulls were painted black, and with their dingy crew and gigantic bulk, they had a gloomy and terrific appearance.'

It was still then a common expression among the old seamen, in reference to the form of a vessel, to say it was 'cat built'.

On the borough arms is found a complete, three-masted ship held by a demi-lion and three demi-ships appear on the panel. Confirmed in 1560 by Wyllyam Herve, Clarenceux King of Arms, two silver seahorses were granted as supporters and represent the horses which hauled Neptune's chariot.

When Isabel Clover chose the subjects for the panels of the Charter Hangings 2000, a set of eight embroidered hangings which celebrate the 800th anniversary of the Charter granted to Ipswich in 1200 by King John, one of the components was a Viking boat. The design came from a Viking gravestone in Stora Hammers, Sweden, as did the figure holding the torch.

ALBION WHARF

This wharf is adjacent to St Peter's Dock on the north band of the West Dock and south of College and Key Streets. With the demise of the working docks it seems to have lost its name lately (except to the locals) and now forms part of the Common Quay. The towering silo of R & W Paul Limited, currently home to quantities of feral pigeons, marks the site of the maltings which closed in November 2004. It is a reminder of a firm that has contributed to the town's commerce since the early 19th century and many can still recall the sweet smell of the malting grain permeating across the docks and surrounding streets.

Pauls Agriculture was founded in Ipswich in 1850 by Robert Paul (1806–1864), initially to trade in malt and barley for the town's several brewers.

Robert and his two sons, Robert and William, became not only maltsters but also grain merchants and cattle food millers. R & W Paul Limited was incorporated in 1893 and the brothers set up a new company, The British Oil & Cake Mills Limited.

By the early 1900s cheap imported cereals, especially maize from America, allowed the company to diversify into animal feeds on an industrial scale. Wheat, too, began to arrive from America and Canada, soya from the US and South America, groundnuts from Africa and cottonseed from East Africa and the Far East. Distribution from the port mills was by rail, and the company opened branches all over the country. They owned large granaries, provender mills and maltings, and for most of the 20th century they relied on sea-going transport for the movement of goods.

Robert Simper writes:

'R & W Paul needed barges to bring raw materials from the London Docks to their Ipswich mills so they bought the Dock End Yard at Ipswich and built their own wooden sailing barges. The last of these, "Ardwina", was launched in 1909. Ipswich became the first port in northern Europe to have fleets of sailing barges. Pauls operated the "Marjorie" and "Anglia" until 1960 while the Ipswich millers, Cranfield Brothers, used their "Spinaway C", "Venture" and "May" to carry some freights under sail until 1963.'

The last freight delivered under sail was by the Pin Mill-owned *Cambria* in 1970 to Eastern Counties Farmers' mills at Ipswich. After this, Pauls and Cranfields operated motor barges and, in 1974, Pauls converted their barge *Ena* back to sail for their employees to sail on. When the *Ena* was sold in 2000 she was the last Ipswich-owned barge.

Barges can still be seen moored alongside Common Quay, usually in front of the Customs House. One is the Thames barge, the *Thistle*,

Sir John Mills, accompanied by Dulcie Gray, was awarded a Doctor of Letters by UEA/Suffolk College in October 2000. John Mills worked for Pauls during the 1926 General Strike and has a theatre named for him on Gatacre Road. (photo: Warren Page)

designed with a flat bottom to enable horses and carts to unload straight off the barge. The *Thistle* was built in 1896 of steel and loaded 180 tons. She is now owned by Topsail Charters.

During the General Strike of 1926 things became fraught on the Ipswich dockside, not least on Albion Wharf. The Strike began at midnight on 3 May and ended at noon on 12 May. It was nine days in British history akin to a civil war when society was thrown into the melting pot and people forced to take sides. When the mine owners announced that they intended to reduce the miners' wages the General Council of the Trade Union Congress (TUC) promised its support in the forthcoming and inevitable dispute. On 1 May the TUC met to agree that a General Strike would begin two days later.

The *EADT* told readers:

'We have to inform our readers that unless there is some change in the attitude adopted by the Unions concerned in newspaper production, this issue of "The East Anglian Daily Times" will be the last until some settlement is reached.'

The next day the Manchester Typographical Society sent notice that all members were to withdraw their labour. The General Strike had reached Suffolk and it remained to be seen how it would affect the companies working out of the docks. Although Ipswich was unlikely to see much in the way of extreme uprising, the docks were a potential source of malcontent.

One of the borough's first actions was to form a body of Special Constables, called Specials, to release the regular police for any trouble that might occur. In the first issue of the *EADT* special strike issue (the National Union of Journalists was one of the few unions not called out) it was reported that Specials had enrolled in their hundreds in both East and West Suffolk.

Dockworkers intended to prevent lorries being unloaded, but the borough police managed to maintain order at the point of loading with the help of the Specials and by providing escorts for the vehicles leaving the dock area. One of the main operators at Ipswich docks was R & W Paul, whose flat barges discharged their cargoes into the warehouses spread along the quayside.

Among those in the R & W Paul shipping department in 1926 was a young man named Lewis Ernest Watts Mills, better known as the internationally famous actor of stage and screen Sir John Mills (1908–2005). He remembered his time there as both 'deadly' and 'monotonous,' enlivened only by the exciting few days of the General Strike when the white-collar workers were required to help keep the goods flowing. In his autobiography *Up in the Clouds, Gentlemen Please* he wrote:

'A notice appeared on the board stating that the police needed volunteers to act as special constables, and one of our directors had added a rider to the effect that any of the staff who felt it their duty to answer the call to arms would be granted indefinite leave from the office on full pay.'

About 30 staff applied and reported to Ipswich Police Station where they were instructed by the sergeant in charge and told that should violence break out they were not to retaliate but remain calm. 'And mind out for the women' he added.

John's first taste of 'the women' came when about 150 strikers were reported to be assembling on the dockside. The shipping office staff were armed with short, wooden truncheons with leather thongs attached and led down to the warehouse. Grain was being unloaded from one of the barges, and they were instructed to line up to prevent any disruption.

Soon the women followers began to arrive with sandwiches and flasks of tea for the strikers; John Mills and the other office workers looked in horror at the group gathered before them. The women were clad in corduroy trousers, waistcoats and leather belts and 'any one of them looked as if she could have eaten us for breakfast!'

After a two-hour stand-off, each side doing little

more than glaring at each other, the deadlock was broken by a one-woman attack on the shipping department.

'After glancing in our direction [a woman] detached herself from the group and advanced towards us like a large, black barge in full sail. She paused at the end of our front line, proceeded slowly along it and came to a stop opposite me. She was huge – built like an all-in wrestler, with a large wart on one side of her nose.'

After a few heated moments, during which the young Mills caught the sharp end of her tongue, the constable called the men off and everyone dispersed for lunch.

The effects of the Strike were short lived and Pauls continued to thrive, through the Depression, the war years and beyond. Until the 1970s the barges were still carrying away malt, although they were by then fitted with engines. In 1992 BOCM Pauls was formed by the amalgamation of two businesses operating in the animal feed industry. The maltings continued until 2004 but by then BOCM Pauls was almost unrecognisable and had been the subject of acquisitions and buy-outs over the years, although the company headquarters is still on Key Street.

The Sir John Mills Theatre on Gatacre Road was named to commemorate Sir John's association with the town when, in 1988, the newly formed Eastern Angles theatre company took over an old drama centre studio.

BACK HAMLET

This street is named for its association with the ancient four wicks (or hamlets) of Ipswich (see also Wicks Bishop Street). Fore Hamlet runs south of Back Hamlet. *Hunt's Guide* described Back Hamlet as 'a dim and murky place where Ipswich low life presents itself almost at its worst'.

Throughout the 18th and 19th century there were several pubs along Back Hamlet associated with Ipswich Racecourse (held at Nacton). One of

them, The Earl Grey, stood at the junction of Back Hamlet and Fore Hamlet but was demolished in the 1950s to make way for the Duke Street roundabout.

Holy Trinity Church was the first Anglican church to be built in the town in the 19th century and is one of the 'docklands' churches. Its exterior looks somewhat grubby as the Woolpit brick façade has not aged well, but it is nevertheless very much part of Back Hamlet and contains a World War One memorial. Roy Tricker said of it in 1982:

'Holy Trinity occupies a fine and commanding position on the hillside, overlooking the town at its eastern end, and it is rather a pity that the exterior is so plain and uninspiring. It is built of 'white' Suffolk bricks, which have considerably darkened over the years. The walls are pierced by large semi-circular headed windows and there is a plain oblong tower at the west end.'

It was erected in 1835, at a cost of £2,000, by the Revd J.T. Nottidge, who also endowed it with an annual income for the support of the minister and the reparation of the building. It is built in a style popularly known as Carpenter's Gothic(k), a whimsical and unscholarly design derived from pattern books and typical of many 19th-century, low budget churches.

At the Duke Street roundabout stands the Grimwade Memorial Hall, currently undergoing conversion into 32 loft-style apartments with 'contemporary open plan layout'. Built in 1869, originally as a chapel, it has long been in decline and in 2005 was renamed the GM Building. It stands opposite the St Clement's Congregational Church, which was constructed 'in memoriam' of Edward Grimwade (1812–1886).

CLIFF QUAY

Cliff Quay extends down the Orwell from the southern end of the Wet Dock forming the extent of the navigable channel. This extension of the port took place in the 1920s on land previously known as

The three power chimneys were landmarks for nearly 40 years and were seen for miles from both land and sea. They were demolished on 27 November 1994.

Hogg Highland and became the site for the power station. Ipswich had enjoyed an electricity supply since 1903, maintained by the Corporation out of the power station in Constantine Road, which by the 1930s was increasingly inadequate. Planning for the new power station began but World War Two prevented the work from beginning. It was not until 1947 that it was operational, only to be nationalised by the British Electricity Authority the following year.

Cliff Quay Power Station served the town until September 1982 when an accident occurred; an oil pipe burst, showering employees with oil. The oil burst into flames and thick, black smoke engulfed the site, damaging it so badly that it was never restored. It was finally demolished on 27 November 1994, the three chimneys being toppled by high explosives. Sentinel Terminal now occupies the site.

In the 1970s Esso Petroleum, Cory Brothers, Shell Mex & BP, Gabriel Wade & English and Fisons Fertilizers occupied Cliff Quay, with HM Customs and Excise next to the Cliff Quay Generating Station. The quay is still used commercially and is

Cliff Quay from the deck of HMS Grafton *with the waterfront in the background.*

deep enough to accommodate Ipswich's 'adopted' warship, HMS *Grafton*, when she visits.

On the opposite bank stood the rendering sheds where whales from Greenland were processed. In the 1780s two ships, the *Ipswich* and the *Orwell*, began whaling, though it was a short-lived operation and not commercially viable. On her first trip the *Orwell* caught seven whales, which netted 4cwt of whalebone and 150 butts of blubber, but subsequent ventures were unsuccessful.

CLIFF ROAD

This road leads from the Duke Street roundabout southward to the old Tolly Cobbold Brewery, a symbol of the town's considerable malting and brewing industry, and combines two of the greatest names in brewing – Tollemache's Breweries Limited and Cobbold & Company Limited.

The first Cobbold to make his mark was Thomas Cobbold (1680–1752), who set up a brewery in Harwich in the 1720s. In due course he took over an existing brewery in Ipswich and in 1746 he set up business at the Cliff, close to the Holy Wells, from where the water was piped straight into the brewery. The Cliff Brewery was a 'green field site' in those days, and with Cobbold's expertise and the sweet water of the Holy Wells the business prospered. When Thomas died his son, another Thomas, continued the business. A memorial in St Clement's Church reads:

> 'To the Memory of THOM. COBBOLD Common Brewer who departed this life April the 21st 1767 in the 59th year of his life.'

The Cobbolds developed other interests besides brewing and malting. They became corn and coal merchants and as ship owners imported goods to Ipswich from all parts of the globe. John Cobbold (1746–1835), grandson of the founder, had a house on St Margaret's Green and it was his second wife, Elizabeth, who befriended Margaret Catchpole and inspired her son, the Revd Richard Cobbold, to write the legendary novel *The History of Margaret*

In the 1980s the brewery tours were still popular but the museum collection was dispersed when the brewery closed.

Catchpole, A Suffolk Girl. John lived to the age of 89 and had two wives, both called Elizabeth, and 22 children. The name Cobbold, therefore, is a familiar one in the civic, commercial and banking affairs of the town.

It was John Cobbold who built the Holywells mansion in the grounds of what is now Holywells Park, overlooking the wells (see Holy Wells Road).

Thomas Cobbold's brewery lasted until the 1890s when it became clear that new premises were needed. The family called in a specialist architect, William Bradford, whose modern building was erected in 1894 and were extended and added to over the next 50 years.

In 1957 the Cobbold brewing operations merged with that of the Tollemache brothers, who closed their downtown brewery in what is now the car park behind Woolworth's (see also Brook Street). During

The old brewery is a familiar, but now sad, sight for those who view it from the river, or from across the water at New Cut West. Harmony II *is on the slipway. (left)*

the 1970s the modernised Cliff plant could fill 1,500 dozen bottles of beer in an hour and the company's transport fleet of more than a hundred vehicles were supplying over 380 Tolly Cobbold public houses and over 50 off-licensed premises throughout Suffolk.

In 1977 the Ellerman shipping group took over Tolly Cobbold, selling it on to David and Frederick Barclays, who sold it again to the Brent Walker leisure group. The days of the local brewery were waning and even the bigger groups found it hard to maintain premises such as the Cliff Brewery. The inevitable happened in 1989 when the town heard that the brewery was to close and that Tolly Cobbold ales were to be brewed in Hartlepool.

Robert Malster records:

'After Ipswich Borough Council had failed to persuade George Walker to reconsider, the brewery was listed as a building of historic and

architectural interest. The listing included equipment such as a 1723-vintage copper and the Turner steam engine.'

A management buy-out extended the life of the Cliff Brewery for a few more years, during which time it opened a brewery museum and a sampling room for those on the brewery tours. Finally, though, it was taken over by Ridley's in 2002 and the brewery is now closed, though the Brewery Tap public house opened for business in March 1992 and is still open for trade. The official address for the Brewery Tap, formerly Cliff House, is 1 Cliff Road, though there are cottages and associated brewery buildings nearby.

For several years customers at the Brewery Tap had a view of the rusting shell of the *Harmony II*, a 189-foot 'mega-yacht' displacing 650-tonnes, undergoing massive restoration on the slipway below the Cliff. In June 2005, as a reminder of the glory days of the port's shipbuilding era, it was finally launched as a transatlantic showroom for Pedley Furniture International.

COMMON QUAY

The Common Quay, formerly Key or Cay, was also known as the Old Quay and is one of the three small quays of mediaeval Ipswich – the Common Quay, Bigod's Quay and one owned by the Harney family. The wharves of Common Quay (part of which is now encompassed by Neptune Quay) were known as St Peter's and the Albion. Dr Taylor's description of this important part of the waterfront in 1888 cannot be bettered:

'A few years ago the site of the [Common] dock was the junction of the Gipping and the Orwell – before the 'new cut' was made, and the upper reach of the Orwell estuary imprisoned to form the dock. The river then came directly up to the warehouses. Some of the latter are very ancient, and are now being pulled down or modernised.'

The ducking chair is in remarkably good condition and suggests that it was a prized possession of the Corporation. On a particular day in 1597 three women were subjected to a ducking. (drawing from G.R. Clarke's History of Ipswich)

Custom House. (ITM Collection)

Dr Taylor might well be awed by the changes taking place in the 21st century as the warehouses, silos, feed mills, coal quays and breweries are either demolished or converted into apartment blocks and hotels. In an extraordinary foretelling of things to come, *A Grandfather's Tale* was published in 1875 by the *EADT*, where the old man says:

'That's where Ransomes used to be. They employed a large number of hands and did a lot of good to the town. It was a bad day for Ipswich when their Works were taken away … How do you like this beautiful piece of ornamental water? Is it not pretty in the sunlight? It's the old dock.'

While it is still possible to see what remains of a Tudor warehouse and merchant dwelling, with 'nogging' brickwork, beside the yard behind the art gallery in Wherry Lane, the character and nature of Common Quay changes almost daily. A driver with the now defunct Euston Transport, who used to visit the docks regularly with loads of coal from the Nottinghamshire and Leicestershire pits, remarked 'If someone had told me ten years ago this would be full of yachts you'd have called them a fool'.

The Custom House (now the Old Custom House) flanks Common Quay and is described by Nikolaus Pevsner in his book *The Buildings of England – Suffolk* as 'remarkably original'. The style is classical 'and the front towards the river monumental and symmetrical, with a bold raised four-column portico carrying a far-projecting pediment'.

The Old Custom House was an important component in the development of the Port, which commenced with the Ipswich Dock Act of 1837, one of the first acts to receive the Royal Assent of the young Queen Victoria. It was built in the 1840s and replaced an older Custom House described by G.R. Clarke as 'a low, ill-shaped, isolated building, supported, on the south, next to the water, by a numerous range of pillars, reaching the whole

Old Custom House by George Frost. (Ipswich Borough Council Museums and Galleries)

Sailor's Walk, Old Custom House by F.B. Russell. (Ipswich Borough Council Museums and Galleries)

length of the front, which is about a hundred and twenty feet, forming a colonnade, under which the masters of vessels and other seafaring people delight to perambulate, excursion, as being, we suppose, more similar to the agreeably-varied amusement of walking the deck.'

This was echoed by the author of *Hunt's Guide* who wrote of its paved colonnade being called 'Mariner's Walk, in which seamen used to "walk the deck" and gossip of their voyages'.

The earlier Custom House was said to have been tumble down and patched with brick; in 1830 it was 'in a very crazy condition'. It had served as a place of civic administration and customs for between four and five hundred years but by all accounts it was nearing the end of its life. The dockside, though, was heaving with activity. Robert Malster writes:

'The dock was in those days full of sailing ships whose spars and rigging wove a delicate pattern against the sky. There were collier brigs and brigantines which brought coal from the ports of the north-east coast, "onker" barques bringing timber from Scandinavia and the Baltic; little schooners which carried goods of all kinds coastwise to and from London.'

Coal was a significant commodity until the late 1950s and most of it came from northern England and was unloaded at the Isaac Lord wharves. Later it came in from Russia, South Africa and Poland. The first vessel to pass through the new lock in 1842 was the big *Zephyr* with a cargo of coal from the Tyne.

In 1840 it was announced that the Corporation would pull down the wooden custom house and a young architect named John Medland Clark, who died in 1849 at the very young age of 36, was commissioned to draw up plans for a new one. The new building was opened on 21 July 1845 as the New

Hall of Commerce, H M Customs and Excise Offices, and was intended to be a meeting place for merchants, shippers and captains. The Hall of Commerce formed the central room, with Customs in the west and Excise in the east wing. *The Ipswich Journal* said it was 'a remarkable instance of how much may be done with judicious and economical use of materials, where funds are comparatively scanty.'

In celebration there was a public dinner, boat racing and other sports, the day concluding with a 'brilliant display of fireworks on the Dock'. Lieutenant Colonel White and the band of the 7th Hussars were in attendance, the iron paddle steamer *River Queen* moored off Common Quay providing a floating bandstand. All the great and the good of the town were assembled, writes David Barton of the Ipswich Maritime Trust:

'The day ended with a brilliant firework display … the centrepiece was a ship 22 feet long by 20 feet high complete with masts and rigging. Above it were the words "Hall of Commerce" … and beneath "Prosperity to Ipswich". With the band of the Hussars playing, cannons firing and the populace cheering, the occasion had been a splendid one.'

It was from the quayside in front of the custom house that the famous Ipswich ducking stool was used to subdue 'the quarrelsome female-kind' and as a punishment for women convicted of prostitution. Now kept at Christchurch Mansion, the ducking stool is a strong-backed oaken armchair with a wrought-iron rod fastened to each arm in front and meeting in the segment of a circle above. A strong iron ring and chain is connected for the purpose of 'ducking' the chair – and the unfortunate female sitting in it – into the river.

The chair was found in the Custom House at the beginning of the 19th century, 'amongst a quantity of lumber stowed away in an apartment little used', but it might not always have been kept there since

there is evidence that porters were paid for carrying the stool down to the waterside and 'ducking the scolds'.

It was from the Common Quay that the adventurer, Bartholomew Gosnold, set off in 1602 to the New World as leader of an expedition aboard 'Concord' to what was then called 'the northern Parts of Virginia'. He landed near Cape Cod and named Martha's Vineyard after his recently deceased daughter. Five years later Gosnold returned with shiploads of emigrants to create the first permanent settlement at Jamestown (Virginia).

In 1630 John Winthrop left for Massachusetts. He founded the city of Boston and became the first Governor of the State of Massachusetts. Four years later Nathaniel Ward emigrated to Ipswich, Massachusetts, and was author of a code of laws for use in the new colony.

COPROLITE STREET

This tiny street, which links Duke Street with Neptune Quay, bears one of the most interesting 19th-century street names in Ipswich and one that recalls an important aspect of its industry. Coprolite is fossil dung nodules, which are contained in the red crag beneath large areas of Eastern Suffolk, formed by chemical concretionary action. The coprolite nodules contain high amounts of calcium phosphate which, it was duly discovered, can be ground up and converted into superphosophate, better known as chemical, or artificial, fertilizer.

Coprolite was first dug in 1817 by a farmer at Levington, Edmund Edwards, who discovered its use as a fertilizer but the practice did not become widespread and he was not destined to be the 'discoverer' of artificial fertilizer. Instead, the idea was taken up by Revd Professor John Stevens Henslow, one-time Professor of Botany and Mineralogy at Cambridge University who had retired to take up the rectorship of the Suffolk parish of Hitcham.

Professor Henslow was Charles Darwin's mentor, and he was responsible for teaching him much of his scientific technique. He had arranged for his place aboard HMS *Beagle*. The Professor put all his knowledge and experience to good use when he became one of the founders of the Ipswich Museum, but he made only a mediocre preacher. He, therefore, decided to help his farming parishioners through science rather than religion, and he encouraged them to take part in artificial fertilizer trials. Henslow had found that the coprolite nodules contained a higher volume of phosphate than the crag in which they lodged and thought that if the nodules could be ground and immersed in sulphuric acid it would release its chemical effect more efficiently. And so it proved.

An entrepreneur, Edward Packard, began grinding the coprolite in an old mill at Snape and by 1850 had become the first to manufacture and sell the new phosphate chemical fertilizer.

It was during a holiday in Felixstowe that Henslow met Joseph Fison who was so impressed with Henslow's ideas that he, too, set up a fertilizer company at Bramford and Ipswich with offices near to Stoke Bridge at Eastern Union Mills.

Coprolite was dug along the Orwell and Deben Rivers from the 1840s to the 1890s, during which time barges bringing goods to the quays left loaded with coprolite. By 1877 10,000 tons (10,161 tonnes) were sold annually, although by then they were no longer relying on local supplies but were bringing in the raw materials from further afield. By 1880 it was manufactured not just by Packard and Fison but by four other firms including Henry Chapman, whose head office was on Cornhill, and William Colchester, who operated from Griffin Wharf on the Stoke side of the river.

Eventually, in 1929, three of the original firms united under the name of Fison, Packard and Prentice Limited, which was to form the basis of the internationally-renowned firm of Fisons. The new company bought up over 30 other British fertilizer companies and in 1942 adopted the name Fisons Limited.

Edward Packard and the subsequent manufacturers laid the foundations of a profitable, high-volume industry that provided the docks with one of its most exciting ventures of the 19th and 20th century. Towards the end of the 20th century local fertilizer manufacture declined, and while Fisons continue to service the agricultural industry it diversified into other areas.

Coprolite Street commemorates a time of immense progress. The Victorians viewed coprolite as a great benefit to home agriculture and it provided employment for thousands not only on the docks and in the factories but also in all the ancillary businesses.

CRANFIELDS YARD (Bigod's Quay)

The Cranfield Brothers founded their flour mills in 1884 on the site of the ancient Bigod's Quay. The entire Cranfields Mill complex has become part of the Wharfside Regeneration programme, dubbed The Flour Mill Project, and is currently undergoing dramatic change.

The mills occupied the site of what was once called Bigod's Quay, one of the three mediaeval quays of ancient 'Gipeswic', which owes its name to Roger Bigod, the son of a Norman Knight, who distinguished himself at the Battle of Hastings. He held 'Gipeswic' for William I and was responsible for building Ipswich Castle when work began in 1101 (see also Elm Street). He was described as 'small of body, but brave and bold, [who] assaulted the English gallantly'.

In 2005 the Ipswich Archaeological Trust reported that a dig around the remains of a late 15th-century, stone cellared house, on what was Bigod's Quay, shows that it was located beside the point where the brook that ran down Brook Street joined the river. There was also evidence of two separate wooden-posted structures, possibly Saxon in origin, which await dendrochronology or carbon dating.

DUKE STREET

Both Ogilby's 1674 town plan and Pennington's 1777 map show Duke Street as Duck Street. Since it is so close to the water, could this be where the ducks congregated, perhaps encouraged by spillage of edible cargoes, or even where ducks were bred for

A lunchtime scene in Duke Street just before World War One. Workers from Ransome's Orwell Works pass the Anchor inn and (right) the Packard Chemical Manure Works.

market? Alternatively, since it is so close to the quayside, duck might simply be a mistake for dock.

In Pigot's 1830 Directory the Anchor public house is shown in Duck Street (and run by Hannah Hambling), as is the Three Compasses (run by John Bromley). By 1844 the Anchor was listed in Duke Street (run by John Cornwell); the Three Compasses is not listed but there were two beer houses, run by

William Seagriff and Elizabeth Worth. Duke Street was, therefore, known for some time as Duck Street.

In the 19th century the pubs in Duke Street were renowned for providing Ransomes' workers with their 'dinnertime' pints, lining up full glasses along the bars to save time.

FELAW STREET

Richard Felaw, born about 1420 to John and Agnes Felaw of Ipswich, was deeply involved in 15th-century civic and national affairs, as well as being a successful merchant, Member of Parliament and brewer. His ships brought 'salt and fish from Scandinavia, wine from Gascony and iron from Spain'. The Felaw brewery buildings are now converted to offices but still remind us of the former brewing and malting industries that were the main stays of the local economy during the 18th and 19th century.

The name Felaw is closely linked with the 15th-

The Steamboat Tavern on Felaw Street.

The SS Essex *and landing stage, with the Steamboat Tavern in the background, at the beginning of the 19th century.*

century history of Ipswich School, which provided him with an education sufficient for a career as a parliamentarian and a man of influence in maritime and naval matters.

FORE HAMLET

Fore Hamlet is an extension of Fore Street, running eastward off the Duke Street roundabout and towards Bishop's Hill, which in the last century rose so steeply that 'no heavy vehicle could descend it without a drag'. It is associated with the four ancient wicks (or hamlets) of 'Gipeswic' (see also Wicks Bishop Street). Hunt's 1864 uncomplimentary description of those who frequented Fore Hamlet is of people who were 'a coarse speaking, noisy race of seamen and labourers.' The inhabitants had lived there for several generations, and 'seem like a separate race from the population of other parts of the town' prone to uproarious jollity one hour and to fighting the next. They were 'good-hearted but improvident people, with doubtless much of the blood of old Saxon fishermen and sailors in their veins.'

Because of its proximity to the docklands, and Ransome's wartime munitions works, Fore Hamlet

sustained bomb damage in World War Two. Ransomes built nearly 800 aircraft in hangars in a disused clay pit beside the old brickworks and, therefore, attracted enemy fire. On 2 June 1943 11 people were killed in nearby Myrtle Road and several bombs fell in neighbouring Cliff Road.

One of the outstanding landmarks of modern Fore Hamlet is the long-established Mortimers Seafood Restaurant, occupying the 'V' between Fore Hamlet and Duke Street. Mortimers was originally at the end of Wherry Lane and called 'Mortimer's on the Quay'. It is now to be owned by the Loch Fyne seafood restaurant chain that plans to refurbish the interior with the Loch Fyne 'look' of wooden floors and themed artwork.

FOUNDRY LANE

This takes it name from the foundry of Bond, Turner & Hurwood, which became Turner's Foundry and moved to Foxhall Road in 1922. Wodderspoon writes that foundations of priory buildings were discovered when the foundry was built in 1837 and yet more found in 1848 close to St Mary at Quay.

The route of Foundry Lane is generally thought

to be the site of an Anglo-Saxon river crossing, in line with Great Whip Street on the south bank.

GAINSBOROUGH LANE

The great Suffolk artist Thomas Gainsborough (1727–1788) spent seven crucial years of his professional life in Ipswich. He moved here in 1752 with his wife and two small daughters and lived in Foundation Street until 1759. An Ipswich Society commemorative plaque is seen on number 32 Foundation Street. In fact, he rented number 34, a similar house to number 32, which was demolished in the early 1960s. Gainsborough drew much of the inspiration for his paintings from the wooded banks of the Orwell, and Gainsborough Lane perpetuates his memory. Another Suffolk artist, John Constable, wrote in 1799 'I fancy I see a Gainsborough in every hedge and hollow tree'.

In 1888 Dr Taylor described the Lane:

'Just after leaving the "Brewery" and the "Ship-yard", on the left is a sandy road, which winds up the irregular hill-side to the high ground above. Then we easily make our way to the locally famous Gainsborough Lane, which crowns the high land (as seen from the river) with an avenue of huge ancient oaks.'

Many of the oaks that had been there in Gainsborough's time were by then gone but the lane was still 'the dearest walk in the "environs" to Ipswich people', so that they could ramble down to the water through thickets of gorse bushes.

A couple of miles down the Orwell, 'best reached by following the lovely road known as Gainsborough's Lane', was Priory Farm. The farm was famous as one of the places were Margaret Catchpole was employed as a servant and, as its name implies, has monastic associations. In 1845 Richard Cobbold wrote in his semi-fictional *Margaret Catchpole*:

'The site of this old house is still a most romantic and sequestered spot. In front of it,

along a pleasant green slope to the shore, runs a rippling stream, which having passed through the moat, meanders along the meadow down to the Orwell, whose broad waters look here like a magnificent lake'.

Time has badly eroded Dr Taylor's 'dearest walk' and the Orwell Bridge now traverses it.

GREAT WHIP STREET

This was the ancient route into 'Gipeswic' and it may be that the river was forded at this point before that of Stoke Crossing. Great Whip Street meets Dock Street close to the crossing and was one of the two mediaeval routes to London through Stoke Hamlet.

Muriel Clegg writes that the early name (first noticed in 1285) of Great Whip Street was Losegateway, or Lousgateway, and the street forded the river at the present Foundry Lane, just south of College Street. Whether this came before or after Stoke Bridge is unclear, but the two crossings are very close and no doubt evolved at much the same time (see Bridge Street).

How it became Whip Street is unclear, but it could relate to the place where criminals were taken for whipping (as in York) or have connections with the craft of whipcording.

In 1836 the Ipswich Union purchased a three-acre site, from Christ's Hospital, for the purpose of erecting a workhouse. The land cost £525 and was known as St Peter's Workhouse. It had accommodation for 400 inmates. The entrance was on Great Whip Street and a chapel and infirmary were added later.

A famous resident of nearby Little Whip Street was Emma Hunt, who has a plaque put up in her memory outside Debenhams on Cornhill that reads 'Emma Hunt, a Real Suffolk Landmark, Rest in Peace, Debenhams'. For 20 years Emma was a familiar sight, sitting in a chair surrounded by the flowers of Tower Flowers under the street overhang and passing the time of day with customers leaving and entering the store. When she died in January 2005 Debenhams paid for the plaque to be hung in memory of the 82-year-old 'as a mark of respect' for what many considered as much a part of Ipswich as a Giles cartoon.

Emma was born in Norfolk but came to Ipswich after marrying Douglas Hunt, and the couple made their home in Little Whip Street. After her husband died she moved to Burrell Road where she lived until her death.

In her latter years Emma was accompanied by her dog, Benjam, who was always at her side and was as popular – if not more so with the children – than Emma herself.

HELENA ROAD

Helena Road is another small road that runs south alongside South West Quay onto Ship Launch Road but is now somewhat overwhelmed by the frenetic changes taking place on that part of the embankment. It owes its name to the *Helena*, a 16-gun sailing sloop of war that was moored near the

lock gates and served as the Seaman's Church. A footbridge was constructed and a porch built onto the side of the ship. The Admiralty gave permission for such use in November 1869 and it continued in service until June 1880. The *Helena* had seats for a congregation of over 500.

HOLY WELLS ROAD

This road takes its name from the Holy Wells that were found in the Anglo-Saxon hamlet of Wicks Bishop and near the site of a palace of the Bishop of Norwich, who stayed here when his duties brought him to Suffolk. It is so named because the springs or wells, 'haligwille', thereabouts were believed to possess miraculous powers. At the time of the Norman Conquest a 480-acre farm lay to the southeast of Holywells Park, occupied by 24 families with 48 oxen between them.

Holywells Park (for some reason the two words are united for the park but separate for the road) is

Holywells Park, Ipswich, by Thomas Gainsborough. (Ipswich Borough Council Museums & Galleries)

nearby and is one of the town's most popular green areas.

A mansion, built by John Cobbold in 1814, became the Cobbold family home throughout the 19th century. It was presented to the town by Lord Woodbridge, Arthur Churchman of W.A. and A.C. Churchman (see Westgate Street) in the 1920s but sadly neglected during World War Two. The 60 acres of undulating parkland was opened to the public in 1936. By 1962 the mansion was in a dilapidated state and was demolished, though the stable building, clock tower and conservatory were saved.

ISLAND, The

A piece of land between the Wet Dock and New Cut was called The Island. Laid out in the 1840s, it had a promenade and close to the lock gates was a shelter known as the umbrella. There was also a cottage 'for the keeper of the Promenade' and a statue of a winged horse.

The Island was a favourite place for families to take leisurely walks and general recreation, especially on a Sunday, with good views of the docks. In 1900 there was an avenue of lime trees where the Edwardians sat and nannies pushed their perambulators on fine afternoons. Rowing boats could be hired by the hour and a little way down the river, at Stoke, there was a bathing place.

The Dock Commissioners wanted to end public rights of way to The Island in 1912, although it was not until a few years later that they laid a railway line down over what had been the Promenade. The trees were removed in the 1920s, and although the shelter remained there until the 1950s by then the surroundings had been taken for industrial use.

KEY STREET (also Quay Street)

Key Street might well be thought to lack the peace and quiet expected of an ancient thoroughfare but the fact that it echoes to the almost constant roar of traffic is not unfitting for an area of town that has always been busy and noisy. It runs parallel with the river and at one time extended further westwards along what is now College Street. Both streets now

seem to exist for the sole purpose of getting traffic in a one-way direction from east to west, but this has been its purpose all along since its origins were as a pathway from the river to the town. It makes for an uncomfortable and fume-soaked walk along the narrow pavements, rubbing against high, blackened walls and the last remnants of the massive industrial structures of the 20th century that are gradually disappearing from the quaysides. Its one redeeming feature is the 15th-century Church of St Mary at Quay.

The spelling of Quay as Key is due to a corruption of the Danish 'Kaai' (meaning quayside), which over the years became 'Key', and a second derivation from the similar Norman word 'Quai' (meaning quay or wharf). There is no tradition of a key in the context of a lock, although, as pointed out by Dr John Blatchly, 'the church weather vane has long had a key on it'. St Mary's, however, retains Quay, while the street is Key (Wodderspoon has it as 'Kay'). On Ogilby's 1674 map the waterfront 'quay' is named 'key' and so is the street, though the former is the root word and the latter a corruption thereof.

As well as associations with the wealthy Tudor merchants of Ipswich, such as Henry Tooley and Thomas Pownder, St Mary at Quay (called St Mary Quay) has long been a place of refuge. In the 14th century two murderers, John Bryd in 1338 and Nicholas Soweband in 1341, 'fled to the church of St Mary de Caye' for sanctuary, and the iron closing-ring on the 15th-century door is almost certainly a 'sanctuary ring', grasped by those fugitives from the law who claimed the right of sanctuary afforded by the confines of the church building.

Built in the centre of dockland, it once stood behind the 'barricade' of warehouses that mushroomed up between it and the old dock, though it is now on what is effectively an island on the inner ring road with waste ground, destined for development, on two sides. The surrounding industrial silos dwarf its 73ft tower which was once topped by a wooden cupola containing a Sanctus bell. Many of St Mary's treasures, including the 16th-century Pownder and Tooley brasses, are now

Entrance to St Mary Quay, between Star Lane and Key Street.

in the borough collection, and the church has been in the care of the Churches Conservation Trust since 1973.

St Mary's is one of the 12 mediaeval churches of Ipswich and, while the present edifice was built during the late 15th and early 16th century, it took the place of an earlier church on the same site (thought to have been Stella Maris, Our Lady Star of the Sea). Among its many patrons and benefactors was Henry Tooley (see also Foundation Street), who added the north transept and aisle. Tooley's table-tomb in the north transept is a reminder that this church was once the place of worship for the merchants whose trade and enterprise made Ipswich a centre of maritime commerce.

The magnificent double-hammerbeam roof of St Mary's has apostles and other figures standing beneath canopies on the wall posts. The spandrels have carvings on both sides and portray birds drinking, human faces and a little man reclining on his elbow. Binoculars are useful for spotting the naked man (perhaps Adam waiting to lose a rib to make Eve?) and the heads of a man with a flowing beard and headband and another with his tongue stuck out!

Although the original 1525 Pownder brass is now in the borough collection, there is a fibreglass replica made by William Lack, which shows Thomas and Emme Pownder and their eight children in what is considered to be one of the most beautiful brasses in England. Although William Dowsing visited the

church in January 1644 to 'brake down 6 superstitious pictures', he left the Pownder brass untouched.

East Anglian churches, especially those in coastal areas, have a preponderance of fine brasses, attributed to easy contact with Europe and to the great wealth of the 'merchant princes' of Ipswich. They are recognisable as being of foreign workmanship; English brasses have the figure cut out to the outline and inlaid with stone, while foreign brasses have the figures engraved in the centre of a large rectangular plate. Invariably the background is filled in with diapered work of great delicacy. The Pownder brass was made in Bruges (or by a Flemish craftsman) and has the peculiarity of a blank space in the top left hand border. This was to have been filled in with the date of Emme Pownder's death, but she outlived her husband by almost 40 years, by which time Henry VIII's Reformation had occurred and it was, no doubt, impolitic for the new Protestants to commission such an engraving.

Another interesting aspect of the Pownder brass is the engraving of the arms of the Merchant Adventurers, incorporated in 1296, a reminder of the great Merchant Companies of Tudor England. The Merchant Adventurers were merchants and other important tradesmen who were free to trade or 'adventure' their money at any port and on any market. They operated along the lines of guilds, or trade associations, and were formed in the 13th century to promote the cloth trade. Although the Merchant Adventurers were strongest in places like York, where there survives a rare example of a considerable Merchant Adventurers' Hall, there is no doubt that there would have been a strong following in Ipswich. The merchant's mark of Augustin Parker (1590), Grocer and Merchant Adventurer, can be found in St Nicholas' Church, and at St Peter's is a merchant's mark on the ledger stone memorial of Adrian Waywell (1620).

The Tooley family worshipped here throughout the first half of the 16th century and Henry Tooley had an inn, which for nearly three centuries stood on Key Street, The Half Moon. It was famous for its unusual carved corner post, which depicted a fox preaching to geese and was a satirical comment on the clergy of the time. Although it was on the official list of buildings to be protected, the borough council authorised its demolition in 1960.

In 1898 flooding, which for many years had caused damage to the floor and the vaults beneath, rendered the church unsafe and – to the distress of parishioners – extremely smelly as the dampness got worse. It had been built on marshland and had, presumably, always suffered from water damage. The church was closed but after an appeal it was restored and reopened in 1901.

St Mary Quay was one of the places that sustained damage in World War Two, when a bomb fell east of the church in 1943. The windows were shattered and damage caused to the chancel roof and floor. There was a move to have the church demolished but with help from the Friends of Friendless Churches it was restored in the 1960s.

On the corner of Key Street and Fore Street is the lingering representative of R & W Paul Limited, whose name is emblazoned on the huge silos, which still (just) towers above the blocks of apartments that are mushrooming up along the wharfside. The Pauls complex is currently being redeveloped but the offices at 47 Key Street are still the Head Office of BOCM Pauls, who now operate only in the United Kingdom but was at one time the centre for its national and global operations (see also Albion Wharf).

The Bull inn, which stood in Key Street, was damaged in World War One, when a Zeppelin bomb fell close by, demolishing the cottage next door and killing a man. The inn closed in the 1970s.

NEPTUNE QUAY
Neptune Quay is the old Ding Quay and one of the earliest recorded shipyard sites in the country. Here a galley was built for Edward I in 1295. The king ordered galleys to be constructed in 26 towns along the east and south coasts, Ipswich being chosen to build both a galley and the barge that was to be its tender.

Neptune Quay is now in the ascendancy with its marina that has berthing facilities for the increasing number of craft using the 26-acre Wet Dock, the deep water controlled by 24-hour lock gates.

NEW CUT WEST
New Cut West is also called Stoke Quay and is a continuation of Dock Street. Felaw and Purplett Streets both run off it and the whole area is undergoing 'regeneration' on a considerable scale.

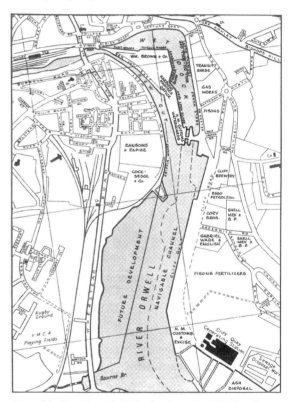

Map of the New Cut and Wet Dock as it was in 1973 when the docklands were thriving with trade and industry. (Ipswich Borough Council)

From 1895 to 1930 the Great Eastern Railway Company operated three paddle steamers to Felixstowe and Harwich from New Cut, the *Suffolk*, *Norfolk* and *Essex*. Passengers embarked at the Steamboat Tavern at the end of Felaw Street and the booking office was in Purplett Street. (Purplett should be Puplett, after Richard Puplett who was a bailiff during the time of Cromwell.) The 'Steamboat', which hosts live music gigs, is overlooked by the Felaw Maltings which were converted into offices in the 1990s. One of the newest ventures is the IP-CITY Centre in nearby Bath Street (the disused industrial site). Part of the building had a brief life as Spoils Kitchen Rejects but is now a complex of business units with conference seating, audio-visual equipment and promised rail access to the rest of the waterfront.

RAPIER STREET

This tiny street is a miniscule reminder of the huge industrial legacy of Richard Rapier who, in 1862, became manager of Ransomes railway department. In 1869 Richard Rapier and Robert James Ransome formed a new company – Ransomes & Rapier – that played a leading role in providing equipment for the Welsh narrow-gauge slate railways, built railways on sugar plantations in far flung parts of the Empire, and negotiated a pioneering contract to help build the Shanghai and Woosung Railway in China. Some years later they were supplying railway equipment for lines in India and began manufacturing sluices for the Aswan Dam.

ST CLEMENT'S CHURCH LANE

On the town maps this is now a mere line of dots linking Fore Street with Grimwade Street, and the lane has obvious associations with St Clement's Church.

The lower parts of Grimwade Street and Waterworks Street were connected and known as Church Lane. The middle section of the lane is now known as St Clement's Church Lane (incorporating the defunct Church Lane) and runs close by the historic church dedicated to the Patron Saint of merchants, fishermen and lighthouse men.

Hunt's Guide described Church Lane thus:

'It is an old, unpaved thoroughfare, where the generally squalid appearance of the houses and courts on the left hand side are in striking contrast to the large and handsome flint-built church and extensive graveyard half full of trees, only divided from the road by a low wall on the opposite side.'

Known as the Sailor's Church, St Clement's is erected on the former site of the Church of St Osterbolt, said to have stood near the lost East Gate of the town. Nothing is known of St Osterbolt and very little about the East Gate, though there would have been such an entrance at one time and it could well have stood on a site now occupied by Suffolk College. The perpendicular tower of the present church is seen mostly from the car window, though close up it still has a wooded churchyard that surrounds it providing a glimpse of what was once its rural setting.

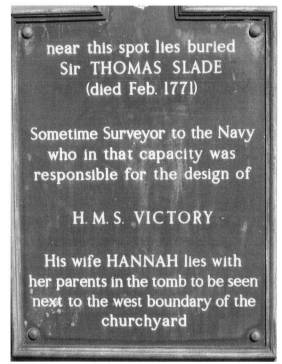

Sir Thomas Slade plaque beside the tower of St Clement's.

It would be surprising if there were not a church dedicated to St Clement in one of the oldest quaysides in England. St Clement was the third successor of St Peter in the see of Rome and governed the church as Pope for about 10 years. After various political upheavals he was exiled to the Crimea and was killed by being thrown into the Black Sea with an anchor round his neck. Angels were said to have made him a tomb on the sea bed, which was uncovered once a year by an unusually low tide. Thus St Clement's symbol in religious art is the anchor, examples of which can be found in the church. There is also one halfway up the tower outside, close to the memorial to Thomas Slade.

There are several monuments inside the church, including one to John Tye, merchant and portman, who died in 1583, and here is the burial place of two famous seamen: Thomas Eldred (died 1622), who accompanied the explorer Thomas Cavendish (1560–1592) on his epic voyage around the world in 1586, and Sir Thomas Slade (died 1771), the surveyor who designed Admiral Nelson's flagship the *Victory*.

The 16th-century Ipswich merchant and circumnavigator Thomas Eldred lived in Eldred House on Fore Street. It is probable that his father, a chandler, lived there before him in what was one of many such merchant houses in and around the parish of St Clement's. The Eldred family was considered one of 'great respectability' and several held offices in the town. Dr Taylor wrote:

'Close by [the Neptune inn] are the houses believed to have been once occupied by Cavendish, Eldred, and others. The old navigators loved to dwell beside the salt water when ashore'.

Dr Taylor thought, however, that Eldred House did not 'offer any external characters to distinguish it from its equally quaint neighbours. It is nearly opposite the Neptune inn and is remarkable for the painted panels over the fire-place.'

The chimney piece and three panels from Eldred House can be seen in Christchurch Mansion, one of the panels containing Eldred's portrait. In another is a ship and globe carrying the legend:

'He that travels ye world about
Seeth Gods wonders and Gods works.
Thomas Eldred travelled ye world about;
And went out of Plimouth ye 21 of July 1586, and
Arrived in Plimouth again the 9 of September, 1588.'

Thomas Cavendish was 20-years-old when Drake arrived back on the *Golden Hind* and took inspiration from his achievements. He first sailed under the patronage of Sir Walter Raleigh and made plans to emulate his hero. Having finally got together a small fleet of ships, with Thomas Eldred as navigator, they left Plymouth in the *Desire* heading for the Straits of Magellan. After a difficult passage they sailed to California, where they captured a Spanish treasure ship, and returned home via the Moluccas and the Cape of Good Hope.

Sir Thomas Slade spent his early career working on ships built in Ipswich for the Navy, but in 1758 the Board of Admiralty in London placed an order for the construction of 12 new battle warships, among them a 100-gun 'first rate'. The following year it was decided to call the ship *Victory*, and Sir Thomas Slade was commissioned to submit draft designs. The cost was £63,175 (equivalent to around £30 million today) and the plans required 200 trees. The keel was laid on 23 July 1759 at No.2 Dock, Chatham Dockyard. The *Victory* was launched in 1765 and her greatest hour was to be under the command of Nelson at the Battle of Trafalgar in 1805.

Having been acclaimed for the *Victory* Sir Thomas was asked to design the famous HMS *Agamemnon*, launched in 1781, which Nelson called his favourite ship. He commanded her between 1793 and 1796, although it was on board the *Agamemnon* that he lost the sight in his right eye. The same ship was at the centre of events in 1793 where Nelson first met Emma, Lady Hamilton.

Sir Thomas died in 1771 at Bath, but his body was brought back to St Clement's for burial. His grave is lost but a memorial was put in the churchyard, and Slade Street, which runs between Star Lane and Key Street, is named after him.

Beside the church is Sir Thomas Slade Court, which stands where the Rectory did before it was bombed in 1941. The Victorian glass in the east window of the church blew out, smashing into small fragments apart from one piece which remained whole and depicted the head of Christ.

While Sir Thomas is renowned in his own right,

his association with the great hero of Trafalgar, Admiral Horatio Nelson, undeniably enhances his fame. Although Nelson never lived in Ipswich, his wife Frances had a house, Roundwood Place, close to the Woodbridge Road. Nelson installed her there in January 1798 with his father, the Revd Edmund Nelson, his agent having bought the house at an auction held at the Great White Horse. Nelson was already intimately acquainted with Suffolk. His mother, Catherine Suckling, came from Barsham, and it was her brother who took the young Horatio for his first voyage and taught him the rudiments of seamanship.

The borough authorities welcomed news that the Admiral's wife, Francis but called Fanny, and father had moved to Ipswich, and when the Earl of Dysart died in 1800 they appointed Nelson as High Steward of the town, a post he held until his death. In October 1798 Lady Nelson attended the ball at the Assembly Hall in Northgate Street to celebrate her husband's victory at the Nile. Admiral Sir Richard Hughes and Admiral Reeve greeted her and the Revd Edmund Nelson, their arrival being announced 'by the ringing of bells, and the loud huzzas of a vast concourse of people in the street'.

They were accompanied by Miss Berry, sister of the 'Vanguard's Captain Berry, and found the ball-room 'lighted up with transparencies, and variegated lamps interspersed amongst a variety of evergreens', with upwards of 300 people of 'distinction and fashion' present. The evening was said to have passed off with 'universal hilarity and eclat'.

Nelson visited Roundwood Place only twice. On the second occasion Sir William and Lady Hamilton accompanied him (Emma Hamilton at the time pregnant with Horatia, Nelson's daughter). Finding his wife out (Fanny having gone to London, thinking, to greet her husband there), he and the Hamiltons spent the night at the Great White Horse and returned to London the following day. The unorthodox relationship between Nelson and the Hamiltons was well known and this exotic 'ménage de trio' was dubbed the 'gleesome threesome' by the satirists.

News of Nelson's arrival spread rapidly and the people mobbed his coach. Although Nelson was used to such adulation, he was, by all accounts, in a very bad temper at finding his wife not at home and wanted to be on his way. He was reunited with Fanny in London but by that time the marriage was over and not long afterwards Roundwood Place was sold.

Ipswich rejoiced when news came of the victory of Trafalgar. G.B. Clarke records:

'November 29, 1805. On the arrival of the news of the victory of Trafalgar, large collections were made at all the churches here, in aid of the patriotic fund at Lloyd's; but the rejoicings were greatly damped by the loss of the gallant hero, Nelson, who was peculiarly connected with this town, as high steward, and whose amiable lady had long resided in its immediate vicinity.'

In the 1960s Ipswich enthusiastically embraced the prevailing fashion for renovating or removing old buildings and so, in 1961, the council demolished Roundwood Place and built St John's Primary School on the site. There are, however, memorials in the streets thereabouts – Nelson Road, Victory Road, Trafalgar Close and Roundwood Road – and the Lord Nelson public house survives on Fore Street.

Bequests and charitable donations that benefit seafaring families are a feature of St Clement's parish. In 1723 Captain Samuel Green, mariner, left £50 for 'the relief of the widows and children of seamen', and in 1719 Captain Robert Cole also left £50, this time to provide a distribution of bread 'among poor widows of seamen' once a fortnight at the church.

Captain John Dorking, in 1727, left £100 to be used, among other things, for 'poor seamen's widows and children' in gratitude that he was 'remarkably delivered from shipwreck, and preserved in a storm at sea'.

In 1818 a subscription was raised for the widows

and orphans of the crew of the *Endeavour* of Ipswich, lost off the coast of Scotland, and the *Unity* of Ipswich, lost off the Lincolnshire coast with all hands on board.

One of the more colourful entries in the St Clement's registers is that of the burial of Grace Pett, fisherman's wife, said to have been a witch and to have died from 'spontaneous combustion' in April 1744. The coroner discovered that Grace had been drinking 'plentifully of gin' the previous evening and had gone downstairs in the night where she was apparently burnt to ashes. No fire was in the grate and the candlestick stood on the table with the candle burned out. The resulting sensation came to the notice of Dickens as the demise of Grace Pett is mentioned in *Bleak House*.

St Clement's has a special place in literature as it was where the Dickens character Sam Weller sat staring at 'the old brick houses'. He was deep in thought, 'bestowing a wink upon some healthy-looking servant girl as she drew up a blind, or threw open a bed-room window'. Then:

'Mr Samuel Weller walked forth from the Great White Horse when his father had left him; and bending his steps towards St Clement's Church, endeavoured to dissipate his melancholy, by strolling among its ancient precincts. He had loitered about, for some time, when he found himself in a retired spot – a kind of court-yard of venerable appearance – which he discovered had no other outlet than the turning by which he had entered.'

Dickens must also have strolled 'among its ancient precincts' though most of the 'Church Lane' – and certainly the green gate – described in 'Pickwick Papers' has gone (see also Tavern Street).

In 1966 fire destroyed the late 19th-century roof and St Clement's was declared redundant in the early 1970s and became, for a while, a prop store for the Wolsey Theatre. As a result of its isolated position it suffers continuous vandalism.

In August 2005 a statue of Our Lady of Lourdes

was found in a box that had lain hidden for years. Her original home could not be found so the statue has a new home at the Catholic Church of St Pancras. The last surviving churchwarden from when the church was open is John Andreasen, who is still on hand to welcome visitors to the church, which is now in the care of the Ipswich Historic Churches Trust.

ST PETER'S QUAY (and DOCK)

This is the quay closest to the Stoke crossing and stands between the river and St Peter's Church, from which it takes its name, and is sometimes called Stoke Bridge Wharf. The old rail track and colonnade that once shifted commodities from one end of the quay to another still runs along the quayside.

Colonnade running along St Peter's Quay with the start of the wharfside railway.

Above the quay, on the dock side of Stoke Bridge, is the large red and white buoy of Trinity House, which marks the division between two channels of the river.

SALTHOUSE STREET (and Salthouse Lane)

Salthouse Street was created in 1878 and was a completely new road, although it celebrates the long and illustrious salt trade that was once so important to the port's prosperity and the everyday needs of the people. The street formed a 'communication from the lower part of St Clements, passing the Salt Office to the Common Quay' and cost £1,848 to lay down. It took the path of an established quayside route.

Salthouse Lane once ran off the street but, like many other byroads or links, was closed and amalgamated into the prevailing development. It led to the Jews' Cemetery, started in the 18th century by the local Jewish community, which was then behind the Green Man inn (on the corner of Key Street). Although the lane is gone and the cemetery no longer used for burials, it is still surrounded by a brick wall that forms part of BOCM Pauls yard. It

has 36 gravestones with Hebrew inscriptions, though most have been made illegible by weathering, and there are parish boundary stones in the east and north walls. The synagogue was in Rope Lane but was pulled down in 1877.

Salt had numerous uses, of course, and was acquired from various sources. It was not only a vital ingredient in the preservation of food; indeed in mediaeval times it was the only means of preserving meat throughout the long winter months. In the 13th century Ipswich merchants took goods to Brittany in return for salt, and the great Henry Tooley often bargained for 'weys' of salt when negotiating the hire of his vessels to Iceland. The *Mary Walsingham* was often fishing in Icelandic waters, and the fishermen would pack the fish with salt for the return voyage.

The use of salt and spittle in the mediaeval sacrament of baptism is illustrated on the font at St

Cobbold's on The Quay was originally a Malt Kiln of brick and converted into a public house in 1980. It stands on Neptune Quay beside the Salthouse Harbour Hotel, opened in July 2003.

Margaret's Church, where a scroll holds the legend 'Sal et Saliva' (salt and saliva). Blessed salt was, and still is, used in the preparation of holy water to ward off evil.

Robert Malster writes that much of the salt, also used in the tanning process, brought into the port came from the Tyne:

'North and South Shields formed the greatest centre in Britain for the manufacture of salt in the early 18th century, with almost 200 saltpans in which seawater was evaporated using the cheap local coal'.

The Green Man inn was the scene of a scuffle between a group of sailors and the men of the Impress Service – or Press Gang as it was commonly known – that ended in the murder of Thomas Nicholls, the master of the Ram inn. The Navy always had trouble recruiting enough men for all its ships, especially in wartime, and it gained seamen by three means: volunteers, the Impress Service and (from 1795) the quota acts. The press gangs covered every port in Great Britain and they knew all the inns and taverns where seamen drank. Merchant ports like Ipswich were obvious targets afraid that they would take their best men, some merchant captains built hideaways on board, in case the gangs went aboard in search of 'recruits'. On the night of 12 December 1778 a fight broke out in the Green Man as the gangers attempted to take two 'recruits' and were challenged by Thomas Nicholls, who had tracked them down after they had caused an affray in the Ram. Nicholls was so badly hurt that he died the next morning. Seventeen of the gang were caught and detained in Ipswich gaol. They came up for trial the following year but were freed due to lack of evidence.

Running battles were often fought in the streets between the press gang and locals trying to retrieve men taken. Although there were supposed to be rules about the taking of men, the scope for corruption was enormous and the gang operated largely with impunity.

There were two other pubs in Salthouse Street in the 1880s, the Ocean Queen, on the corner of Salter's Lane, and the Original Ocean Queen. The latter was frequented by sailors and at one time was kept by William Webb, known as Bulldog Webb on account of his breeding bulldogs, and sold from his address at St Bernard's Place, Salthouse Street.

The Salthouse Harbour Hotel, which stands high on the Neptune quayside, takes the place of the old merchant warehouses and is a landmark clearly visible from both the river and the quayside itself. Opened in July 2003, it is owned and operated by the well-known Suffolk hoteliers the Gough family, who have kept The Angel at Bury St Edmunds for over 30 years.

On a warm summer's day the water in front of the hotel is an ideal place to spot swarms of jellyfish (*Aurelia aurita*). Although widespread along the British coast, they seem to particularly like the warm waters of the Wet Dock, as do the swans.

SHIP LAUNCH ROAD

The name of the road is self-explanatory, and it was just north of the St Clement Ship Yard. It is uncertain which came first, the road or the inn, but the Ship Launch inn was once very popular as a venue for political and trade union meetings, held on the grassy area known as the Knoll. It once stood at the entrance to the Island, was also used by the dock workers and is one of the few pubs in the area still in business. Indeed, the modern Ship Launch Road consists of little other than the inn, though it was different in the 19th century.

Trevor James writes:

'Before the lock gates were constructed in 1881, Ship Launch Road had a double row of lime trees which joined those of the promenade at right angles. The 'Umbrella' shelter and the statue of Pegasus, the winged horse, were at the point where the two avenues of trees met. It was one of the most popular places in the town at this time but when the Dock Commission proposed closing to the public there was little protest.'

Ship Launch Road. (ITM Collection)

In fact it stayed open, although the lime trees, 'whose scent had drifted down the river on warm spring evenings', were cut down in 1914 and the footpath closed.

The Knoll has yielded early clay tobacco pipes, but archaeologists are uncertain whether the bank is a 'virgin mudflat' or an old spoil heap. It had been silting up since it was bypassed in 1822 and is not far from what is known as Nova Scotia, so called because it was where the piles of timber arrived from Canada.

In the 1970s Ship Launch Road was the point where the rail line went across the river at the south end of the South West Quay, where William Brown's Timber Yards were. The swing bridge still operates across the river.

VERNON STREET

This is named in honour of Admiral Edward Vernon (1684–1757), Member of Parliament for Ipswich in 1741–1754, obviously a favourite with the town's publicans as in Lower Orwell Street was the

'Portobello', commemorating the Admiral's famous engagement in 1739 in Spain. He was, however, known as 'Old Grogram' and is famous for being the first to introduce the practice of watered rum into the Navy. On 21 August 1740 he ordered that the quarter pint of neat rum, issued daily to each sailor, be diluted to 1 gill of rum to 3 gills of water to prevent drunkenness. The mixture was called 'grog' after the Admiral's nickname (he wore grogram breeches and clock, grogram being a mixture of silk and wool or mohair). Admiral Vernon was cashiered in 1746 and lived on his estate at Nacton. His portrait, painted by Thomas Hudson in around 1750, is in Christchurch Mansion where the attack on Portobello is depicted in the background.

WHERRY LANE (and Wherry Quay)

This street and quay name is a reminder of the days just prior to the ferry steamers when the wherries ferried passengers and cargo between Ipswich and Harwich and other points on the Orwell. The Wherry inn once stood nearby. The lane is now a

A Tudor merchant's house at Isaac Lord's Wharf. The river would have come up to the bottom of the steps and through the walkway.

tiny cut through from the quayside to Key Street and consists of the John Russell Art Gallery, Broadblue Catamarans and The Cotton Tree, a firm of interior designers, yet it has a special, vibrant atmosphere all of its own. At the base of the Broadblue Catamarans wall is a pile of black stones, known as Sarsen stones, put along the wall base to protect the building from horses and carriages as they passed along the narrow lane.

Suffolk has long been a Mecca for artists, Gainsborough and Constable among them, and the John Russell Gallery's stated aim of showing the work of contemporary East Anglian artists came from Anthony 'Tony' Coe's idea of tapping into this rich vein of talent and bringing it to as wide an audience as possible. Proprietor of the gallery for over 30 years, Tony Coe has exhibited the work of countless local artists and has around 12 different exhibitions a year of original prints, paintings and sculptures by both established artists and the new

and promising talents. The gallery, a name derived by adding John to Tony's middle name of Russell, is housed on the 18th-century Isaac Lord wharves, and beside the yard behind is an example of one of the Tudor merchant houses that once lined the quaysides.

Tony Coe is a man of many talents, among them stand-up comedian, dancer, compere, DJ-ing and touring the world as a jazz guitarist with some of the best known names in entertainment such as The Who and Jimi Hendrix. In the 1960s he played with the American 'soul shouter' Geno Washington, an American serviceman stationed in England. Geno fronted the Ram Jam Band, which had a series of chart hits during 1966–67 and led to Tony and others founding the Ram Jam Club at the Gardeners Arms in 1962, which was the first jazz club in Ipswich.

In the 1980s Tony returned to Ipswich to realise his dream of running an art gallery. He formulated his policy of showing work by contemporary local artists and in 1994 moved to Wherry Lane, the 'opening rites' being performed by the jazz musician George Melly.

Part of the old Isaac Lord wharf has lately been renovated, when steel columns were inserted underneath to keep it standing. It once had its feet in water as the barges came right up into the yard, alongside the house, to unload into the warehouses. The exposed brickwork is an example of 'nogging', where bricks are used to fill in the open space in a wall between the studs or other frames and are set at diagonal and right angles, making a distinctive pattern.

The John Russell Gallery on Wherry Lane.

WYKES BISHOP STREET

Now only a tiny street close to the Duke Street roundabout, the name has associations harking back to when St Clement's parish was divided into four hamlets, one of which was the Bishop's Wick, or 'Wicks Episcopi' (the others were Stoke, Brookes and Wicks Ufford). The Anglo Saxon word 'wick' could also be part of the original name for Ipswich, 'Gipeswic', and simply have meant a hamlet near the Gip(ping). The hamlet and manor of Wykes Bishop were granted by Richard the Lionheart to John Oxenforde, one of the founders of Trinity Priory in the town, and it came within the jurisdiction of the Bishop of Norwich, in whose hands it remained until Henry VIII's Reformation.

In pre-Conquest days it was held by Queen Edith, wife of Edward the Confessor, and extended from the south of Felixstowe Road (part of which is called Bishops Hill) and across to Holywells Park (where the Bishop's Palace once stood). Wykes Bishop stayed in the jurisdiction of successive bishops until Henry VIII granted the hamlet and manor to Sir John Jermie. Left without an Episcopal residence, the new, post-Reformation Bishop of Norwich, John Parkhurst, bought Curson House on Westgate Street.

In Anglo-Saxon times there were two chapels, Wykes Bishop's and Wykes Ufford, the latter named after the famous family of de Ufford, Earls of Suffolk, who owned the manor in which the chapel was situated, though its precise whereabouts is unknown. St Clement's eventually replaced the two chapels. When these early chapels were built, the area was almost entirely agricultural and an old guide recalls:

> 'Where today we see rows of small houses reared in narrow streets was once fruitful soil, while the good citizens of Ipswich found this region, then outside the walls of the town, a place of leafy lanes and shadowing trees, and therefore a pleasant and convenient part in which to stroll and to breathe the salt air from the Orwell on a bright summer's evening.'

Wicks Bishop was particularly known for the quality of its water and within the hamlet were wells, known as Holy Wells, where the Cobbold family began their brewing empire (see Holy Wells Road).

FURTHER READING

The History of Ipswich, 1500 Years of Triumph & Disaster. Peter Bishop, Unicorn Press, 1995.

A Famous Antient Seed-Plot of Learning: A History of Ipswich School. John Blatchly, Ipswich School, 2003.

Early Country Motoring: Cars and Motorcycles in Suffolk 1896–1940. John F. Bridges, The Wolsey Press, 1995.

The History & Description of the Town and Borough of Ipswich. G.R. Clarke, 1830.

Streets and Street Names in Ipswich: Their Origin and Development. Muriel Clegg, Salient Press, 1984.

The Way We Went: Streets in Nineteenth Century Ipswich. Muriel Clegg, Salient Press, 1989.

Justice in Ipswich 1200–1968. R.L. Cross, Ipswich Corporation, 1968.

Tour Through the Eastern Counties. Daniel Defoe (originally published in 1724, republished in 1949 with an introduction by R.A.N. Dixon).

The Official Guide to the Borough of Ipswich. R.A.N. Dixon, East Anglian Magazine, 1946.

Ipswich Inns Taverns & Pubs. Trevor James, Fuller-Davies Ltd, 1991.

Ipswich Events, People and Places over the Last 100 Years. David Kindred, Sutton Publishing, 1999.

A History of Ipswich. Robert Malster, Phillimore, 2000.

The Popular Guide to Suffolk Churches (Central Suffolk). D.P. Mortlock, Acorn Editions, 1990.

Ipswich Through the Ages. Lilian J. Redstone, East Anglian Magazine Ltd, 1969.

The Madonna of Ipswich. Stanley Smith, East Anglian Magazine Ltd, 1980.

In and About Ancient Ipswich. Dr J.E. Taylor, 1888.

Ipswich Churches Ancient & Modern. Roy Tricker, Ipswich, 1982.

Great Tooley of Ipswich. John Webb, Suffolk Records Society, Ipswich, 1962.

Memorials of the Ancient Town of Ipswich. John Wodderspoon, 1850.